THE MORAL STATUS
OF ANIMALS

THE MORAL STATUS
OF ANIMALS

S TEPHEN R. L. C LARK

Oxford   New York

OXFORD UNIVERSITY PRESS

1984

Oxford University Press, Walton Street, Oxford OX2 6DP

London New York Toronto
Delhi Bombay Calcutta Madras Karachi
Kuala Lumpur Singapore Hong Kong Tokyo
Nairobi Dar es Salaam Cape Town
Melbourne Auckland

and associated companies in
Beirut Berlin Ibadan Mexico City Nicosia

Oxford is a trade mark of Oxford University Press

First published by the Clarendon Press 1977
First issued with a new Preface as an Oxford University Press paperback 1984

British Library Cataloguing in Publication Data

Clark, Stephen R. L.
The moral status of animals.—(Oxford paperbacks)
1. Animals, Treatment of
I. Title
179'.3   HV4708
ISBN 0–19–283040–6

Library of Congress Cataloging in Publication Data

Clark, Stephen R. L.
The moral status of animals.
Originally published: Oxford : Clarendon Press, 1977.
With new pref.
Bibliography: p.
Includes index.
1. Ethics. 2. Animals, Treatment of—Moral and ethical aspects. I. Title.
[BJ1012.C58 1984]   179'.3   83–26819
ISBN 0–19–283040–6 (pbk.)

Printed in Great Britain by
The Guernsey Press Co. Ltd.
Guernsey, Channel Islands

PREFACE TO PAPERBACK EDITION

Soon after our marriage my wife and I were staying in a Suffolk village to which my parents had retired. Throughout the night we were woken by the sound of calves lowing miserably in the neighbouring farm, and learned the next day that these calves had only that day arrived from the farm where they had been born, and were to spend the rest of their short lives in a barn. This knowledge, that young creatures were taken from their mothers and prevented from living anything like a decent life according to their kind, tipped us into the decision we had both considered before: not to go on financing such practices. It is necessary to emphasize that the farmer responsible for our conversion was a kindly and honourable man who would certainly never willingly have 'mistreated' his beasts—never beaten or starved them (see p. 56). The tragedy of our times is that decent people, step by step, have come to treat non-human animals as mere material for their own purposes, but there are far worse symptoms of this perverse outlook than my parents' neighbour ever provided. His animals, we believed, were not being allowed the sort of life that they ought to have had, even if it were right to breed them for eventual slaughter, even if they were not exactly 'in pain'.

Our commitment to the vegetarian ideal grew by degrees. Experience taught us that we could not accept flesh-foods from hospitable friends without being ill; enquiry revealed that there were many other practices of which we could not approve that we had, half-knowingly, been financing. But our initial commitment remained largely inarticulate until it occurred to me to prepare lectures on the general topic of the moral status of animals. Elements in this decision were a meeting with Peter Singer, whose *Animal Liberation* was then in press, a conversation with Jonathan Glover, who reported his own surprise and uneasiness when challenged by Roslind Godlovitch (the author of one of the first relevant philosophical articles in recent times), and the usual problem faced by vegetarians of replying politely to the swarm of, usually ill-informed, objections. The research for those lectures was first conducted in the Bodleian Library, and continued in Glasgow when I moved from All Souls to the Department of Moral Philosophy there. I owe a great debt to my colleagues in Glasgow for their kindly attention, even when I have failed to convince them.

This personal history may explain some features of the book which followed. The effort to get to grips with the philosophical problem, and to expiate my own guilts, first took shape as a lecture series, designed for people with some experience of philosophical argument. Some not wholly unfounded criticisms of the work have failed to reckon with its dialectic nature: very often I expounded one partial view, balancing it a little later by a statement of its necessary opposite. Some readers, prompted maybe by their own exasperation with my style or my conclusions, took me to mean only part of what I said—for example, that only the moral intuitions of vegetarians can be taken seriously (p. 183)—whereas I had intended this only as a thesis to be transcended (in this instance, by the realization that all of us are in conflict with our own principles, that none of us can afford to drum anyone else out of the moral community).

Since this book and Peter Singer's were published several philosophical journals have devoted issues to the problems surrounding our relations with the non-human world. Of these the most interesting collections have been *Inquiry* 22 (1979) and *Philosophy* 53 (1978). Several conferences have been held to bring the philosophical and empirical aspects of the case together: the most notable proceedings have been edited as *Animal Rights: a Symposium* (ed. R. Ryder and D. Patterson: Centaur Press 1979), *Self-Awareness in Domesticated Animals* (eds. D. G. M. Woodgush, M. Dawkins and R. Ewbank: U.F.A.W. 1981), and *Ethics and Animals* (eds. H. B. Miller and W. H. Williams: Humana Press 1983). Two journals have been dedicated entirely to these matters: *International Journal for the Study of Animal Problems*, and *Environmental Ethics*. Other collections include *Animals in Research* (ed. David Sperlinger: John Wiley 1980), *On the Fifth Day* (eds. R. Knowles Morris and M. W. Fox: Acropolis Books 1978), and *Environmental Philosophy* (eds. R. Elliot and A. Gare: University of Queensland Press 1983). Amongst the philosophers to consider these issues at book-length are Bernard E. Rollin (*Animal Rights and Human Morality*, Prometheus Books 1981), Mary Midgley (*Animals and Why they Matter*, Penguin Books 1983), Robin Attfield (*The Ethics of Environmental Concern*, Blackwell 1983), and Tom Regan (*All That Dwell Therein*, University of California Press 1982). Cora Diamond has published several useful discussions (see *Philosophy* 58 (1978) and Sperlinger op. cit.). Raymond Frey (*Interests and Rights*, Clarendon Press 1980) and H. J. McCloskey (*Ecological Ethics and Politics*, Rowman and Littlefield 1983) have argued against aspects of the zoophile and environmentalist cases—in my view, unconvincingly. Henry Salt's masterpiece (*Animals' Rights*) has been reissued by the Society for Animal Rights (Centaur

Press 1980), and Charles R. Magel has provided a very thorough *Bibliography on Animal Rights and Related Matters* (University Press of America 1981). In short, a great many philosophers have been taking these issues seriously, and any new edition of the present book would have to be longer and more detailed.

Fortunately, I am under no obligation to provide a thoroughly revised edition. My own further thoughts on these matters may be found in the philosophical journals, in *The Nature of the Beast* (Oxford University Press 1982), and *From Athens to Jerusalem* (Clarendon Press 1984). Relevant articles include 'Animal Wrongs' (*Analysis* 38, 1978), 'The Rights of Wild Things' (*Inquiry* 22, 1979), 'How to calculate the Greater Good' (Ryder and Patterson op. cit.), 'Humans, animals and "animal behavior"' (Miller and Williams op. cit.), and 'Gaia and the Forms of Life' (Elliot and Gare op. cit.).

If I ever do offer a genuinely new edition of this book to the world, it will be a different book. When I wrote it I believed (not wholly without justification) that what was needed was an abrupt and uncompromising challenge to 'orthodox' or 'conventional' wisdom: a cry of 'En garde!' that would have to be acknowledged. 'If I am wrong, refute me,' I declared (p. 198). I do not believe that anyone has made a serious attempt to do so. Such attempts to meet my challenges as I have seen have been scholastic ('Animals don't really have any interests, because they don't have the capacity to understand that they do') or crudely utilitarian (crudely so, because decent and sophisticated utilitarians would not think it right to justify animal suffering by reference to human advantage without taking the degree of suffering, the probability of the advantage, the possibility of alternative techniques into account). Having failed to elicit any solid and credible restatement of the 'humanist' creed, I would now prefer to develop a more systematic version of the moral and metaphysical structure which is my vision of the world.

The apparent lack of system in what I had to say, the way in which I preferred (as Anne Berkeley said of her husband) to pull down rather than build, has been criticized almost as much as my ferocity, my tendency to call foolish arguments and wicked practices by their real names. The ferocity I do not always regret. The supposed lack of system, which I jestingly attributed to my being by turns Aristotelian, Sceptic, and Neo-Platonist (p. 5), has been much exaggerated (even by myself). I have spelled out some of the background to my moral epistemology in *The Nature of the Beast* (Oxford 1982), 'God, Good and

Evil' (*Proceedings of the Aristotelian Society* 77, 1977), 'The Lack of a Gap between Fact and Value' (*Proceedings of the Aristotelian Society*, Supplementary volume 54, 1980), 'God's Law and Morality' (*Philosophical Quarterly* 32, 1982), and 'Morals, Moore and MacIntyre' (*Inquiry* 26, 1984). Briefly, my position in moral epistemology—which should have been no mystery to anyone acquainted with Aristotelian thought—is that what it is right to do is found by considering what someone of sound moral character, equipped with the usual capacities for affection, loyalty and self-forgetfulness, would do. Such a person, as described by Aristotle (and myself), has the habit of being aware of, and delighting in, the beauty and goodness of the world and its members. Correspondingly, the well-being of ourselves and of other creatures consists in our performing well what is the 'work' of our kind: human beings do well when they choose well, when they live as social and rational beings who know that they are not the most important of the things that are; other creatures live well when they live out the pattern of their lives, when (being deer) they run and joust, or (being fowl) they stretch and dust-bathe and secure their places in the peck-order of their tribe. If they are not allowed to live in the way that fulfils their natures, they are deprived: and we, who do not allow it, are deprived as well—for we have failed to appreciate the glories of the created universe, and imagined that there is something called 'our welfare' that requires us to oppress others. Naïve egoists imagine that 'their welfare' requires them to cheat and exploit and terrorize all others: mistakenly, since the only welfare they can ever have depends on having real friends and a just community. Naïve 'humanists' imagine that 'their welfare' depends on exploiting creatures who chance not to be of our species (not of our own breeding-group) or without rational capacity: mistakenly, since 'human welfare' rests in obedient enjoyment of the world, sharing what can be shared, delighting in the dance of time. This is only another way of expressing Plotinus's rebuttal of the Gnostics, that if the world was empty of value so too were they: 'if God is not in the world, He is not in you' (*Enneads* II, 9.16). I have developed the thesis further in *From Athens to Jerusalem* (Oxford 1984).

It is a sad reflection on the philosophical education of a generation that this vision should appear to be either revolutionary or eccentric. Those who think that the ill-conceived 'humanism' of the Research Defence Society (see p. 6) or the convolutions of 'social contract theory' (on which see Midgley op. cit.) constitute decent philosophy have failed to grasp the extent to which these transformations of the *philosophia perennis* are products of particular social changes within Western society. True humanism, which I would not wish to attack, is constituted by an appreciation of the proper place of humankind within a created universe more reliable, more lovely, than the ersatz products of our factory farms and scientific laboratories.

My supposed lack of system was a consequence not only of the necessities of debate (what good would it do to argue only from premises that are in dispute?), but also of my conviction that it is a vision, not a rule, that stands at the heart of any way of life. To change the way that people live it is necessary to change the way they see things, to bring a new vision to light in them. If I am right to think that the 'orthodox' view of nature and humanity is deranged, people will not be cured of it by scholastic argument (however important it may be to set out the implications of the new covenant). The deranged are cured when they can remember how to see: argument is not enough. It was for this reason that I invoked poetry, humour, and polemic rather than relying—as it has been fashionable to do in recent times—upon cool, philosophical analysis. Such analysis has a vital part to play, but it can only set out the options, not determine the conclusions. Either non-human animals 'have rights' (which is to say, 'have moral standing') or human infants and imbeciles do not. there are moralists who have chosen the latter hypothesis, though they usually pay tribute to the decencies by providing some reason or other to treat such creatures well. Either the laws forbidding cruelty to animals (unless one has a licence from the Home Office, or a commercial interest) are an admission that such animals have at least some rights, or else liberal democrats ought to seek their repeal, as wanton interferences in the private pleasures of the subject: there are those who accept the latter hypothesis, while themselves disclaiming any interest in badger-baiting. If the zoophile case is one that all honest reasoners must at last accept (as I believe it is) this is not because it follows incontrovertibly from logically undeniable premises. I know of no moral or scientific conclusions that do. It is because being an honest reasoner involves a willingness to be moved by laws not of our making, a readiness not to insist on one's own way all the time, to see through the eyes of others, to prefer friendly relations to hostile ones. This willingness, when purged of ignorance about the natures of our kindred and the practices of our time, must surely issue in zoophily. Such zoophiles may still find much to disagree about, and they will not imagine that there is some simple rule to resolve their disagreements. The project of being a good mammal, a good animal (p. 182), a good participating member of 'the odyssey of evolution' (p. 31), is one that allows many variations, and requires the cultivation of moral and intellectual virtue (as Aristotle described it): it stems from a vision of the world that can be shown to be rational, but not to be the only logically coherent possibility.

Those who regret these conclusions, wishing it to be the case that there is some one logically compelling principle that will enable all of us to be 'moral experts', without any need to cultivate the moral and intellectual virtues and with the certainty of there being one unequivocally right action in all our uncertainties, sometimes fall victim to utilitarianism. Though I reject this creed, I freely acknowledge that its greatest exponents have done much to alleviate animal and other suffering. I have no wish to re-establish all the moralistic regulations that the utilitarian acid helped to corrode. But it remains a subterfuge: a principle that purports to be a clear and unequivocal way of deciding what is best to be done ('what results in the greatest net surplus of pleasure to pain') turns out to be as obscure, as ambiguous, as difficult to apply, as the traditional morality it was invented to replace. Actually, despite the offence I apparently caused some critics by saying so (p. 74), it does not seem to me that utilitarian calculation is ever more than a rationalization of conclusions reached on the basis of sentiment. I am aware that some zoophiles, including Peter Singer, wish to be regarded as rational utilitarians, according 'equal respect' to all pleasures, all desires, and arguing that this respect must issue in a commitment to animal welfare. The trouble is that as there is no way of spelling out what constitutes a 'net surplus' of pleasure, nor any way of tracing what the consequences of any given action may in the end be, it is open to other theorists to say that (for example) bankruptcies amongst those professionally involved in factory farming, in the breeding of experimental animals, in cosmetics, and in the fur trade; the restrictions on alteration of land use; the increase of guilt-feelings amongst the liberal classes—all these constitute a reason not to press for massive reforms in our present practices, even if a world run on zoophile or environmentalist principles might show a higher surplus (if such a surplus could ever be calculated). Consistent utilitarians must take account of the pleasures and pains of exploiters: even the pleasures of sadistic cruelty can only be outlawed if there is reason to believe that they are surpassed by the pains of the victims, and that the attempt to suppress such iniquity would not distress the villains just as much. Finally, it is difficult to believe that one's own refusal to engage in iniquity will have much general effect: despite Peter Singer's insistence to the contrary, it is (I fear) unlikely that I have relieved any animal, or diminished the gross total of animal suffering (if such a total has any real existence), by not eating flesh-foods. My point here is not merely that vegetarians are unwise to base their project on utilitarian calculation, but that no-one can really base any project (except that of mere convention) upon such a figment. Any departure from conventional behaviour causes distress that would not otherwise be caused, and is unlikely in practice to relieve the pains which the utilitarian (rightly) deplores. Utilitarianism, in short, remains what I called it: 'the dead end of argument' (p. 75). Individual utilitarians, moved by nobler and more immediate considerations than they suppose, are often to be found on the side of decency, insisting on giving each creature—in imagination— one vote, and none more than one. There are, unfortunately, as many professed utilitarians who deny in effect that anyone should have a vote except themselves, who hold that everything 'belongs' to the social engineers, in the sense that they alone can calculate the 'greater good' (which is not the same as what those affected would now want). Utilitarian defences of vegetarianism jostle against utilitarian defences of factory farming and of crass experimental practice: which side one picks is a function not of a supposedly objective utilitarian calculation (when has anyone ever performed such a thing?), but of one's moral character and purposes.

Utilitarian zoophiles are, I believe, on better ground than the 'orthodox' who refuse to reckon with animal pains and pleasures at all. Bentham (see p. 21) and J. S. Mill (*Dissertations and Discussions* (1859), Vol. II, p. 485: 'Granted that any practice causes more pain to animals than it gives pleasure to men: is that practice moral or immoral?') alike, from their rather different positions, rejected what has come to be called speciesism, and were vigorously attacked for so doing. Their intellectual heirs, professing merely utilitarian standards, have until recently forgotten that there are other sentient beings in the world who make their own contribution to the totalities of pleasure and pain: some have forgotten their own intellectual forebears so thoroughly as to accuse me of misrepresenting Bentham and J. S. Mill. Doubtless this makes them happier, and hardly injures me: self-deception is, accordingly, a utilitarian obligation! More seriously: though Bentham and J. S. Mill denounced such practices as (they had convinced themselves) caused more pain to animals than pleasure to humans (how could they calculate it?), this would not satisfy ordinary standards of justice in the human realm. What of practices that cause considerable pain (say) to women, but still more pleasure to men? Must not a utilitarian allow, or even advocate them? Must not a decent regard for the 'rights of women' forbid them? How can such a prohibition be coaxed from the utilitarian pseudo-calculus? Similarly, must not a decent regard for our 'fellow-voyagers in the odyssey of evolution' render it unthinkable to hurt the non-human even if we do manage to convince ourselves that 'our' pleasure somehow exceeds their pain?

If the utilitarian calculus is a figment, and if decency within the human realm requires us not to use others merely for our own purposes without regard for their purposes, their proper modes of life, then the way is open to remember that there are other creatures than the human, that the terrestrial biosphere constitutes a genuine community, even if not all its members are self-consciously such (see pp. 31, 160). Our present human civilization seems dedicated to ruining that community, not even for the sake of humankind (many of whom now starve because of the corrupt farming practices we have preferred): 'by consuming meat, which wastes the grain that could have saved them, last year (1973) we ate the children of the Sahel, Ethiopia and Bangladesh. And we continue to eat them this year with undiminished appetite' (R. Dumont, quoted by S. George, *How the Other Half Dies* (Penguin 1976), p. 53). What mode of life we may develop when enough of us take seriously the real existence of our kindred, and our real membership of Earth's Household, is something I do not know. That there is a better way, and that we are obliged to seek it, I remain convinced.

If I were rewriting this book I should speak more softly, and allow more virtue (in particular) to Stoic and Thomist moralists. In this, perhaps, I show more worldly wisdom, as well as an improved acquaintance with the better side of those traditions, but I am not sure that the man I was ten years ago was entirely incorrect. Righteous indignation, as he knew (p. 191), is dangerous: is it better not to care, or not to make clear the extent to which one loathes the pretended arguments and iniquitous conclusions that were unchallenged in professional circles for too long? Once again: if I am wrong, refute me. If I am right, is it not up to all of us to change our ways?

September 1983

PREFACE

In composing this work I have sought to convince: that is, I have sought to face squarely any argument that friends or opponents have suggested, and have not relied on any single argument without striving to see what might follow if my first premises be denied. It may be that, as a result, my readers seeing so many bolt-holes stopped may paradoxically be convinced that there are as many more still open: the peril of philosophical debate is that it may seem doomed to perpetual motion. In this situation it may often be tempting to abandon any serious commitment to moral enquiry and relax upon the second-nature of contemporary custom.

Lest the central issue of my discourse be lost in the tangle of a hundred codicils, I therefore state it here: whatever else be true, whether there be gods or only atoms, whether men are significantly superior to non-human animals or no, whether there be a life to come or this poor accident be all, this at least cannot be true, that it is proper to be the cause of avoidable ill. There may be other moral principles than this, but this at least is dogma. And if this minimal principle be accepted, there is no other honest course than the immediate rejection of all flesh-foods and most bio-medical research.

The point, whatever its later complications, is a simple one, and the attempts of our hypocrisy to evade the issue provide a fascinating case-history of the corruption of our moral and philosophical sense. I say, and mean, 'of *our* moral sense'. That my manner must often pass from the academic to the polemic, and thence to the prophetic, is no sign of a clear conscience. 'Cursed is he that taketh reward to slay the innocent': so have we all.

There are many who deserve my gratitude for moral and philosophical support while I was working on this theme: I thank especially Graham and Athelyn Haydon and Gillian, my wife. Others have earned it rather against their will, by offering opposition or a gentle tolerance of my idiosyncracies. If I have travestied their careful offerings, I beg their pardons and also that they show me my mistake. And finally I thank most willingly the Delegates of the Oxford University Press for undertaking such a consciously outrageous publication.

April 1976

ACKNOWLEDGEMENTS

I would like to thank authors and publishers for permission to reproduce the following copyright works:

'The Animals' by Edwin Muir from his *Collected Poems* (London 1963). Copyright © 1960 by Willa Muir. Reprinted by permission of Faber and Faber Ltd and Oxford University Press, Inc. N.Y.

Extract from 'Memorial for a City' by W. H. Auden from his *Collected Shorter Poems 1927–57* (London 1966). Reprinted by permission of Faber and Faber Ltd and Random House, Inc. N.Y.

'Take one home for the Kiddies' by Philip Larkin, from *The Whitsun Weddings* (London 1964). Reprinted by permission of Faber and Faber Ltd.

'The Gallows' by Edward Thomas from his *Collected Poems* (London 1922). Reprinted by permission of Mrs. Myfanwy Thomas and Faber and Faber, Ltd.

'Student Taper' by James Stephens from his *Collected Poems* (1954). Reprinted by permission of Mrs. Iris Wise and the Macmillan Company of London and Basingstoke. Also © 1938 by Macmillan Publishing Co., Inc. N.Y.

Extract from 'Jubal and Tubal Cain' by Rudyard Kipling, from *Songs from Books*. Reprinted by permission of the Executors of the Estate of Mrs. George Bambridge and the Macmillan Company of London and Basingstoke and Doubleday and Co., Inc. N.Y.

CONTENTS

Eternal God! Maker of all
that have lived here, since the Man's fall;
the Rock of Ages! in whose shade
they live unseen, when here they fade.
Thou knew'st this paper, when it was
mere seed, and after that but grass;
before 'twas drest, or spun, and when
made linen, who did wear it then:
what were their lives, their thoughts and deeds
whether good corn, or fruitless weeds.
Thou knew'st this tree, when a green shade
cover'd it, since a cover made;
and where it flourished, grew, and spread,
as if it never should be dead.
Thou knew'st this harmless beast, when he
did live and feed by Thy decree
on each green thing; then slept (well-fed)
clothed with this skin, which now lies spread
a covering o'er this aged book,
which makes me wisely weep and look
on my own dust; mere dust it is,
but not so dry and clean as this.
Thou knew'st and saw'st them all and though
now scatter'd thus, dost know them so.
O knowing, glorious Spirit, when
Thou shalt restore trees, beasts and men,
when Thou shalt make all new again,
destroying only death and pain,
give him amongst Thy works a place,
who in them loved and sought Thy face.

    Henry Vaughan, 'The Book' (*Silex Scintillans*, 1655.)

I

INTRODUCTION

Academic and critical values

Academics are professionally committed to objectivity. That is, they are required by the ethical standards which define their craft to be ready to submit their most cherished doctrines to the scrutiny of their peers, and themselves to stand a little apart from these doctrines even in their own privacies. This is not to say either that they have no settled doctrines for which they might in other phases of their existence be prepared to suffer, or that academicity is separable from judgements of value. On the contrary, the academic tradition of critical enquiry embodies extremely rigorous standards, and any who do not accept those standards—which are admittedly rather difficult to number—are self-exiled from the academic community.

Nonetheless, it is difficult to escape the suspicion of treason to other and perhaps higher values if one pretends to debate with proper detachment questions which hardly seem open to debate. It may seem merely foolish to engage in philosophical, and insincere, discussion, say, of solipsism or of the existence of the material world. Not because these are empty questions, but because those who actually experience their full challenge, for whom they are living options, are unlikely to be assisted by the rhetoric of disputing philosophers. It seems more than foolish, rather it seems disgusting, to pretend to disinterest in certain moral affairs. We are committed to decency in argument, but there are other decencies than those of logic. 'By entering the arena of argument and counter-argument, of technical feasibility and tactics, of footnotes and citation, by accepting the presumption of legitimacy of debate on certain issues, one has already lost one's humanity.' (CHOMSKY p. 11.)

This tension between one's responsibilities as Christian, citizen, self-committing person and academic must always be a source of profound disquiet. Tertullian's question 'What interest can Jerusalem have in Athens?' was not a parochial one. The philosopher inhabits a world without maps, where any contest may go on for ever:

there are no fatal strokes in philosophy, nor any final answers. In
other forms of living it is otherwise. That there is a resolution of
this crux, and that it lies in the serious acceptance that academic
virtue is self-submission to a Truth and Beauty that is always greater
than any words of ours could tell, is a matter outside my present
brief.

Chomsky's difficulty, of course, lies in the temptation to fight
upon ground chosen by one's opponent rather than in the fundamental requirement of philosophical insincerity. But that temptation would not exist were it not assumed that no thesis can be
accepted that cannot be deduced from any premise one's opponent
cares to take. The philosophical duty of taking one's convictions
lightly all too often means that other, and less scrupulous, debaters
set their own limits to the argument. 'If we attempt to controvert
a vivisectionist by showing that the experiment he has performed
has not led to any useful result, you imply that if it had led to a
useful result you would consider his experiment justified. Now I
am not prepared to concede that position.' (SHAW p. 23.) The result
must be that works of philosophy, if they were read as sincere
searchings for truth or righteousness rather than as proper perform-
ances within the academic tradition, would richly deserve criminal
prosecution as incitements to riot and depravity. How can we
accept, or pretend to accept, theses which in ordinary life we would
consider worthy of the asylum, or the prison, or the hangman's
rope? There is, of course, the hope that by accepting them we shall
reveal their inner incoherence—but to confess to that hope may be
a betrayal of one's academic trust.

Perhaps the best we can do is simply to offer ourselves, our biases
and sincere beliefs, to the debate of reason, in the faith that the more
clearly and honestly the opposing theses are stated the easier it will
be to see where they collide, and where our hearts are given. I therefore confess, at the start, that my temptation is to modify Chomsky's
words and say:

'There may have been a time when our behaviour to the non-
human creation was a debatable matter. This time is long past.
... The war is simply an obscenity, a depraved act by weak and
miserable men, including all of us, who have allowed it to go
on and on with endless fury and destruction...' (after CHOMSKY
p. 12.)

I have deliberately retained the expression 'the war', for I believe it to pinpoint a major theme in our psychology, as I shall argue later. My concern is not with the events of that war, save as examples of what our assorted principles may imply, but with the principles, the presuppositions which make it difficult even for decent and intelligent men to grasp the real nature of what we regularly, and unblushingly, perform. I shall attempt to treat these principles with understanding, but my attempt must often be a failure: many of them I can no more countenance than could most likely readers of this book stomach the suggestion, let alone the bland presupposition, that it was permissible or even obligatory for 'Aryans' to torture Jewish children to death. I cannot seriously pretend to think that some of the principles I shall discuss are any worthier of rational acceptance than that, but I believe it incumbent upon us all to attempt to understand the world-view within which decent men have convinced themselves that they obey 'the decencies'. In understanding that we may at last understand ourselves.

In return for my effort I would ask that even my opponents should be prepared to listen to my case. The pursuit of truth and righteousness is not assisted either by zoophiles who forget that, despite the enormity of the war, there are also other wrongs to be remedied and other rights daily defended, or by the orthodox who appear to believe that all vegetarians and anti-vivisectionists are motivated by Manichaeanism and anti-human sentiment (as HÄRING I, 544 f.; III, 230 and 244; after AUGUSTINE (1) 35 f.). I repeat that I am not engaged in any pretence of standing above the fray: I am a committed crank and zoophile, and my hope is to convert my audience. If I am prepared to fight my prejudices to the extent of giving my enemies a hearing, though I may often fail to give them a fair hearing, I hope that they in their turn may do me the courtesy of not dismissing me with a casual sophism, and of forgiving any outbursts of rage and indignation which the vileness of the war may occasionally excite in me. I ask them to forgive: I do not ask them to forget.

All argument must take place within a tradition of agreed rationality and courtesy. Without such a tradition no argument can be more than a brawl, but it may sometimes be that the convictions and indignation of a participant are such that no mere modification or adaptation of the tradition seems likely to satisfy his demands. He finds that the whole heart of man is evil from the beginning, that the only hope of truth and righteousness is to leap beyond the tradition, to refuse proffered compromises, to insist on a new perfection. What traditionalists can say to such a man I do not know: to deny the possibility that he is right is in the end to deny the possibility of truth. The voice of honest indignation may not always be the voice of God, and most of us find our first escape from self in the service of a tradition, but it should be no part of a decent orthodoxy to believe that orthodoxy is inviolable. To be successful the prophet must appeal past the surface orthodoxy of his audience to the hidden, guilty, nebulous convictions of the heart. It is to these convictions that I hope to appeal, and by their standards that I aim to convict us all of sin. If you are not convinced I hope at least that you may be rid of that strange delusion of the orthodox that zoophiles cannot be serious, and must have some hidden and disreputable motive.

Statement of prejudice

I have already, for those with sharp enough ears, defined much of my own philosophical background: to do so in detail would be a task even more arduous than the treatment of the single, ramifying topic of my present concern. Most of my basic beliefs will be obvious from what follows, though I shall not restrict myself to arguments that I myself think relevant: I do not myself believe, for example, that we men are contingently evolved entities within a naturalistically describable universe that is inevitably heading for final catastrophe. I believe that the concept of the natural universe now popular amongst the most vocal segment of the educated public is a contingently evolved idea within a spiritually describable history. But to make this and this only an axiom of my argument would be very unprofitable, and very misleading. There is a story that a German vet insured good sanitation for a village's cows by pronouncing that 'if the windows were left open so that witches could go in and out freely, the demons would not enter into the cattle'. (E. P. EVANS (1) p. 9.) I am similarly prepared to accept for purposes of conviction premisses with which I cordially disagree, where these premisses are not themselves iniquitous. In this I follow tradition: Seneca's Neo-Pythagorean master, Sotion, was similarly more concerned with the practical conclusion than with the precise argument that led there (Seneca, *Epistulae* 108. 27 f.): to forswear flesh.

For the record, however, and with apologies for what must seem frivolity in the absence of a systematic exposition, I am an Aristote-

lian on Mondays and Wednesdays, a Pyrrhonian Sceptic on Tues-
days and Fridays, a Neo-Platonist on Thursdays and Saturdays and
worship in the local Episcopalian church on Sundays. And if I add
that I am strongly influenced by Mahayana Buddhism I hope that
you will not mistakenly infer that I despise the material world or
believe myself a member of some spiritual elect.

More helpfully, perhaps, I will mention some of the groups with
whom I am most out of sympathy. So much so that I find it unusu-
ally difficult to understand how they could mean what they say.

First of all, the Thomist or Roman tradition of moral philosophy,
for which animals are effectively things, owed no duties of justice,
charity or religion 'as neither are stocks and stones'. (RICKABY p.
248 f.) Rickaby's view is no more extreme than that expressed by
other such writers (see ADDIS AND ARNOLD, MURRAY), save that
he even denies that 'we are bound to any anxious care to make (the
pain we cause animals in sport or science) as little as possible'. Most
other writers do make a nominal genuflection in the direction of
'avoidance of unnecessary suffering'—a caveat recognized as effectively meaningless and irrelevant even by such orthodox as GURNEY
(1, pp. 210 f.).

> ' "I know", said Herr Stricker on one occasion, "that this experi-
> ment will seem cruel; but it is *necessary* that my hearers should
> have its effects impressed on their minds".' (LEFFINGWELL p.
> 50 f.; see SALT (1) p. 30 f.)

It is only fair to add that there have been zoophiles amongst
respected figures of the Roman church, including Cardinal Manning. Cardinal Heenan has expressed the kindlier, though I think
still inadequate view, that animals, who have no rights 'in their own
right', nonetheless have rights as God's creatures (AGIUS; see also
ROCHE(1)pp. 17 f., RAMBURES p. 148). I anticipate my later discussion by remarking that the view is inadequate not because animals
do have rights in their own right, but because nothing does, save
as God's creature. In general, however, the Thomist tradition has
helped to harden men's hearts and to substitute an enormous mass
of casuistical gallimaufry for the word of God, and for the common
sense of Aristotle.

My second antipathy is formed by such groups as the Research
Defence Society, which has had, historically, much support from
Thomist morality. BENDER p. 73, for example, contends that all

experiments are humane, all legal limitations should be abandoned, and that the vivisection of His creatures is pleasing to God.[1] Spokesmen for such groups will blandly announce that little suffering is caused to experimental animals, that the humane instincts of the experimentalists would restrain them from wanton experimentation, that the situation is far worse in countries which lack such restraints as the Act of 1876, that this Act works well 'because of the sympathetic understanding and cooperation of the authorities and the good sense and humanity of the licence-holders' (R.D.S.), and that 'there are certain anomalies and inconvenient provisions in the 1876 Act which might with benefit be altered'. In the face of the smugness and incoherence of such reports it is not surprising that some zoophiles have concluded with SHAW (p. 12) that 'when the witnesses begin by alleging that in the cause of science all the customary ethical obligations (which include the obligation to tell the truth) are suspended, what weight can any reasonable person give to their testimony?'[2] It is not surprising: it is also perhaps not entirely fair. Many, though certainly not all, experimentalists have been decent men after their lights. And whatever the inadequacies of the Act of 1876, which are many, this Act has served to restrain the worst excesses of experimentalists, though not without cost. The Act is so framed that prosecution is effectively impossible, and the Research Defence Society display a startling lack of integrity in basing their defence upon the lack of prosecutions under the Act. They would, and often do, condemn much non-British practice as barbarous: they show little awareness of the iniquity of nineteenth-century practice, and make no attempt to distinguish scientific from merely commercial exploitation of the experimentalists' victims (see RYDER). I shall touch on the main points of their defence later: my point here is to express my contempt and hatred of the use made of such assertions as that 'science is more concerned with evidence and logic than with emotion' (MCDONALD): from which naïve falsehood it follows, if anything, that scientists *qua* scientists have no right to take ethical decisions, still less to overbear those non-scientists who have the impudence to question their methods. 'Let anti-

---

[1] 'From which it follows that a "divine Father" is one who approvingly permits the stronger and craftier members of His family, for their own selfish ends, ruthlessly to torture the weak and the simple.' (KINGSFORD AND MAITLAND (1) p. 172).

[2] POWYS ((1) p. 263) cites William James as saying that 'vivisectors ought never to be trusted, either in what they are doing or in what they brag of doing'. Certainly the sort of utilitarianism which vivisectors sometimes invoke may often *demand* that they tell lies.

vivisectionists coddle themselves and leave men of good will to work in peace.' (Morali-Daninos: cited, approvingly, by LECOMTE p. 142.) Science is an activity of men, and is as subject as any other activity to moral debate: the substitution of expert, technical debate for moral debate is one of the most vicious of rhetorical fallacies. Experimentalists have a right, perhaps, to a fair hearing: they have no more right than other and more public figures first to conspire in concealing the evidence and then to denounce their critics for ignorance and injustice.[3] This is not to deny that some experimentalists, and such liberal zoophiles as are prepared to cooperate with them (e.g. RUSSELL AND BURCH; see HUME (1)), have in the short term done more to benefit laboratory animals than more radical zoophiles: the same, *mutatis mutandis*, may be said of certain concentration camp guards.

The third group whom I cordially detest are the transcendental humanists, whatever their mythology. When I am told that 'man's destiny is to be sole agent for the future evolution of this planet' (HUXLEY p. 165), or that 'man is come of age'[4] I am baffled that anyone could take such grandiose nonsense seriously and terrified at what might happen to a world wholly delivered to the tender mercies of such a god. Even less transcendentally inclined humanists, such as PASSMORE, are in my view warped by their adoration of humankind, to the extent that the non-human creation is regarded as one asset amongst many, to be weighed against other human wishes. The world which such men seem to themselves to inhabit is a purely human world—everything else being merely material for our scheming. One's ethical, as well as one's ontological framework is determined by what entities one is prepared to notice or take seriously. Admittedly, there is something extremely odd about the human species as it now exists—though not as it existed, so far as we can tell, for most of its past—and denials of this oddity, whatever its significance, by the more extreme of zoophiles may be merely obscurantist. But there seems no decent ground in reason or revelation to suppose that man is uniquely important or significant.

---

[3] 'No institution of value can forever shroud its activities in secrecy without the danger of abuses creeping in' (RULAND p. 376): still less a worthless institution.

[4] The sub-Hegelian gibberish of the R.D.S. journal *Conquest* (January 1970, quoted by RYDER pp. 146 f.) that 'on earth there is nothing great but man; in man there is nothing great but mind' demonstrates the extraordinary naivety of too much scientific moralism—scientists should really consult their philosophical colleagues before committing themselves to such inexpert fooling.

Certainly there seem no such grounds within the context of the naturalistic universe such transcendental humanists espouse. 'To the biologist this is not even the age of men ... it is literally the age of insects.' (ALLEE p. 199.) It may be true that all flesh shall be blessed in our seed: this seems no good reason to denigrate other flesh than ours. And I see no reason beyond caprice and sentiment for always preferring our own species if that promise is not true.

The topics and arguments at which I have glanced in describing my three most detested groups of moralists will be occupying me later. In brief, what I detest is humanism, which so far from being a humane and civilizing influence has, in the enormous area of man's relation to the non-human, served merely to darken counsel. It has perhaps helped to lessen man's persecution of his fellow-men, but at the expense of substituting yet more innocent and defenceless victims. Fantasists have occasionally imagined the nations of the earth united by extraterrestrial threats—the assumption being that we should unite against such a threat. This is not, in essence, a fantasy: humanism is precisely such an attempt to replace intra-human antagonisms by an imaginary war against the world of plants and animals, creating an *ersatz* reality within which we may come to feel ourselves at home, beleaguered by the threatening hordes of the animal creation. Humanism is a dangerous game: if we condemn acts of injustice and cruelty because their victims are human it may always be open to our enemy to deny the title of 'man' to his chosen victim—and what then can we say except to reiterate a superstitious respect for those we have taken to be our kin? If it is right to torture and kill for the sake of those for whom we feel a sense of kinship, why is it wrong for 'Aryans' to torture Jews? Kindly do not accuse me, as would that vile and unhappy man, AUSTIN (pp. 37 f.), of callousness to the sufferings of humanity. Doubtless man is born to trouble, but it is no more obviously true that we should not be concerned with non-human suffering until all men are perfectly happy than it is obviously true that we should give no money to Oxfam until there are no beggars in Britain. Much practical zoophily, in any case, involves no expense at all. Doubtless we must have priorities: what are our grounds for them, and what actions do they license?

Finally, let me rebut the charge of sentimentality. Most of us are liable, and indeed eager, to live our lives in willing ignorance of what is done, often in our name, to non-human animals. We cloak our actions and the actions of our agents with fine-sounding names, pretending that our food-animals are grateful to us for eating them (see SALT (1) pp. 41 f.; (2) pp. 70 f.), that our experimental animals are overjoyed at the prospect of sacrificing themselves for the good of humanity: 'Today he basks in the glow of his memories among the peaceful surroundings of the National Zoological Park in Washington: astronaut Ham, the space chimpanzee.' (American Acro-Medical Research Laboratory: quoted by DEWAR p. 29.)

'Can we doubt', asked SALT ((1) p. 73) ironically, 'that the victims themselves, if once they could realise the noble object of their martyrdom, would vie with each other in rushing eagerly on the knife?' William James, I fear, had already answered 'yes': 'all these diabolical-seeming events are often controlled by human intentions with which . . . all that is heroic in [the dog] would religiously acquiesce'. (JAMES (1) p. 58.) But he at least did not suppose that the dog *did* acquiesce.

Everything is, of course, perfectly all right: 'we wish to believe that all is well with the existing system and that its only critics are cranks. We have no wish even to listen to the evidence.' (Dowding: *Hansard* 14 October 1952.) I suggest that any of my readers who are under this happy delusion take steps to educate themselves. When they have done so, and have recovered from their nausea, they may understand why zoophiles become a little impatient with 'the noodles who can give no wiser reason for the infliction of suffering on animals than that it "is better for the animals themselves", the flesh-eaters who labour under the pious belief that animals were "sent" us as food, the silly women who imagine that the corpse of a bird is a becoming article of headgear'. (SALT (1) p. 89; on the history of the corpse-fashion see DOUGHTY.)

Certainly, sentimentality is our enemy: the inability to see the real, suffering animal for a haze of aestheticism, misplaced piety and emotional projections. The inability, or rather the unwillingness: to see the reality is to stand defenceless before the Judge. There is no shortage of evidence; you need only read the morning papers with attention and consider what realities are hidden behind the news and the advertisements (see also HUTCHINGS AND CAVER; VYVYAN (2); HARRISON; RYDER; GODLOVITCH AND HARRIS).

If, on the other hand, 'sentimentality' means merely a concern for the well-being of my fellow-creatures and an unwillingness to torture them for my own satisfaction, whether of greed or sport or curiosity or extravagance, then I willingly subscribe to it. And since my concern is one with the most impressive part of our ethical tradition I think it is up to my opponents to prove me in error.

'"In that day", said the Lord God to and through the prophet Hosea, "will I make a covenant for them with the beasts of the field and with the fowls of heaven and with the creeping things of the ground: and I will break the bow and the sword and the battle out of the land, and make them to lie down safely."' (Hosea 2:18, see Isaiah 65:25; PRIMATT pp. 78f.)[5]

The days of that covenant are doubtless far hence; it seems to me a nobler vision than the ancient heresy of man as god. Shelley went further, in speaking of the coming splendour:

> No longer now
> he slays the lamb that looks him in the face,
> and horribly devours his mangled flesh,
> which, still avenging Nature's broken law,
> kindled all putrid humours in his frame...
> All things are void of terror: Man has lost
> his terrible prerogative, and stands
> an equal amid equals. (*Queen Mab*, 8. 211-18.)

And even for Pope 'man's prerogative' was once 'to rule, but spare' (POPE 3. 160: p. 109). If we are equals, what shall we say to them? If we are gods, or as gods, to the non-human animals, 'we are obliged by the same tenure to be their guardians and benefactors'. (HARTLEY 1, 415.)

'The fear and dread of you shall fall upon all wild animals upon earth, on all birds of heaven, on everything that moves upon the ground, and all fish in the sea; they are given into your hands.' (Genesis 9:2.)

---

[5] The Lord Christ's being 'with the wild beasts' in the wilderness (Mark 1:12f.) refers to this restoration of paradise (see JEREMIAS (1) pp. 69f.). SCHAPIRO has discussed the later use of this motif, suggesting that it was overlaid by the treatment of beasts as 'the enemy'. The Lord who preached, in opposition to the Rabbinic tradition of His day, that God's care extended even to sparrows (Matthew 10:29f.; JEREMIAS (1) p. 182) has been ill served by His disciples. The angels of the little ones stand by the throne of God (Matthew 18:10): what was last, shall be first (Luke 13:30). We cannot say that we have not been warned.

As Barth remarks 'it is surely obvious that the possession of such powers confers upon man a very definite responsibility towards non-human life.' (BARTH III pt. 4 p. 350.) It is also obvious that we have abused our powers and neglected our responsibilities, and the cry of our victims goes up before the Bull of the Zoroastrians in the court of heaven, and before the Lamb (ZEND-AVESTA II, p. 245; PORPHYRY (1) III, 16; MARTINENGO-CESARESCO pp. 144 f.). 'It is the pity of God that is bound upon your tables; it is the justice of God that lies helpless under your racks. But it will be the vengeance of God that will descend upon your children's children...' (POWYS (1) p. 205.) And again: 'What we men run a risk of being damned for is our barbarity to those creatures who have been given into our complete dominion, and for our conduct to whom we shall be fearfully answerable.' (HELPS p. 117.) If you think I exaggerate the wrong, you must either be ignorant or at odds with my principles. Your ignorance you must correct yourself, and cloak the truth no longer with sentiment and fantasies of cruel necessity.

Salt's puzzle

I shall conclude my introduction with a simple puzzle. Henry SALT ((1) pp. 5 f.) believed that the laws offering protection against cruelty, even against cruel owners, amounted to giving or recognizing animals' *rights*. RITCHIE (pp. 107 f.) contended that as laws protecting, for example, ancient monuments, do not assign rights to the monuments, but rather remove them from the owners, so also animals have no rights in law, although it is admittedly wrong to mistreat them. Salt seems to have misunderstood this argument (see SALT (3)), and Ritchie is generally thought to have won (as PASSMORE p. 116). Technically I think he did, but Salt's exasperated response that the *reasons* for these laws are quite different is entirely apt. The mere fact of legal protection implies nothing about the rights of the thing protected, but Salt's point was rather that the laws had been passed because animals, or some animals, were seen to be deserving of protection. We protect ancient monuments because they are part of our heritage; we similarly protect, on some views, certain rare species of plant or animal. But no-one can claim that the individual Fido, Hannibal or Jemima is part of our national heritage. Nor, indeed, is there anything in law to prevent my killing my pet: I *am* barred from torturing it—unless I have a licence from the Home Office or a commercial interest.

'If one person is unkind to an animal it is considered to be cruelty, but where a lot of people are unkind to a lot of animals, especially in the name of commerce, the cruelty is condoned, and, once large sums of money are at stake, will be defended to the last by otherwise intelligent people.' (HARRISON p. 144.)

I am not allowed to torture my pet, nor even to neglect it. Why not? It's mine isn't it? 'You bought the animal with your money, it is true, and he is your property ... You could not purchase the right to use him with cruelty and injustice. Of whom could you purchase such a right? Who could make such a conveyance?' (LAWRENCE; NICHOLSON p. 92.)

Lawrence introduced the concept of *ius animale*, the recognition that animals could be and were being *wronged*, and it was in part by his influence that the protective laws were eventually made. But there were other supporters with other ideas, such that COBBETT (pp. 626 f.) was moved to join with Windham (see TURNER pp. 110 f.) against those who wished to interfere with the pleasures of the poor. The 1833 Act against bear-baiting was particularly moralistic, though the 1835 Act restricts its principle to an attack on cruelty as such. Whewell's judgement is typical of this school: these laws are laws of manners, to teach virtue, as the ancients had supposed the office of all law: 'Such Laws are enacted to prevent what is repugnant to the general feeling of the English public ... They cannot give Rights to creatures which are not Persons.' (WHEWELL p. 594; see p. 494, and pp. 592 ff.) We might equally, he says, have laws against lying, as particularly shocking to the truthful. NICHOLSON (p. 17) comments further that 'we should have to fine and imprison a man for wasting his own money or smashing his own window—lest by and by (in a moment when his ideas of "meum" and "tuum" had got muddled) he might waste the money or smash the windows of other people'.

There is the puzzle. Either those laws, from Martin's Act of 1822 to modern legislation against gin-traps and spring-traps, recognize that animals can be wronged or else they are laws of manners, dealing with the vice or virtue of the state's citizens. Either the evil they seek to prevent is the suffering of animals, as HART supposes that he supposes (p. 34),[6] or it is the moral corruption of human beings.

---

[6] For if Hart truly believed that avoidable suffering should be avoided, and the law invoked to insure this, he would be an advocate of vegetarianism: in fact he plainly disapproves not

If it is the latter we must decide whether we are willing to retain such illiberal laws at the price of abandoning any objection of principle to further moralistic legislation. If it is the former, if animals are wronged—a wrong is committed—when they are treated with cruelty or negligence, how can we pretend to excuse the present fate of those creatures tortured for their flesh, their fur, our pleasure, our convenience? My own opinion, indeed, is that a community has as much right to protect its moral as its material heritage, but most modern humanists seem to disagree. In that case 'if these laws have not been founded on a silent recognition (that *some* animals have at least *some* rights), they are unwarrantable curbs on the rights of men'. (NICHOLSON p. 16.)

And if some animals have some rights, even of this negative sort, to be spared wanton ill-treatment, on what grounds do we deny them other rights, to life and happiness within their kind? On what grounds can other animals be fair game?

of the infliction of *unnecessary* suffering, but of suffering inflicted in the course of human practices of which he disapproves for other reasons.

II

MAN'S PREROGATIVES

Salt restated

In restating Salt's puzzle I may seem to have entered upon a dialectical maze: for there has been no fully satisfying account even of human rights, let alone animal. All sorts of problems might arise: men can waive their rights, but animals either cannot do so or at least cannot be assumed to have done so; some human rights at least are positive, embodying the rightfulness of some claim upon society's resources, yet animals, perhaps, can make no such claims.[1] If animals have rights that can be disregarded, are they not disregarded also by other non-human animals, and do we not therefore have a duty to protect each creature's rights against all comers? And where do such *rights* lie in the relation of prey and predator? One law for the lion and the ox is oppression, and to save the ox may be to affront the lion. To the extent that these queries embody real issues I shall attempt to deal with them in what follows, but it is as well to remember that they may too easily be mere devices to distract attention from the main point. I therefore restate that point.

There are laws to protect animals even against their owners, laws which some judges at least have interpreted as according rights to the animals (TRIBE p. 1342). It may be, however, that better legal opinion would hesitate to speak of *rights* in this context, or would wish to make some subtle distinction between different varieties of rights. Such distinctions may be useful, but they do not contradict the simple claim that it is *wrong* to treat animals badly: *wrong*, not because of some consequent damage to the human psyche (though such damage may indeed be grave) but for the very same reasons

---

[1] Though Graham Haydon has remarked to me that if the right to an education is founded upon the possession of certain educable capacities it seems to follow that chimpanzees, dolphins *et al.* have a right to an education. It also seems likely that experimental animals in particular have a claim in natural justice to care and protection at society's expense. An earlier version of this chapter was read to a history of ideas seminar in the University of Glasgow, and owes much to the criticisms and suggestions of David Bell, Paul Jeffreys-Powell, Dudley Knowles, Andrew Lockyer, Richard Tur and others.

that it is wrong to treat human beings badly. Animals can be
wronged, *injured*, not merely metaphorically but in fact. The very
fact that we do speak of *injuring* animals, whereas we can only
damage the inanimate, is a symptom of our recognition that animals
are proper objects of moral concern. If we are mistaken in this, as
Thomists and Kantians must suppose, and our relations with animals are without moral significance, then the protective laws are
indeed merely laws of manners. If on the other hand Thomists and
Kantians are merely the mistaken heirs of Stoic thought, and animals *are* moral objects, how can we excuse our treatment of them?

Justice and mercy

The Stoics, for whom non-human animals were defined by
extrinsic teleology, believed that plants were for animals, and animals for men (Cicero, *De Natura Deorum* II 14, 37), following in
this a loose remark of Aristotle (*Politics* 1256b17: see CLARK p. 46).
Pigs were locomotive meals, with souls in lieu of salt (PORPHYRY
(1) III 20). As such, being dependent entities without even lives
of their own, they assuredly had no rights. Beasts have no share
in reason; beasts are not persons; beasts cannot be members of our
community (see Cicero, *De Officiis* I 50-1) It is this tradition to
which AUGUSTINE ((2) I 19) appeals in denouncing vegetarianism,
and which AQUINAS consolidated as the main line of Roman doctrine (*Summa* Ia 2ae q102 art 6 ad 8). Animals are subject to and
mere instruments of Man. Only those things can have rights which
can have duties 'for right and duty are correlative terms'. (ADDIS
AND ARNOLD; see RITCHIE p. 108.) Only those creatures which
can lay claim to property or to actions can be allowed to have any
rights. 'Brutes are things in our regard ... They exist for us, not
for themselves.' (RICKABY pp. 244 f.) In fairness of a sort to Rickaby
I should add that he also declares that everyone is a thing to the
Creator, apparently because we can make no claim against Him.
We can only hope that God treats His things better than we do ours,
and wonder how one thing can own another (for to be able to 'own'
is to have admitted rights).

The Stoic tradition also appears among non-Thomist philosophers. Kantian ethics decree that we should choose our acts from
the point of view of those who can be supposed makers of laws of
action. (KANT (1) 438; (2) pp. 239 f.) Beasts, being irrational, cannot
be ends-in-themselves: 'they are merely means to an end. ... The

end is Man'—a doctrine which Paton, being a humane man, does his best to alleviate, and over which even Kant seems to have wavered (BROADIE AND PYBUS). Contractual theorists of a Rawlsian type are also variously convinced that beasts, being unable to enter into contracts with us, cannot have rights: 'it does seem that we are not required to give strict justice to creatures lacking the capacity (for a sense of justice)' (RAWLS p. 512). RICHARDS attempts a modification of this (pp. 182 f.), suggesting that 'the original contractors' whom Rawls envisages as theoretical arbiters of justice would wish to avoid possible mental misgivings if they should turn out to like animals, and also to avoid cultivating dispositions towards cruelty. By a strange coincidence this is very much the attitude of Thomist orthodoxy in its kindlier phases. GRICE (pp. 147 f.) firmly denies all rights not only to animals, but also to children, lunatics, embryos, and our posterity, on the familiar grounds that they are in no position to enter into contracts with us. It is not in our interests that they should—and Grice seems very sure that he knows who *we* are. I do not believe that these exclusions strictly follow even from his principles, for to speak of 'children', 'embryos' or 'lunatics' as creatures of a distinct kind from human beings is a clear case of pseudo-speciation (see LORENZ (1) pp. 48 f.). One might as well conclude that 'sleeping men' have no rights, for they too are in no position to enter into contracts with us: certainly they have potentials, realizable on condition of waking up—children must *grow* up. It is nonetheless entertaining to find a philosopher who is willing to accept the obvious moral of Roman law, that children have no rights against their parents, although he attempts to lessen the practical effect by an extraordinary piece of special pleading to the effect that other adults might have an interest in the welfare of other people's children.

Humane men, of course, are always eager to mitigate the viler effects of their suggested principles, or even to suggest that their principles, properly understood, are of better effect than is at first supposed. RICKABY himself declares (p. 250) that 'a sedulous observance of the rights and claims of other men, a mastery over one's own passions, and a reverence for the Creator, give the best assurance of a wise and humane treatment of the lower animals'. I do not agree, nor do I know why he is concerned to believe that this is so, if 'brutes are *things* in our regard'. But I would not deny that men are often better, or worse, than their principles, and that kindliness is always creeping into the most unlikely hearts. I do not myself think that such evanescent sentiments are enough: even the Roman populace was so impressed by the dignity and intelligence of Pompey's elephants that they found the spectacle of their torment vile (Cicero *ad Fam.* VII 1.3; Pliny *N.H* 8.21 : 55 B.C.).[2]

But suppose for a moment that all this is so: that animals, and children, and the old, the sick, the defenceless and our posterity have no rights at all. Are we, or Grice, or Thomists ready to assert that we may decently do as we please with them? If they should come to man's estate they may justly resent our conduct when they lay at our mercy. Lawyers under the pressure of liberal hypocrisy may invent such legal fictions as allow a man to sue for pre-natal injuries which, had they been more effective, would have been no wrong at all—pretending that only that is *injury* which is rationally known as such. But are we prepared to apply such principles throughout? Let us say such creatures have no rights, and wait upon our mercy: shall we not give it them? GALSWORTHY was content if animals should be as well treated as children or as imbeciles, and 'rights' reserved for some more technical discourse: 'Rights or no rights I care not ... Once admit that *we* have the right to inflict unnecessary suffering, and you have destroyed the very basis of human society, as we know it in this age' (pp. 59 f.). Zoophiles have generally held to talk of *rights*, for they supposed that it was not charity but bare justice that was owed the animals we have enslaved, and tortured, and slain. But suppose that we do not owe them justice: yet do we owe them mercy. PLUTARCH ((3) Cato 4.5) rightly insists that a good man cares for creatures grown old and sick in his service. Suppose that neither animals nor our posterity have any claim in justice upon us: what claim have we on them?

The Stoic tradition has always had its opponents, and Stoics have perpetually been stepping down from their high principles to arguments of the most blatant sophistry and self-interest to deal with them. The plaint 'what about plants, then?' reiterated by AUGUSTINE ((2) I 19) is plainly a Stoic slogan—it is remarkable how sympathetic the orthodox become to tomatoes when asked how they excuse the torments to which we put a veal-calf—mentioned and answered by PORPHYRY ((1) I 4, 18; II 13). Similarly the plaint 'what would happen to civilization?' As PLUTARCH commented in works which orthodox editors persist in regarding as *jeux d'esprit*,

[2] Cicero says that people felt that there was a sort of *societas* between men and elephants.

foibles of early youth, life would not come to an end if we were
to forswear our platters of fish, our *paté de foie gras*, mincemeat and
kid's flesh ((1) 964d ff.).

> 'It has been said that the world could not have either gold, sugar
> or coals but at the expense of human blood and liberty. The world
> in that case ought not to have either gold, sugar or coals. ... But
> the assertion was fallacious and unfounded.' (LAWRENCE:
> NICHOLSON p. 91.)

And the same, *mutatis mutandis*, is true of the supply of food, clothing, perfume, entertainment and medical knowledge, which is now
at the expense of animal blood and liberty. To those who speak of
necessity, I only say 'there is none'.

The more interesting ethical dispute, however, lies at a higher
level. On the one hand are those who deny reason to brutes and
therefore deny them rights. On the other, those who query one
premise or another of the implied syllogism. PLUTARCH ((1) 962e;
see PORPHYRY (1) III 23) observes that we do not speak of a tree's
being more intelligent than a bush, whereas similar judgements on
brutes may be entirely apt. To argue that they have no reason
because men have more is like arguing that partridges cannot be
said to fly, because hawks fly higher (PORPHYRY (1) III 8). Even
if we grant that there is a hierarchy of ability, and allow the ancient
principle of hierarchic sovereignty—which egalitarians, as Thomas
TAYLOR pointed out with a subtler irony than is commonly supposed (e.g. by PASSMORE p. 115),[3] should be slow to admit—still
that hierarchy should not be a tyranny.

> 'We confess [Man] is a tall creature and has mighty privileges.'
> (DEAN pp. 76 f.)
> 'But when a man boasts of the dignity of his nature, and the ad-
> vantages of his station, and from thence infers his right of oppres-
> sion of his inferiors, he exhibits his folly as well as his malice.'
> (PRIMATT p. 22; see NEMESIUS I 70.)

AUSTIN, of course, did not agree:

> 'Animals should be treated with personal indifference; they
> should not be petted, they should not be ill-treated. It should

---

[3] Taylor's work is thought a mere parody of Paine and Wollstonecraft, but he translated
Porphyry with approval and is clearly uneasy about the exploitation of our brothers. His
point is simultaneously an assertion of the principle of hierarchy and a reminder that that
principle does not license tyranny.

always be remembered that they are our slaves, not our equals, and for this reason it is well to keep up such practices as hunting and fishing, driving and riding, merely to demonstrate in a practical way man's dominion over the brutes.' (p. 32.)

Austin's psychological state will engross me later: it leads him (p. 36) even to the point of accepting, despite his profession of Christianity, that Thrasymachus was right to define justice as the interest of the stronger. We may note NICHOLSON's remark that he knows of 'no theory of right and wrong, except might is right, which would not equally allow a proof of animals' rights'. (p. x.) I mention Austin now to make clear why zoophiles sometimes speak so fiercely. The denial of rights to animals is in practice to leave them defenceless against man's greed: Ritchie's claim to believe it wrong to 'mistreat' them is the merest hypocrisy.

Similarly SCHOPENHAUER: 'Spinoza's contempt for animals, as mere things for our use, and declared by him to be without rights, is thoroughly Jewish, and in conjunction with pantheism is at the same time absurd and abominable.' (11, p. 645; see SPINOZA IV app. c27.)

In fact it is not Jewish at all, any more than it is a relic of Neo-Platonism as C. W. HUME supposes ((2) and (3)). Neither Jews nor Platonists could feel contempt for brutes, for whose sake God spared Nineveh (Jonah 4:11) and with whom He made his covenants as much as with the children of men. It is the fact that concern for our animal cousins has so often had a Neo-Platonic background that impels the ignorant to equate zoophily with Gnosticism or Manichaeanism (which Plotinus, incidentally, attacked as fiercely as did Augustine).[4] Though it must be admitted that our attitude to 'the beast within' has influenced our treatment of the 'beast without' (see MIDGLEY), and that Iamblichus's urge to defend and explicate animal sacrifice led him to deny souls, and moral significance, to brutes: both are significant corruptions.

There has been a tradition of concern for animals, of belief that there are bars against our mistreatment of them which are of much

---

[4] I emphasize that I have not forsworn flesh because I think 'the flesh' is evil or because I feel contaminated by its passing my lips. But I really have nothing to say to those who express their love and respect for God's creation by enslaving, torturing and killing His creatures, and then have the impudence to accuse me of despising those same creatures.

the same kind as those bars against our mistreatment of our fellow men: a tradition more widespread, perhaps, among those nations influenced by Hindu or by Buddhist thought (whose record is somewhat marred by doublethink: see KIPLING; FÜRER-HAIMENDORF), but one not unknown even in the European sub-continent. In the Middle Ages of Europe it was not necessary to be wilfully ill-intentioned to be thought worthy of punishment or reciprocal injury (as RITCHIE p. 109 has apparently forgotten). We have abandoned this principle, at least in theory, as far as it touches human beings. We continue to hold powers of life and death over the non-human: by taking away the *name* of punishment, we have made the *thing* infinite. Liberal zoophiles (e.g. BROWN p. 6) tend to speak as if such mediaeval practice was inhumane: they forget its corollary, that animals were also thought to deserve fair trial. 'Even rats have a right of counsel.' (B. Chassenée at Autun in the sixteenth century: E. P. EVANS (1) pp. 18 f.) Certainly they could not appear to put their own case: no more can children, or (once upon a time) could women. But their interests were also to be weighed: a Savoy case of 1587 concluded with the ceding of pasture-land to its native flies (MARTINENGO-CESARESCO pp. 348 f.). Doubtless RULAND is right to declare that the 'errors' of animals deserve pity more than punishment (pp. 367 f.), but at least those who condemned might also acquit, and those who claimed might also cede possession. St. Kevin is reported to have rejected a brand new monastery offered him by an angel of God with the words, 'I have no wish that the creatures of God should be troubled because of me.' (WADDELL p. 136; see ROCHE (2).) This attitude has been overwhelmed by Stoicising philosophers at the public level, but many men still find it altogether natural to think of animals' interests as worthy of respect. *Because* they have interests, they have rights (NELSON; see GODLOVITCH AND HARRIS).[5]

'Wild nuts are crucial to the survival of many wild birds and animals, who have just as much right to them, and considerably more need!' (MABEY p. 29: Mabey is certainly not a consistent zoo-

[5] PASSMORE (p. 116) contends that they do not have interests in any sense that implies their having rights—they have no *legal* interests. But this is to mistake the argument. They have needs and things which advantage them and wishes for those things. It is not a logical but an ethical truism that if a creature benefits from having, and suffers from not having something, it has to that extent a claim upon that thing. Certainly a creature may have wants without having wishes: it is also certain that mammals, birds, squids, reptiles and fish (and probably others) have both.

phile.) As *much* right: if any have a right to nuts wild animals do. The success of Adams's *Watership Down* is a slight sign that people are, however inadequately, inclined to be uneasy at the exercise of man's dominion.

It was to this background of uneasy respect that the major British zoophiles have appealed. SALT wished simply to declare that 'if man, as a sentient and intelligent being, should be exempt from all avoidable suffering, it follows that other beings who are also sentient and intelligent, though in a lower degree, should have, in lower degree, the same exemption.' ((1) p. 95; see (4).)

He linked this thesis to Utilitarian doctrine as stated by Bentham: 'The question is not, can they *reason*? nor, Can they *talk*? but, Can they *suffer*?' (BENTHAM p. 310 n.) This introduction of the hedonistic calculus raises problems that are not peculiar to the present topic, and which I shall defer, but it serves once again to reveal why Salt found Ritchie so irritating. What is wrong with treating men in certain ways? What can it be that is wrong which would not also, and for the same reasons, be wrong (even if *less* wrong) in inflicting such treatment on non-human animals? Certainly it is no oppression not to grant bears political liberty (HARE p. 223): it cannot in reason follow, as RICHARDS apparently believes (p. 326 n.) that it is no oppression needlessly to deprive bears of things they actually want, or inflict upon them disabilities and conditions which they actually find painful. That animals have other, or fewer, or weaker desires than men (if they do) cannot in reason be a ground for disregarding the ones they have. Similarly it is no injury, and therefore no injustice, to cut up a sponge: it *is* an injury to cut up a cat. All Ritchie, and those who have followed him, would reiterate to this was that animals, not being persons, could have no rights. If this is a statement of positive law, according to which corporations are persons if we choose to say so and human embryos are not, it is the merest irrelevance, for it simply declares that animals, having no rights in law, have no rights in law (which is, in any case, questionable). If it announces some absolute metaphysical distinction between the human and the non-human (which I shall discuss later), it is still irrelevant: maybe it is wrong to accord *personal* respect to animals (or children), to hold them responsible for their actions and allow that they can even waive their own best interests (maybe: though it is in fact an insulting error to suppose that animals—or even children—are significantly childish), but it does not follow that animals deserve no respect at all—those that are weak deserve our especial care.

What is at issue here? In part, there is a real worry about adopting any form of utilitarianism, and Salt himself was unwilling to adopt it wholeheartedly. Utilitarian theory is notoriously ill-suited to a defence of *rights* which are precisely the individual's defence against factitious calculations of the greater good. Utilitarians deserve credit for espousing the cause of animals, but it is by a dishonest application of utilitarian rules that we commonly defend our behaviour to the non-human.[6] Zoophiles should be wary of such associations, and Salt was merely using the Benthamite thesis as a simple introduction to what he felt to be obvious, namely that it was wrong to multiply suffering beyond necessity, wrong to kill beyond necessity, and that torturing, killing, imprisoning and overworking animals were alike acts of injustice. Stoicists have found the opposite equally obvious: only persons have rights.[7] That is to say, only rational beings of our own kind present any bar to our self-interest as individuals, nations or professional groups—though what this bar may be has yet received no coherent or convincing answer.

Reason, community and tacit understanding

Justice can hold only between individuals who can share and recognize each other as sharing certain values of fair-dealing. Justice only holds in fact where the individuals in fact live up to their shared values; where they do not do so, they ought to, and any observers of recognized authority may assist in bringing justice to pass. Greeks dealing with barbarians, and Europeans dealing with natives have frequently revealed by their actions that they do not believe their opposite numbers to be members of such a potentially contracting community. In betraying any explicit oaths or implicit debts of gratitude they have shown themselves less honourable than their victims. Convinced, or willing to be convinced, that their victims do not understand or appreciate honour, truth-telling, promising they have anticipated what would be treachery in their equals by

[6] NOZICK (p. 35) simultaneously demonstrates the absurdity of such calculations and the moral necessity of vegetarianism.

[7] That is, only those with duties have rights, as BRADLEY (pp. 31–2) thought obvious—though he suspected that beasts might reasonably be thought moral beings, with both. Like MACIVER, I think it entirely unobvious that only 'responsible' beings should have their needs and feelings considered.

what must always seem, and be, treachery in the eyes of their victims.[8] An Australian judge recently ruled that aborigines had no
claim on their ancestral land because they had lacked a European
concept of land-ownership—the proof being that they had *welcomed*
traders and missionaries within their seeming-territory (my thanks
to Philip Lewis for this story). These historical betrayals should,
I think, make us very nervous when one group of living creatures
declares another to be wholly devoid of any understanding. The
time may come when accounts of dealings with the dolphin, for
example (on intelligence of cetacea see LILLY (1); BATESON pp.
334 f., FICHTELIUS AND SJOLANDER), will be, most properly, the
object of horrified stupefaction.

But it may be true that non-human animals are incapable of
understanding or abiding by the common values of humanity. If
this is so, the Stoics say, there is no possibility of justice between
man and animal (see Cicero, *De Officiis* I 50–1; BALDRY p. 185).

> 'The man who breaks a cat's back breaks a cat's back; the man
> who breaks a man's back, breaks an implied treaty. The tyrant
> to animals is a tyrant. The tyrant to men is a traitor. Nay, he
> is a rebel, for man is royal.' (G. K. Chesterton: cited by SALT
> (1) pp. 110 f.)

Tyranny towards men is injustice, for there is a possible state of
justice in which such acts are outlawed. Tyranny towards animals
is not injustice, for no such covenant could be made with the con-
fessedly irrational. Injustice is a breaking of an implied treaty,
whether that treaty was historically concluded, or whether it is a
mere device of thought. There can be justice only where there can
be friendship, and friendship only where there can be a shared
understanding (Aristotle, *Nicomachean Ethics* 8.1161b).

Our eagerness to believe the worst of beasts' morals, as it were,
is a matter of great significance, to which I shall return (see MIDG-
LEY). ROCHE, for example, speaks of 'the general demoralisation
or disorder of the animals, their ferocity, their predatory instincts'
(1) p. 28). Such creatures do not merely stand outside justice, but
are justly to be attacked: the just war against beasts is a familiar
thought (Isocrates, *Panathenaicus* 163; PORPHYRY (1) I 14; see also

---

[8] As Maitland remarked: 'Our rule of conduct is to be, not our own sense of right and
wrong, but the sense of right and wrong we ascribe to those with whom we happen to be
dealing.' (KINGSFORD AND MAITLAND p. 171.)

Plato *Protagoras* 322b3), and a very revealing one, which still appears in such slogans as 'man's animal enemies'.

> 'Because a wolf will seize upon a man is a man therefore warranted to whip a pig to death? ... What is this but to say that cruelty in Britain is no sin because there are wild tigers in India?' (PRI-MATT pp. 30 and 36.)

In fact, there seem excellent reasons for believing that animals live lives that are by no means unstructured, that they spare the defeated and even assist the endangered (LORENZ (2); HOWARD pp. 74 f. and 149 f.).[9] Doubtless this is all a matter of instinct, not the true self-determination of the ethical being, though I do not know why we are so sure. But this is to say, as PLUTARCH remarked ((1) 489 f.), that beasts are virtuous without effort, that in some measure they enjoy that condition which we regret and pray for when the Lord shall write His covenant in our hearts. We are their 'superiors' because we can make mistakes—and when *they* do, that is their stupidity. As Primatt said, beasts very seldom hurt us, at least in comparison with the amount we hurt them: 'One would be almost tempted to suppose that the brutes had combined in one general scheme of benevolence to teach mankind lessons of mercy and meekness by their own forbearance and long-suffering.' (PRIMATT pp. 29 f.; see TRYON p. 127.) Though I hesitate to emphasize this point—such an attitude to the non-human is enshrined for the Christian West in the figure of the lamb (once *our* symbolic beast par excellence: see below pp. 124 f.), and the lamb's supposed long-sufferingness and symbolic associations has reconciled too many to his slaughter.

The lamb thy riot dooms to bleed today,
had he thy reason, would he skip and play? (POPE I. 81: p. 23.)

We cannot even be certain that a man-animal community of interests and values is impossible. The shared interests of shepherd and sheep-dog are an obvious example, and so is the sidelong friendship of human and domestic cat, but there are even stranger apparent compacts. The stories of the saints are full of agreements between saint and beast, as Rose of Lima and her choruses of mosquitoes

---

[9] Darwin somewhere mentions a blind pelican's being fed by other pelicans (and see CAR-RIGHAR p. 125 on gibbons' feeding an elderly and arthritic gibbon). MAIMONIDES 3.48 too observed that a mother's love for her children is no product of a uniquely human reason. He concluded from this that one should not kill calves *in the presence of* their mothers.

(ROCHE (2) p. 61). Doubtless these are mere apocrypha. There is an extremely amusing account by BOONE (pp. 124 f.) of how, goaded to tearful exasperation by the ants who had occupied his house and supper, he addressed them 'gentleman to gentleman' to offer a compact of mutual non-interference, stormed off to visit the cinema, feeling a complete idiot, and returned to find a house entirely empty of ants. He was never again invaded. WEIL, a less flamboyant American, also records (p. 132) that he has never again been troubled by bees since he eliminated his negative feelings about them (see also NIALL p. 140). For those who relish the investigation of chemical correlates it seems perfectly possible that glandular effusions of the same sort that govern intra-species behaviour may also provide for inter-specific relationships. Those who are not greatly concerned with the pursuit of such correspondences may be content to note that we may have real, even if puzzled, friendships and associations with creatures not of our species.

Why, after all, should we find the principle at all surprising? I do not deny that some of the recorded examples of its action are pretty surprising, but the principle itself is entirely obvious. Justice, say the Stoics, is possible only between those who share values. But the rational understanding of those values, on which Stoics place such emphasis, is, as Socrates observed long ago, entirely beyond most of us (see PORPHYRY (1) III 2 f.).[10] We forget this fact in this context because we are always comparing our ignorant conception of animal being with an overdrawn picture of a very cultivated man (E. P. EVANS (2) pp. 22 f.). Most of us are content to rely upon the same sort of tacit recognitions and abilities as those with which we walk, ride bicycles, recognize friends and the like. And it is these non-verbal recognitions, abilities and judgements which we share most certainly with the non-human animals, and particularly with our mammalian next-of-kin (see HARDY (1) pp. 276f.; BIERENS DE HAAN).[11] We, dogs, cats, rabbits, sparrows,

[10] THORPE (p. 364) denies that animals can have any general concepts of right and wrong, and may be correct in this Aristotelian judgement (though I do not know how we can tell). Few philosophers pretend to such general concepts, and have rarely convinced any others of their truth. Doubtless only men can recognize, e.g., that equals taken from equals leave equals behind as an absolutely general (and empirically dubious) rule. I think it equally obvious that most men recognize no such thing.

[11] It was a legal commonplace in Greek thought that beasts and men have a common law, particularly with reference to the treatment of kindred, parents and children (see JONES pp. 61-2). Indeed the Stoics themselves recognized as much, and that our ethical values take their start from animal affections and ritual (see PEMBROKE, WILLIAMS (3)).

jackdaws, snakes, tortoises, frogs and fish may, variously, share quite enough of a common perception of the world, common curiosities, common disinclinations to betray or injure travelling or working companions, common affections for the small and defenceless—witness the many recorded cases of, e.g., dogs looking after small cats, hares, geese—for a sense of community to be entirely possible. When Stoicized thinkers affirm that 'attachment to animals is a compensation for lack of social satisfactions, and the loss of a sense of responsibility towards fellow-humans' (DEWAR pp. 155 f.)[12] they display an unbearable smugness, a pathological distrust (as I shall argue later) of personal emotion, and a frankly racist attitude toward living creatures. It may be easier to imagine that one has understood a cat when one has not than it is to imagine similar fantasies concerning our closer kin: it *may* be so. Animals may frequently serve us as screens on which to project our own fantasies: to do so is not 'to be attached to animals' nor to enter into any sort of community with them. On the contrary.

'We may feel friendship and a proper sense of duties to kindred natures'. (PORPHYRY (1) II 22.)

And again: 'There is a kind of respect and a generall duty of humanity, which tieth us not only unto brute beasts that have life and sense, but even unto trees and plants. Unto all we owe Justice, and to all other creatures that are capable of [receiving] it, grace and benignity.' (MONTAIGNE II.11, p. 126.)

In short, we are moved on the one hand by a covert racism, and on the other by an overweighting of our linguistic abilities at the expense of our non-verbal capacities. The latter error is understandable: language, human language, is a very great and a very mysterious gift, and our single advantage over the non-human. Without it, human children even lag behind the chimpanzee. Few of us would perform much better than rats at the non-linguistic intelligence tests commonly set them (see HARDY (1) pp. 276 f.). And it is difficult to see how language could even get started without an appeal to the common, tacit appreciation of our situation which we share with the animal creation and which is most probably the basis for our capacity for ethical discrimination. It is the mark of man as a reasonable creature that 'he can find or make a "reason" for

---

[12] KLINGENDER pp. 139 f. offers the same explanation for the friendship shown to animals by Celtic and Northumbrian saints.

anything he has a mind to do' (Benjamin Franklin, cited by SALT (4) p. 12): man is a rationalizing animal. It is the mark of man as an ethical creature that he recognizes what is to be done before he has thought of a reason. This capacity we share with the beasts, and may fairly rely on our shared values to defend our compacts— compacts which the beasts are more likely to keep than we.[13]

'Touching trust and faithfulnesse there is no creature in the world so trecherous as man' (MONTAIGNE II.12, p. 173.)

Assigned rights

But suppose all this is false. Suppose that non-human animals are such that no compact can be made with them: nothing can be reasonably expected of them whether of commission or omission. Suppose that they cannot be given 'moral credit' for any of their actions, or rather for their behaviour: does it follow that they are owed no respect at all? Surely the reverse—it is impertinent to be angry or indignant with beasts, as also with babies, and for that very reason they must be given greater toleration. I will assume for a moment that animals are still to be reckoned sentient: what is lacking in them is any capacity to act on principle, any capacity to call something their own or another's on the basis of agreed codes of conduct. I do not believe that this can be true in any clear sense— the very songs of birds are, in a sense, declarations of an agreed property—but I am willing to concede that there are important differences, or may be: animals perhaps cannot decide to *exchange* their 'property' (FOX AND TIGER pp. 146 f.), though even this is debatable (see HOWARD pp. 50 f.). It is likely enough, though I suspect often false, that they do not stop to think. Must they then be denied all rights? Are they fair game? Positive rights, let us suppose, they do not have: they have no *right* to claim any share of the world's or of our resources, because they are unable to *claim* such a share. They may of course seek to get it, but they cannot be said to be *claiming* it, because (we are supposing) they have no notion of a claim.

Now on absolute terms it is plausible to say that nothing has any positive rights: all is gift, whether to us, or to jackdaws, or to the young lions that seek their prey from God. But such a philosophy

---

[13] KROPOTKIN ((2) p. 59) interestingly suggests that the sense of justice originated in a guilty feeling that animals would revenge harm done their kin.

is obviously not the best basis upon which to erect our present tyranny. It is possible to believe that amongst other gifts we are given the flesh of our fellows, though even ROCHE ((1) p. 33) comments that this permission is given, after the Flood (Genesis 9:3), with the same sort of 'eery sarcasm' with which Israel is given a monarchical system. Nor is it obvious that a concession given in a time of natural disaster and extreme indigence is of much relevance to *our* situation (see HILDROP II pp. 13 f.), but it is possible to believe that we have been licensed to use animals for our need. God forgives us our necessities (PORPHYRY (1) III 18)—it is He after all that creates them. But such permission does not amount to the ceding of a *right*.[14] Animals perhaps have no positive rights: it is difficult to see on what basis *we* have any either.

But let us agree that we are not required to go out of our way to supply the necessities of animals, that they have no positive claim on us—though St. Francis and Meister Ekhart, long before GOD-WIN (p. 38), pronounced that not to give to one in need was tantamount to theft. Does it follow, because a beggar has no *right* to our money (if he has not, and if in any clear sense it *is* ours) that we are therefore in the right if we take away what little he seems to have? Surely not: and neither does it follow from the 'rightlessness' of animals in the present sense that *we* have or should be expected to have any rights to their flesh or their service, or are in the right if we torment them.

Necessity may sometimes drive us, as it drives them: 'But if it really is necessary, we shall kill in pity and sorrow, not degrading and torturing it—which is the current practice, some thrusting red-hot spits into the throat of swine. ... Others jump upon the udders of sows about to give birth, sew up the eyes of cranes and swans, shut them in darkness and fatten them, making the flesh appetising with strange compounds and spicy mixtures.' (PLUTARCH(1)996 f.) And again: 'We are degrading animals in our day by the methods of reproduction and rearing we are now employing. De-beaked hens, cooped-up calves fed on antibiotics, and our growing denial of the personal association to our domesticated animals, which is their *right* if we domesticate them, constitutes a degradation not only of the animals, but of ourselves.' (DARLING (1) pp. 80 f.) Let no-one think that factory farms are something strange and new: they

---

[14] The Lord allows us flesh, but not the blood in which is life: 'this bond doth give thee here no jot of blood' (Shakespeare, *Merchant of Venice*, IV.1).

are but the logical conclusions of our old iniquity. An iniquity that even Barth recognizes: 'Man must not murder an animal. He can only kill it, knowing that it does not belong to him, but to God, and that in killing it he surrenders it to God in order to receive it back from Him as something he needs and desires.' (BARTH III pt 4, p. 355.) Barth's error is to suppose more necessary than is.

In short, perhaps animals can make no rightful claim on land, on food, on the air they breathe, on human care, on their own bodies. It does not follow that *we* can make any claim on them that our fancy pictures. If they have no positive rights, yet they have negative. A drowning man has no absolute, unfocused *right* to life, nor even (in law) a right to be rescued by whoever passes by: it does not follow that he had no right not-to-be-pushed-in—which is simply to say that no-one else had or has the right so to push him. Let it be that animals have no *rights*—they can still be wronged.

Stepping down from such heights, it is surely possible to say that property in land or food or other natural goods may be assigned even to those who have not, or could not have, demanded such an assignment. In a household a dish or chair or food may be assigned to an animal, and it is thereafter that animal's. The animal's rights to it are protected by some member of the household powerful enough to get away with doing so. Why should anyone do so? Equally why should a Homeric chieftain be moved to assign rights to the powerless, the stranger, the orphan, the widow? Zeus Timios, god and guardian of suppliants, guaranteed their rights—rights for which they could not be expected to fight. And the general acceptance of this guarantee reflects more than any simple calculation about 'supporting the system so that I may benefit in my turn from some other host or ruler'. Rights are places in the sun guaranteed to the defenceless under some generally accepted system which represents our mutual concern. As such, offences against the protected entity are counted as, are truly, offences against the guarantor. Or in more familiar terms: 'Whatever you did for the least of these My brothers, you did it for Me' (Matthew 25:40).

Historically those who could not claim a place of their own power were protected, in the system of their day, by the God. Those who still espouse such a tradition are ill-advised to imagine that the rights of man are on any different footing from the rights of animals, and ill-advised to stand upon their rights to another's hurt. Those who do not adhere to the faith of their fathers, but have adopted or seek some secular attempt to defend the individually defenceless, should still, I suggest, retain the feature that individuals to be respected, not to be interfered with, to be permitted at the least a place of their own, are in no case to be thus respected because they can make good their own claims. A powerful, amiable, useful male citizen is in little danger of oppression: it is the unamiable, the powerless, who need protection against the strong.

Why should we agree that beasts merit such protection? The only reasons for assigning it to the weak of our own species must in the end either be the command of God, which is equally a reason in the case of animals, or else our own sense of kinship towards them. One may similarly feel such kinship towards the beasts. Our common parents are earth and heaven, as Theophrastus said (POR-PHYRY (1) III.25). NICHOLSON was of the opinion (p. 28; see also GODLOVITCH AND HARRIS) that Darwinism would encourage fellow-feeling and kindliness. He was too sanguine, but he should, in logic, have been correct. If we are, if man is 'one of a vast number of evolving organisms' (HARDY (1) p. 29) distinguished in the end only superficially from uncounted myriads of other species who share our world and a common interest in continued living, we might surely be expected to think of our cousins as cousins and not as trash. Unfortunately, the symbolic use to which Darwinism has been put is to exalt Man as heir of the ages, and depress the non-human animals as errors, or backslidings, or material. The genetically programmed sympathies that we feel for the young, the defenceless are as readily extended in us to other species as they are in other species: witness the success of the cuckoo. For excellent psychological reasons we have preferred to repress these sympathies, to pretend that it is man as carrier of the divine flame of reason whom we honour, not merely our kindred, and consequently to deny to our more distant kin any share in the divinity we purport to extol.

> 'Any ground which obliges us to be considerate to human beings obliges us also, *mutatis mutandis*, to be considerate to all other sentient creatures.' (HUME (2) p. 73.)

If we honour men for their place in a rational hierarchy, then other creatures must be honoured too. If we honour them because they are our kin, then others are so too. 'Men are only fellow-voyagers with other creatures in the odyssey of evolution.' (LEOPOLD p. 109.)

And as such we should recognize ourselves as members of an abiding community. Not a community formed in myth or history by a signed contract between adult and autonomous persons, but a community, a biocoenosis which has evolved its own regulating factors, its own enormously varied ways of life over several thousand million years. 'We abuse land (and animals) because we regard (them) as a commodity belonging to us. When we see land as a community to which we belong, we may begin to use it [and our kindred] with love and respect.' (LEOPOLD p. x.)

You are at liberty to regard this as a tale twice-told, to believe and to feel that you are fortunately free of the manifold sympathies which bind men and animals together, just as a cancerous cell is fortunately free of the genetic heritage which would show its place in the organism (see LORENZ (1) pp. 33 f.). You are at liberty to feel so, but be warned: you have several thousand million years of evolution against you, and like the cancerous cell's, your final victory would be your defeat.

There is a last word to say. The community of which I have spoken, which exists even if it contains no tacit compacts and allegiances—though I believe it does—this community is the very same which those who follow the theistic tradition should have found in the Bible.

'This is the sign of the covenant which I establish between Myself and you and every living creature with you, to endless generations: My bow I set in the clouds, sign of the covenant between Myself and earth. When I cloud the sky over the earth, the bow shall be seen in the cloud. Then will I remember the covenant which I have made between myself and you and living creatures of every kind.' (Genesis 9:12 f.; see Romans 8:19 f.)

It is within that covenant and its successors that we must admit that we are not the only creatures to be granted God's attention, and His care. 'We are neither above nor under the rest: what ever is under the coape of heaven ... runneth one law, and followeth one fortune. Some difference there is, there are orders and degrees; but all is under the visage of one-same nature.' (MONTAIGNE II.12, p. 153.) We are 'fellow-voyagers in the odyssey of evolution': there are two nuances in the metaphor that Leopold most probably did not intend—the first, that the original odyssey was a return home; the second, that Odysseus had managed to lose all his ship-mates.

The theist may hope for that return, after long exile, and must pray that we lose none of those our fellow-creatures whom God has put into our hands. 'As the dominant mammal on the face of the earth, as the clever one, the only one as far as we know capable of reflection and of accumulating knowledge, our duty is plain, to serve the lesser creation, to keep our world clean and pass on to posterity a record of which we shall not feel shame.' (DARLING (2) p. 122.)

Moral corruption

And one last supposition: suppose I am entirely wrong, and that animals are not in themselves proper objects of moral concern. Yet Thomists have supposed it sin to *enjoy* their suffering, for this is to corrupt one's moral character, and so at last to come to enjoy the suffering of men. 'According to this doctrine ... it is no worse from an ethical point of view to flay the forearm of an ape or lacerate the leg of a dog than to rip open the sleeve of a coat or rend a pair of pantaloons...' (E. P. EVANS (2) p. 99) so long as one is not enjoying the pain. I shall not harp on the point that the very fact that enjoyment of the torment of a dog is thought to lead to enjoyment of human agony is an admission that animal and human suffering are of the same quality. Do we expect those who enjoy hitting balls to come to enjoy hitting people (NOZICK pp. 35 f.)? Nor shall I rebuke Thomists too severely for setting up such 'fences around the Law' as are specifically denounced by the Lord Christ (Mark 7:7 f.): it shows some slight moral sense that they have done so. Rather I enquire if carelessness about animal distress may not also spread? ADDIS AND ARNOLD indeed admit the danger, and the history of biomedical research over the last century has not been such as to inspire much faith in the sensibilities of experimenters (see PAPPWORTH, FREUND). Shakespeare knew as much: when a wicked queen determines that

> I will try the forces
> of these thy compounds on such creatures as
> we count not worth the hanging

Cornelius replies

Your highness
shall from this practice but make hard your heart. (*Cymbeline*, 1.6).

And JOHNSON comments:

> 'The thought would probably have been much more amplified had our author lived to be shocked with such experiments as have been published in later times, by a race of men who have practiced tortures without pity, and related them without shame, and are yet suffered to erect their heads among human beings.' ((1) p. 39.)

May not the practice of eating animal-flesh spread until we also eat men (see PORPHYRY (1) 1 23)? May we not come to shuffling our fellow-humans as so much trash as we progressively deny our immediate sympathies, progressively employ the non-human creation for our greed and luxury? May we not? Have we not already?

Let us pretend that Thomists and Kantians are not foully mistaken: yet still we should take care lest in seizing our profferred chances we destroy our souls and acquire habits of self-aggrandizement that weaken even human ties at last. Why should we treat animals as we do if we are not already mean-minded and inane?

> On shallow straw, in shadeless glass,
> huddled by empty bowls, they sleep:
> no dark, no dam, no earth, no grass—
> *Mam, get us one of them to keep.*
>
> Living toys are something novel,
> but it all wears off somehow.
> Fetch the shoebox, fetch the shovel—
> *Mam, we're playing funerals now.*
>> Philip Larkin, 'Take one home for the kiddies'
>> (*The Whitsun Weddings*, London 1964, p. 26.)

III

NECESSARY PAINS

Earth household

I have attempted to put, and rebut, the thesis that only those creatures with whom we share a 'community of reason' should be counted as worthy of our concern. It may be that I put the case ill, for most of the orthodox are so contemptuous of zoophiles that they spare no time to expound their principles. I answered, firstly, that the need for language as a medium for effective compact-making has been much exaggerated: common sympathies and purposes, mutual attractions and puzzlements are quite enough to provide a mutual sense of fair dealing at least with our most immediate, mammalian, kin, and according to some, admittedly bizarre, accounts even with members of entirely different biological phyla. I answered secondly that even if this were not so, even if there were no understandings between us and any non-human animal, yet they might still be owed our courtesy. Within an absolute context it is difficult to see how any of us, men or beasts, have any rights at all: and we certainly therefore have no rights upon them. In less absolute terms any principle, or prince, that accords rights to the weak of our own species must also accord them to animals. I added, as an argument *ad hominem*, that even if our treatment of animals were without moral significance, Thomists should in consistency erect further fences around the law which would at least spare our kin some of the torments to which we put them.

Just-so stories about the once-upon-a-time contract between man and beast are doubtless merely stories; but so are stories about primitive contracts between man and man (see INGOLD). Neither we nor our ancestors ever contracted to society: we were social before we were human, and each of us is born into a pre-existent society, which it is a mere conceit of whoremaster man to suppose is made up only of men. Contractual theorists from Protagoras onward have imagined society as a sort of corporation. Stoics employed this analogy to give men a sense of companionship in the whole kin-group of humanity. My suggestion is that society is much more like a household, including different age-groups, ranks and species,[1] and that a similar analogical process reveals the wider Household which is the community of living creatures (see SNYDER). To respect the interests and ways of our fellows is incumbent upon us: to respect, not necessarily to enforce them. Much of nature may often seem to be inextricably involved in a sort of reciprocated injustice, where prey and predator are at once individually at odds and racially symbiotic. There may be little we can, or should, do about this: it is not the world we think we would have chosen, but interference will usually make things worse—tares and wheat must grow together till the Day (Matthew 13:29 f.). Let us abandon our *own* iniquities before troubling overmuch about what is done under necessity by our undomesticated kin. RITCHIE (p. 109) sneered at Salt that if animals had rights we must set about defending them against other animals, and organize proper juries of their peers to try the case: a symptom of Ritchie's imperialistic outlook, that he could seriously suppose that we, the criminals *par excellence*, were worthy as police. Animals rarely kill beyond necessity: beyond, that is, their own necessities. And in general they kill with speed, and cleanly. It may be true that we have no universal moral duty to save the rabbit from the fox, the fly from the spider: neither have we such a *universal* duty to save a man. It does not follow that we ourselves have any right to kill the man, or the rabbit, or the fly. And if, as Salt supposed, animals have a right to be spared such suffering and slaughter as is mere wantoning, a right to have their interests weighed with care, it does not follow that we must indulge sadistic fantasies about hanging cats that catch a mouse too many. Or if some general care for animals does follow from our recognition of their proper standing it will consist in improving the lives of such creatures as we can. God put us into His garden to tend and keep it, and to be the shepherd of His sheep, and though much has changed that office has not wholly lapsed.

I will return to the problem of our relation to untamed nature. For the moment I only claim that zoophiles take seriously our immediate recognition of common pleasures, inter-species friendships, the mutual dependence of all living. I cannot see that it is a less

[1] The fate of such household animals is not always good, but there is the root of decency there (see DU BOULAY pp. 86 f.).

worthy, and it certainly seems a more realistic, view than that which pretends that the relationship of adult, contracting persons is the sole variety of ethical relationship.

Differences and stupidity

There are those for whom the implied approach to questions of value is mere sentimentalism: 'A human life is nothing compared with a new fact. . . . The aim of science is the advancement of human knowledge at any sacrifice of human life. If cats and guinea pigs can be put to any higher use than to advance science we do not know what it is. We do not know of any higher use we can put a man to.' (E. J. Slosson '*Independent*' 12 December 1895: VYVYAN (2) pp. 20–1.) The half-correspondence with Thomist thought— 'If we suffer for our own good, *a fortiori* animals can suffer for man's own good' (BENDER p. 73)—but without even the care for men that Thomists express, is enough to induce nightmares. Indeed it played its part in inducing a large-scale and historical nightmare, known as Nazism (see CARREL; VYVYAN (2) pp. 155 f., PAPPWORTH pp. 61 f.). But I shall leave the dogmatists of science, a late and bastard tribe from Aristotle's loins, till later.

Animals are irrational (and therefore contemptible). Their supposed irrationality may consist in an inability to act according to any set plans—a perfectly ridiculous idea which betrays its origins in our own psychological needs. Any species that has survived in the wild has done so by being able to cope with all its normal situations in accordance with entirely 'rational' principles. Or the belief may be that they do not act with such principles in mind: in Aristotle's terms they act *kata logon* (according to reason) but not *meta logou* (with reason). So, most of the time, do we. Nonetheless we are easily convinced that animals are stupid, preternaturally stupid. 'Their traits that are not after the fashion of man, we call imperfect, stupid and bad. But we should understand that God created animals perfect in their own kind.' (RULAND p. 366.) We should, but we do not. 'When all is done, whatsoever is not as we are, is not of any worth ... Whereby it appeareth, that it is not long of a true discourse, but of a foolish-hardinesse, and self-presuming obstinacie, we prefer our selves before other creatures, and sequester our selves from their condition and societie.' (MONTAIGNE II.12, p. 186.) We think them stupid because they do things differently.[2] We think them stupid, as a young child may his younger siblings, because they have not yet learnt what he discovered yesterday. We think them stupid because they take time to find their way around, particularly in places and problems we have set them from superior knowledge and in accordance with *our* way of seeing things. We think them stupid for normal failures of lateral thinking, which we rarely surpass. We think them stupid because we are ill-informed. Gladstone commented of some sheep he saw going out onto the hillside in the threat of snow that 'if I were a sheep I should remain in the hollows'. The shepherd replied 'Sir, if ye were a sheep, ye'd have mair sense'. (BUCHAN p. 154.) We think them stupid, finally, because we have bred them so that they may confirm our secret wish, and keep them in confinement that they may stay that way: sullen, stupid, incurious, irresponsible, profligate and dumb. 'This is not the only instance in which tyranny has taken advantage of its own wrong, alleging as a reason for the domination it exercises, an imbecillity which, as far as it has been real, has been produced by the abuse of that very power which it is brought to justify.' (BENTHAM p. 268 n. of women; see LORENZ (1) pp. 40 f.) Consider only the difference between L. WILLIAMS's monkeys ((1), (2)) and the pathetic prisoners of a provincial zoo.

Animal sentience

STRATO of Lampsacus observed that without intelligence animals could not even perceive. If the Stoics were right to say that animals only behave *as if* reasoning, understanding, calculating (as also BENNETT), then strictly one should say that they only behave *as if* seeing, hearing, smelling—all of which activities must involve recognitions, comparisons, judgements. We can go further: animals only move *as if* they were behaving—for behaviour requires that there be some sort of inner life, and of *that*, once we have denied our own immediate, programmed empathy, we have no proof at all. This irredeemably fatuous belief, for which Descartes rightly earned the derision of a Continent (see ROSENFIELD), has been bolstered up by a confusion of methodology with ontology. Ethologists of the 'objective' school prefer to restrain their own automatic recognition of behaviour-patterns, knowing that we are often

---

[2] DEVEREUX ((1) p. 185) mentions a number of similar perversions, like that of the doctor who performed unnecessary hysterectomies upon his wife and daughters, under the subconscious delusion that all points of difference from the self are defects.

mistaken and believing that much can be gained from as nearly materialistic an account as possible (see TINBERGEN). It is natural enough to discount the existence of things in which one does not permit oneself to have an interest, and this natural disposition is here intensified by the passion to find some wholly physico-chemical account of all phenomena.

'The living organism is nothing but a wonderful machine.' (BERNARD (1) p. 63.) My own view is that if such an account were ever forthcoming, to demonstrate that the whole universe and everything in it is a mere complex of machines, we could only conclude *'Machinis maxima debetur reverentia'*. For we know, by a route enormously shorter than any scientist's, that *we* are conscious, loving, behavioural entities, even if our thought and behaviour is embodied in the motion of lesser particles. If we are machines— though as I shall argue later mechanicists are often strangely disinclined to take *this* identification seriously—so much the better for machines.

But the mysteries whereby we spirits strangely cooperate in uttering the material world are beyond my brief. In this context it is enough to emphasize that no science properly intends, or could succeed in so intending, to deny inner life to animals. *We* are conscious beings, and this 'we' does not refer only to those of us later delimited as men. We may often be wrong in our immediate judgements, and rightly restrain ourselves from them for a while, but our recognition of some characters and behaviour patterns is untaught, undeniable and the perceptual basis of science itself. A chemist who informs us that it is an illusion to suppose a difference between free-range and battery eggs, because he cannot yet distil the physical essence of that difference, is a fool: for the human organs of taste are still the basis of much chemical differentiation and cannot thus be called in question. The biologist, testifying before the U.S. House of Representatives in 1963 (cited by VYVYAN (2) p. 190), who announced that 'science has not yet proved that animals suffer. To think they suffer is anthropomorphism. We believe that any reflex or reaction is instinct and is not induced by any sensation of pain' is worse than a fool. Here, as so often, K. Lorenz's judgement should be remembered: 'The similarity is not only functional but historical, and it would be an actual fallacy not to humanise.' (letter to WILLIAMS (2) p. 54.) There is no need to ask, with Voltaire, 'has [an animal] nerves to be without pleasure or pain?' Certainly the argument from analogy, though invalid or at least extremely weak in strict philosophical terms, is of some practical effect: we more readily believe that the experiences of mammals or birds are like ours than those of creatures with radically different nervous structures. Those who are certain insects feel no pain, and fish little, usually find it difficult without grotesque hypocrisy to deny the experience to dogs and monkeys. But if an analogy of nervous structure is thought relevant, the analogy of overt bodily structure and behaviour is more obvious, more affecting and even more relevant. More affecting, for good or ill: to imagine that a dolphin is a fish is automatically to count it of less worth. More relevant, for whatever neurological circuits may be found by surgery within my wife's brain, or my cat's, can only add to our knowledge of what may serve as a physical base for experience—such discoveries cannot, in their nature, disprove what I already see to be the case, that such creatures may be in distress.

I see that animals are in distress, and the notional addition of a language would not assist my perception. 'I am in pain', after all, only 'replaces' a cry of anguish, which must be recognized as such before the words may be taught or learned. 'I am in pain' does not explicate, identify or prove the existence of that anguish. Seriously to believe that animals, all animals, are insentient is pathological (RUSSELL AND BURCH pp. 14 f.). It may be that their intelligence, their understanding of and their ability to escape from distressful conditions is less than ours, but this is not to remove them from consideration nor to deny that they may feel distress. 'The conditions of fluctuation in conscious states, when intelligence is rudimentary, are such that lower animals have a special claim on our considerateness. ... No sane person regards a baby as insentient because he cannot talk.' (RUSSELL AND BURCH.)[3]

It may be that animals feel less distress, or fewer distresses, than we do, though we might remember that the same has been said of the human poor, and of the racially distinct. Nor does it make sense to argue that because 'animals do not have desires to the same extent that humans do, or not of the sorts (exactly) that humans have, thus the wants of animals have correspondingly less moral weight'. (RICHARDS p. 326 n.) If A desires few things, and B many things, that is no decent reason why A should lose even those few things

---

[3] Though there is a complacent body of opinion that considers babies' pains to be less severe: there is no evidence at all for this fantasy (see P. LEACH p. 31).

he desires (see 2 Samuel 12). Even if the distress A feels for one particular lack is less than the distress that B feels, this is not of itself a decent reason for stripping A. 'The moral argument (against vivisection) remains, whether the animals suffer as much as we do or only half as much. ... I myself am thankful to believe that even the highest animals below ourselves do not feel so acutely as we do; but that fact does not in any way remove my fundamental disgust at vivisection as being brutalising and immoral.' (WALLACE pp. 381 f.)

What is the evidence that they feel less distress than we do or that their desires are 'of another sort' than ours? Doubtless there are all sorts of distresses, at the way the country is going to the dogs, or at Jones's new car, or the like, which beasts are fortunately spared—though the fact that they most probably do not appreciate our idiosyncratic problems might raise the question as to whether *they* have idiosyncratic problems too. It does not follow, however, from their lack of these distresses that calves cannot be acutely distressed at the absence of their mothers, nor that chickens are not distressed when unable to stretch their wings. It may be true, as Burns supposed, that the mouse whose nest he had destroyed at least was spared the fear and foresight of a worse tomorrow.[4] Animals, maybe, take as little thought for the morrow as human hunter-gatherers (see SAHLINS) or true followers of Christ (Matthew 6:25 f.)—unless, perhaps, they're squirrels. But this can hardly excuse our inflicting present distress on them, merely because they cannot foresee a future *end* of such distress. Doubtless, again 'Death to them is no spectre at the feast, no long-feared visitant' (ROCHE (1) pp. 64 f., after D'Arcy) but I doubt that even for us such emotionalisms are often much more than self-indulgence, or occasionally self-discipline. It does not follow from their alleged unawareness of the possibility of death that they do not fear death, and flee it as the greatest of evils. Nor does this alleged insensibility to death (in which, I fear, POPE believed: III, 1) follow from their lack of understanding of death. We do not, emotionally at least, have much understanding of death: my absence from the world is strictly un-

---

[4] Still thou art blest, compar'd wi'me:
  the present only toucheth thee:
  but, och; I backward cast my e'e,
    on prospects dreer!
an' forward, tho' I canna *see*
    I *guess* an' *fear*. (Robert Burns, 'To a Mouse' (1785).

imaginable to me (FREUD p. 289 see CLARK pp. 166 f.). I am not therefore unafraid of death, and moderately anxious lest I die before my time. A mouse fleeing from a cat is manifestly afraid, and it is more than likely that cattle taken to the slaughter are similarly terrified (see RULAND p. 375; HARRISON p. 28). I devoutly pray that our food animals are not as aware of their species' millenial and hopeless servitude as men similarly placed might be: that they are unaware of their own hopeless servitude I cannot quite believe. Fear of death is not an intellectual disability, though it *may* be (how should *we* know?) that the prospect occurs less often to them than to us. Those orthodox who pretend not to know that a creature is in pain are strangely well equipped to say what dreams and nightmares that same creature has: 'How knoweth he by the vertue of his understanding the inward and secret motions of beasts? By what comparison from them to us doth he conclude the brutishness he ascribeth to them?' (MONTAIGNE II.12, p. 144.)

'But plainly they have less pain. Foxes gnaw off their own feet to escape traps; birds do not object to their wings' being clipped; ants may go on sucking honey though cut in half' (see BIERENS DE HAAN p. 154; LORENZ (2) pp. 22 f.). But these examples—quite apart from their absurd generality—plainly prove very little. Human beings, in desperation or excitement or mere absorption in a task in hand, have endured or ignored pain. It does not follow that they are in general insensible. Possibly animals are tougher than we, accustomed to anaesthesia and comfort, can dare to imagine. It does not follow that they do not dislike and fear the prospect of pain. 'One of the best criteria for distress is that of serving as motivation for conditioned reactions and various forms of learning—in other words, its capacity to serve as punishment.' (RUSSELL AND BURCH pp. 20 f.) Experimentalists and animal trainers are accustomed to use pain and the threat of pain to drive their beasts in the way they should go, to induce hysteria by double-bind experiments and repeated stimulation. It is too absurd even for hypocrisy to claim that they are not really very distressed: the whole point of such procedures is, exactly, to distress them.[5] If they were not like us in this there would be even less reason to use them as analogies to man in psychological experiments. Because we are more intelligent than they—or rather because our distinctive variety of

[5] 'It is a primary condition of circus success that the animal shall abrogate the use of certain higher levels of his intelligence'—particularly the capacity for choice (BATESON p. 339).

intelligence is linguistic and less embedded in immediate instinctive response—it does not follow that we are more sensitive than they. Perhaps mammals are more sensitive than frogs, perhaps chordates more sensitive than starfish—or sensitive to more—but that we men, half-blind, half-deaf, and with no sense of smell, should think ourselves more sensitive than, say, the domestic cat is a frivolity not to be endured.[6]

Unnecessary suffering

Let us admit, then, that animals in varying degrees feel pain and fear, and that we have no general reason to think them less subject to these ills than we: if they have fewer forebodings, if they do, then by the same token they are buoyed by fewer hopes. A burning cat is as agonized as any burning baby. Even where we do have reason to impute a lesser pain, yet pain is painful. It has been urged, in a last desperate throw, that animals, who lack any consciousness of themselves, must find each pang of agony a new thing without past or future, so that they do not seem to themselves to suffer any long pain. Even if we grant the premises—which I do not—yet even pangs of agony are ill to be borne.

To be distressed by something is to find it an evil.[7] We are so constituted that we are inclined to make others' distress our own, the more sincerely the closer these others touch us. Our solidarity in suffering with other sentient life, so RULAND thought (pp. 373 f.; see SCHOPENHAUER I p. 372), was enough to induce in us a respect for the life and dignity of non-human animals. He was too sanguine.

---

[6] It may be that sensitivity to pain is a different feature from sense-discrimination: that cats can discriminate more accurately between sensa may not mean that they 'feel' the sensa more deeply. I agree, for pains are not sensations. But this is to concede a point that I shall argue later: all pains are painful, and how we deal with them is not a matter open to direct observation.

[7] GRAY has used this, that to feel pain or to suffer requires some judgement of present evil, to argue that non-humans do not suffer. I deeply regret that TRETHOWAN, for whose metaphysical views I have some respect, should have given currency to this pitiable nonsense. I repeat: I have as much evidence that the higher animals suffer as that babies, imbeciles and the aphasic suffer. And I have no reason to doubt that all such non-speaking creatures may make judgements at least about their present state. If suffering requires judgement, it does not require speech. As for Gray's attempt to argue from the claim of anaesthetized(?) medical students that they had felt no pain despite having given all the behavioural signs of pain, I can only remark that if all the behavioural signs were there we should more reasonably conclude that the students had forgotten or that pain was felt, but not by them, than that unanaesthetized chimpanzees are merely stimulus-response machines. But there is no depth of self-deceiving stupidity to which mankind cannot sink.

But at least it is very common now to pay lip-service to the thesis that it is wrong to cause unnecessary suffering to an animal (e.g. DOWNIE AND TELFER pp. 34 f.). Necessity, of course (see above, pp. 5 f.), is often defined in terms of human activities that are simply unquestioned, so that (at most) such a rubric merely rules out technical incompetence. Such incompetence, being a symptom of inefficiency, might be left to the technicians' care (see RUSSELL AND BURCH pp. 54 f.), were it not that a fundamental inattention to animals as beings to be taken seriously so often blinds men even to their own profit (see DEVEREUX (1) pp. 234 f. on the technician who cut his rats' eyes out rather than blindfold them). Zoophiles have often supposed that such callousness conceals a real sadism. POWYS (1) depicts torture 'for science' along with torture 'for religion' as hypocritical cloaks upon the honest torture for fun. But this is to read too much of the zoophile into the orthodox: as Powys well knew, sadism is a perversion of sympathy ((2) pp. 35 f.). The toxico-maniac, too, though a closer parallel (E. P. EVANS (1) p. 245), is only occasionally to be found in our laboratories and farms. Much the commonest character trait to work against true competence, let alone compassion, is indifference (which may itself be a cloak for cruelty: DEVEREUX (1) pp. 234 f.). In the face of this the plea for technical competence in the prosecution of a well-defined aim is not out of place.

The difficulty about this slogan (that animals be spared unnecessary pains), minimal as it is, is that it already proves too much for the orthodox to stomach. I emphasize that it *is* a minimal principle, that it makes no mention of rights to life, and indeed allows 'rights' only in the sense that animals are not reckoned mere 'stocks and stones'. As a radical moralizer I would go much further, and will do so: but here for a moment I will take my stand, on the claim that one should not cause unnecessary suffering to animals. Incompetence is to be ruled out, and so also are certain ends which are merely specious, or immoral in themselves. Wanton torture, or torture to impress a friend, or demonstrate man's superiority (to whom?), or to satisfy a particular minor whim for some food-stuff whose production involves enormous suffering, or to save oneself the trouble of taking due care must all, precisely, be counted wanton. The human ends within which we calculate necessity must be of some weight, otherwise the principle is *entirely* meaningless—for it licenses even incompetence: 'if I am to conduct this experiment, run this farm with the minimum of care and attention and without troubling my head or heart about the problematic distress of the lower creatures, a certain undefined amount of suffering in my stock will be *necessary*'.

'It is of little use to claim "rights" for animals ... if we show our determination to subordinate those rights to anything that can be construed into a human want.' (SALT (1) p. 7.)

It is of little use claiming that it is wrong to inflict unnecessary suffering if anything at all will do as a context for calculating necessity.

Consider then: it is not necessary to imprison, torture or kill animals if we are to eat. The laborious transformation of plant proteins into animal protein, indeed, is notoriously inefficient, and wastes a great deal of food that would greatly assist human beings in less carnivorous places. It is not necessary for us to do this: I say nothing of what may be necessary for the Eskimos, for whom (along with tomatoes: see above p. 17) the orthodox display a sudden, strange affection when confronted by zoophiles (though the health of Eskimos might be better served by supplying plant-food). It is not necessary for us, and our affection for other human beings would perhaps be better shown by ceasing to steal their plant protein in order to process it into a form that pleases our palates.

But perhaps flesh-eating, for some reason that escapes me, is held to be an end of sufficient weight.[8] Consider then: it is not necessary to submit animals to their present distress if we are to eat meat. Indeed, it is not strictly necessary to submit them to any distress: now that liberal orthodoxy has apparently decreed that any concern over the integrity of the human corpse is a mere anti-social superstition (witness the demand for transplantable organs), it would seem a simple solution both to our flesh-craving and to the increasing storage problem to cook the victims of automobile accidents. But even if this economical solution is rejected, and our flesh-craving must be satisfied with the death of animals, it is still not necessary

---

[8] The latest pretext known to me is that 'brain development' is dependent on receiving a sufficiency of lipids, which must be built up from leaf and seed and can be obtained in longer chains from herbivores (longer still from carnivores, or men, but let it pass). It seems strange if this were true that there are vegetarian and vegan families of several generations' standing that are not obviously imbecilic. As to an older canard: the vegan diet, which includes comfrey, Barmene and commercial plant - milks such as Plamil, is *not* deficient in Vitamin B_{12}.

to submit them to the foul distresses involved in factory farming (on which see HARRISON). The only case under which these distresses *are* necessary is if we are to go on eating flesh in our present quantities and without attention to their well-being—but that is a reason for changing our habits, not for defending them.

What follows for our obligations? Simply, that if we are to mean what we say in outlawing the unnecessary suffering of animals, we must become, at the least, vegetarians. I repeat that I say nothing here about the Eskimos, nor have I any interest in the desert-island castaway. We are not on a desert-island. Nor have I yet seen an orthodox moralist defend rape or even fornication merely on the ground that most males trapped in solitary and beyond the law with a naked and lubricious female would find their principles a little strained.

The Research Defence Society is fond of observing (R.D.S. MEMORANDUM: W. R. Wooldridge) that intensive farming involves distress far greater than most distress inflicted in the laboratories (though their crocodile tears might be more convincing if *they* were vegetarians) and this is very likely the case (though see also RYDER). It has also been pointed out that intensive farming increases the incidence of infectious and contagious disease, as well as such induced disabilities as rickets and anaemia, in the animals (see HARRISON pp. 75 f., and 110 f.). Further experiments on living animals are then required to cope with these medical problems, not for the sake of the animals, but that the farmer may continue to foster the illusion that he is efficient. RUSSELL AND BURCH, whose principles of humane experimental technique are still, perhaps, insufficiently humane for the thorough-going zoophile, have yet, with the Universities Federation for Animal Welfare (U.F.A.W.: founded by C. W. Hume), done a great deal for the experimental animal. Contingent suffering, defined as distress unnecessary to the success of the experiment, merely demonstrates the experimenter's incompetence (RUSSELL AND BURCH pp. 54 f.). Direct suffering cannot be avoided without questioning the whole principle of animal exploitation, which they decline to do. Within their chosen parameters they advocate the reduction of direct suffering by Replacement (the substitution of insentient material, such as tissue cultures), Reduction in the number of experiments (perhaps by using filmed experiments for demonstration purposes) and Refinement of technique. These measures can, obviously, do no more than reduce the distress we cause animals. It could be still further reduced by querying the use, and therefore the testing, of all manner of cosmetic and merely commercial drugs. Even within this liberal zoophile system, however, it is plain that the present system of intensive farming cannot be defended. We can replace animal-protein by plant protein, even if we preserve some free-range beef-herds and the like. We can reduce the amount of flesh we eat to the point where such whole-food farms can cope with the demand. We can always look for measures that will lessen distress in our animals rather than measures that will give us the least possible trouble.

Let us then be vegetarians, at least. For those who have recognized flesh-eating for what it is, the merest addiction, and one, as SHELLEY saw, to 'kindle all putrid humours in (our) frame' (*Queen Mab* 8. 215: p. 288 and see notes thereto; see also Thomas Love Peacock, *Headlong Hall*, ch. 2—the argument was plainly fashionable)—for such moralists the step is easy. It is not necessary, rather it is incompetent, to kill and torture animals to eat. Those who retain the end of flesh-eating but admit the iniquity of factory-farming and the need to reduce the demand for flesh, are in practice in no better state. Where so many eat so much flesh, there is no 'moderate amount of flesh' that the moralist can decently eat. Until all have reduced their demands to whatever 'reasonable compromise' between the passion for flesh and the distress of the animals the moralist has fixed, he must reduce his demand to zero. Again, he cannot in practice declare that he will eat only decently reared flesh—for he cannot tell what flesh has been decently reared, and if by chance he did he would, by buying it, be putting pressure on the farmer in question to increase his output by increasingly intensive methods.[9] The open iniquity of factory farming has this merit, that it makes self-deception about the horrors caused to animals more difficult. It has this demerit, that by contrast the old ways seem courteous and kind. So the existence of concentration camps acclimatises us to slums.

There is a simple technique for evading responsibility for the things we cause to be done. In the popular morality of the Sherpas 'To kill a living creature is sin ... To kill yak and sheep is sin for the butchers, but not for those who eat the meat.' (FÜRER-HAIMEN-DORF p. 187.) The hypocrisy of this is revealed by the fact that

---

[9] It is worth remarking also that game-birds and the like are preserved for ritual slaughter at the expense of the torture and death of many other creatures thereby defined as vermin.

though exorcizing spirits is also a sin, it is not the exorcizing lama, but the man who hires the lama, who is sinning. There is perhaps a certain sense in the casuistry: Buddhist monks (see GOMBRICH pp. 260 f.), like Franciscan friars, thought it proper to eat what they were given. It was Brother Elias, the Judas of the Franciscan movement, who attempted a total ban on flesh-food, and was rebuked for it by God's angel (St. FRANCIS pp. 9 f.). But however proper this may be for such, who would (in principle at least) surrender their own flesh to those in need, it hardly excuses the average irresponsibility of those who *require* other men to inflict suffering upon animals when, as they know, it is unnecessary.

'The canibales and savage people do not so much offend me with roasting and eating of dead bodies, as those which torment and persecute the living.' (MONTAIGNE II.11, p. 120.)

Eight sophisms

This, of course, cannot be endured. It is not part of the moral philosopher's office to show that we are hypocrites to such an extent. I have noticed, and list below, eight moderately serious devices for avoiding the consequences of the rather innocuous principle I have mentioned. Oddly, some of them have a startling resemblance to once popular theodicy.

The first is not to speak of suffering, or of distress, but of pain, where 'pain' means only painful sensation, as in Edward Heath's dictum (quoted by HARRISON p. 158) that blinded calves could not be said to be suffering unless they had pains in their eye-balls.

The second is to suppose that animals do not miss what they have not got, or what they never had. This is familiar in the annals of political history. It is perhaps true that those who have not got, nor ever heard of, an electric cocktail shaker do not much miss it. It is certainly not true that those who have not air, or sunlight, or room to move, or chance to meet their kind, do not miss these things. The want of them is part of our genetic heritage, even if we have no image of what it is we want.

The third is to invoke the calculation that the victim of our attentions would prefer existence with all its attendant pains to mere non-existence, and that we are thereby licensed to impose those pains. NICHOLSON (p. 50) employs this argument about fox-hunting, though he expresses grave doubts about its validity in the annotated copy in the Bodleian Library. One premise may, in some sense, be true, though I am tempted to reply, with Salt, that 'there is no record of this strange alternative having ever been submitted either to fox or philosopher: so that a precedent has yet to be established on which to found a judgment'. (SALT (1) p. 46.) BOSWELL, at any rate, records against Johnson a somewhat different attitude to the alternative (p. 753). Of course, now that we do exist most of us want to go on living—but that is an odd excuse for murder.

The fourth is to speak of species rather than individuals: 'if all the world were Jews there would be no pigs in existence'. (RITCHIE p. 110; SALT (2) pp. 70–1.) Who benefits by this I do not know. I doubt that even the Great Pig is much delighted by the present condition of His members. Certainly individual pigs are not bene-fited by 'being numerous', and any advantage to the species of its artificially enlarged population is carefully withheld. Nor do I see any reason to believe Ritchie's dogma, that there would be no pigs, no cattle, no sheep were it not for our altruistic and ill-requited efforts. Species have vanished in historical time, but few have done so because man did *not* interfere with them. And finally, the argu-ment is grotesque, both here and in the third device: suppose I would not have begotten my son without the intention of selling him into slavery—do I now have a *right* so to sell him? And again: my present existence is dependent on no-one's having killed me yet. I therefore 'owe' everyone my life—but it does not follow that they may properly enslave, torture and kill me merely because they haven't yet done so.

The fifth device is to balance animal pains against human pleasures in their pursuit, their fascinating physiognomy, their flesh. This is, of course, assisted by the prior assumption that 'they don't feel things like we do'. Even SCHOPENHAUER, Ritchie's 'poodle-loving man-hater', was not entirely innocent in this: he held (1 p. 372) that the pain of the animal was less than would be the pain, to man, of being deprived of its flesh or labour. I doubt if the animal would agree, but its agreement would be nothing to the point: doubtless A's pain at being assaulted might be less than would be B's pain at being restrained from this assault—the rela-tions of zoophile and 'humanist' spring to mind—but this is a reason for re-educating B, not for approving his assault.

The sixth is to ask 'how would I feel about suffering this?' C. W. Hume urges that, leaving the question of death aside, the experi-

menter should ask 'Should I myself be willing to endure that degree
of pain or other stress in order to attain the object in view?' (HUME
(1) pp. 190 f.; RUSSELL AND BURCH p. 59.) But I fear that this,
though ameliorative in intent, is hardly better than the Thomist's
'if we suffer for our own good, *a fortiori* animals can suffer for man's
own good'. (BENDER p. 73.)

The seventh device is also C. W. Hume's, and that of most liberal
zoophiles, namely that it is wrong to hurt, but not to kill. This is
not, in reason, strictly relevant to the case against flesh-eating in
our present circumstances, but its rhetoric does tend to lessen any
sense of urgency the liberal moralist feels. In evidence, Hume cites
the bad consequences to animals of leaving them to end their days
in misery. Which might show that killing is not always wrong (as
Gandhi agreed), but cannot show that it is always right. When a
visitor to a Jaina hospital remarked of the animals that 'the majority
would be more mercifully provided for by the application of a loaded
pistol to their heads' he may have been correct, but as E. P. EVANS
replied ((2) p. 139), the same *might* be said of old persons—and
would that license slaughter-houses? The spleen which some orthodox direct against the doctrine of *ahimsa* is sometimes more a product of their aesthetic sense than a real concern for the animals:
'We shall have the harrowing sights of the East—animals lying on
dust-heaps and taking days to die.' (ROCHE (1) p. 119.) Do the animals mind about the dust-heaps? Or does Roche? Hume also
employs the argument that the death of one cockerel will make little
difference, compared with the death, say, of Lincoln. He may be
right, though it makes a rather marked difference to the cockerel,
but it seems an odd principle. Any historical study quickly shows
that the death, or even the life, of most men has made very little
difference even to the human world. The study of my present topic
has impressed me most forcibly with the realization that the very
greatest names of our great-grandfathers' day were swiftly merely
names, and utterly forgotten, save in the grand mausoleum of a great
library, in a hundred years. Is this to justify homicide?[10]

The eighth is yet another plea of moral irresponsibility. All life

[10] Nor are the exceptions to this rule the ones their contemporaries would expect. It is
the carpenter from Nazareth that shook the world. But in any case to say that death is an
evil solely because of its effects on the survivors clearly implies that to kill everyone (or
everything) would be no crime, for none would be left to suffer pain. It would indeed be
our duty to kill any chance survivor of Ragnarok.

involves some pain, nor can we prevent it all, nor excise ourselves
from all involvement in that travail. Jaina monks may tread innocently, for another man has swept the path. Where all is anguish,
how can we cavil at a little more? And how, in that case, can we
care at all, even about man's suffering?

> There was a weasel lived in the sun
> with all his family,
> till a keeper shot him with his gun
> and hung him up on a tree,
> where he swings in the wind and rain,
> in the sun and in the snow,
> without pleasure, without pain
> on the dead oak tree bough.

> There was a crow who was no sleeper,
> but a thief and a murderer
> till a very late hour; and this keeper
> made him one of the things that were,
> to hang and flap in rain and wind,
> in the sun and in the snow.
> There are no more sins to be sinned
> on the dead oak tree bough.

> There was a magpie, too,
> had a long tongue and a long tail;
> he could both talk and do—
> but what did that avail?
> He, too, flaps in the wind and rain
> alongside weasel and crow,
> without pleasure, without pain,
> on the dead oak tree bough.

> And many other beasts
> and birds, skin, bone and feather,
> have been taken from their feasts,
> and hung up there together,

to swing and have endless leisure
in the sun and in the snow,
without pain, without pleasure,
on the dead oak tree bough.
(Edward Thomas, 'The Gallows' (*Collected Poems*, London, 1922.)

IV

DEVICES OF THE HEATHEN

A righteous man regardeth the life of his beast: but the tender mercies of the wicked are cruel (Proverbs 12:10).

Recapitulation

I have pointed out that even the minimal principle debarring the infliction of unnecessary suffering to animals must, in the present context, require us to become vegetarians, at the least, even if we allow the eating of meat to be an end of sufficient weight to act as the basis of our calculations. If, as seems more rational, we take merely the eating of food as our end, the argument is even simpler. Whatever the necessities of those with no other food available, we have no need of slaughter-houses. We continue to eat flesh from habit, and because our palates are conditioned to an ample supply of animal-corpses. Despite the naïve fantasies of the liberal it is simply false to imagine that 'in our climate' flesh is essential, or that 'only a minority' could ever be supported by the fruits of the earth: on the contrary, it is flesh-eaters who must always be in the minority. 'It is known that the grassland which yields flesh-food enough for one man to live on would yield vegetable food enough for several men.' (NICHOLSON p. 55; see LAPPÉ.) This in 1879 (and see SHELLEY p. 333). If there were no obligations owed the non-human at all, it would still be cruelty and injustice to rob our fellow-men of food in order to pander to our corrupted palates. Doubtless even vegetarians and vegans of the West eat more than their fair share of the world's goods, but they are not so hopelessly in the wrong (see, eloquently but not always accurately, J. WYNNE-TYSON).

The distinction between killing for food and killing for fun is a real one, but in our situation all killing is for fun: not directly so, but the choice of food-stuff is itself luxurious. It has been said of the practice of badger-baiting, where the murdered badger is eventually used as a luxury supper, that 'the defendants can quite rightly suggest that if the end-product can be eaten no-one can now suggest

killing is simply for fun'. (HUTCHINGS AND CAVER p. 91.) So if
we eat our victims any variety of killing and torture, beyond need
and even beyond efficiency, is licensed.

'What claim has man's luxury (for truly it is not his need) upon
the life of the chamois, the seal, the ermine, the auk or the humming-
bird?' (NICHOLSON p. 52.) Is the satisfaction of our imagined
luxury really an acceptable end within which to calculate necessities? Then everything is permissible.

> 'Shut up a young boar, of a year and a half old, in a little room
> in harvest time, feeding him with nothing but sweet whey, and
> giving him every morning clean straw to lie upon, but lay it not
> thick; so before Christmas he will be sufficiently brawned with
> continued lying, and prove exceedingly fat, wholesome and sweet.
> And after he is brawned for your turn, thrust a knife into one
> of his flanks, and let him run with it till he die; others gently
> bait him with muzzled dogs.' (T. Moufet, *Health's Improvement*
> (1746): WILSON p. 89.)

Please note the sinister sweetness of the language, the ferocious
sentimentality—'others *gently* bait him', as some well-meaning
liberals propose, e.g. 'the humanization of whaling'. This is not the
language, nor the custom, of necessity. And yet this young boar was
better off than our veal and beef-calves, who cannot lie down nor
find secure footing upon their mesh. And better off than our broiler
chickens, who are hung by their legs, plucked, sometimes but not
always stunned, have their throats slit and then, still living and perhaps still conscious, pass into a scalding vat (see HARRISON pp. 27 f.,
62 f. and 89 f. And on the condition of some rescued battery birds
see NIALL pp. 128 f.). This is not performed for our necessities.

> 'If you eat meat merely because, as is usual in Tibet, there is no
> other food, or not enough to keep you alive without meat, then
> that is not bad, but neither is it good ... We all pray for a rebirth
> where we do not have to take life in order to live.' (NORBU AND
> TURNBULL pp. 207 f.)

I do not urge, as an immediately practical policy, that all distress
be eliminated from the world: in the present dispensation that could
only be achieved by eliminating all sentient life. I do insist that acceptance of the principle that we should not cause distress beyond
our necessities must, if this principle is to have any meaning, require

us to abstain from all flesh-foods. We are at present in the position of a society that requires a constant supply of condemned criminals to keep up its production of Damascus steel, without even having any *need* for Damascus steel.

'The sufferance of evil, unmeritedly, unprovokedly, where no offence has been given, and no good end can possibly be answered by it, but merely to exhibit power or gratify malice, is cruelty and injustice in him that occasions it.' (PRIMATT p. 5.)

Pains and distresses

The ignoble eightfold path of our hypocrisy is, in truth, a monster more versatile than Proteus and with more heads than the hydra. I do not doubt that however many gambits I enumerate and rebut, more will spring up from the ruins of past argument. I ask only that my readers draw their minds again and again back to the realities I am discussing, back to the battery calf and the syphilitic ape and the debeaked hen, the pet abandoned after Christmas, the muskrat broken on the wheel to make a virtuous matron's coat, the bullock that runs mad to find a flight from death, back always to these things: and ask themselves, before God and their conscience, if this be good.

'A righteous man regardeth the life of his beast: but the tender mercies of the wicked are cruel.'

What more tender mercy could there be, indeed, than to forestall such neurotic pigs as bite their fellows' tails by cutting off the tails of all such battery pigs?

The first device that I mentioned in the previous chapter was to speak not of suffering nor distress, but only of painful sensations. It doesn't matter if it doesn't hurt. Indeed it doesn't really matter if it doesn't hurt quite a lot. 'The sort of distress which human beings cheerfully accept' (RUSSELL AND BURCH p. 59) is not worth bothering about in animals. I emphasize that such 'important pains' are undoubtedly present in a great many of the experiences to which we unnecessarily submit our kin. But this first device ingeniously deadens our concern, by way of the notorious philosophical error of supposing that pains are sensations (see WITTGENSTEIN 246 f.). They are not, as we can see from the fact that if they were, if 'pain' was the name of an incommunicable sensation, we should have no grounds for supposing that anyone else, or we ourselves at different times, meant the same thing by 'pain'. As the imagination of this possibility should instantly suggest, this would make no difference at all to the logic of pain-words. Pain involves sensations, sometimes, but is itself an abstraction from our common experience of distress. Pain is whatever we are distressed by, seek to avoid, squirm at enduring. Pains are not special sensations in the eye-balls. They are frustrations, blockages, threats to certain deeply ingrained natural wants. To say that some creature cannot be in distress, or the victim of injustice, because he has no special sensations (how could *we* tell that he does, or doesn't?), is like saying that one cannot be bored because one hasn't got pins and needles. But even if (some) pains *were* sensations, it does not follow that only such sensations deserve our pity.

What follows from this observation? First, a redirection of our attention to natural wants and ways of behaving as the standard by which distress and injury are judged. To deprive a creature of its proper pleasures is as great an injury, or may be, as to inflict special pains. Second, the beginning of a suspicion whether all talk about 'actual suffering' does not miss the point of injustice. Even to give a man a hair-cut is an assault if he had not implicitly consented to the operation, though the distress, let alone the 'painful sensations', this causes may be and probably is minimal. To interfere with my liberties without lawful authority is an act of oppression; to interfere even with lawful authority may often be properly regarded as oppressive. Any medical experiment carried out on a patient without his informed consent is an assault, and if the patient dies as a result of such an assault the experimenter is guilty of murder: as was the physician mentioned by PAPPWORTH (p. 26). By what right do we claim such lawful authority over the beasts as to decide on their behalf what they would or should mind? Perhaps they shouldn't mind being exploited or exhibited in certain seemingly minor ways: but perhaps they do. Who are we to say what is or is not oppressive interference? Even if they are patient under our interference, are we therefore in the right? Have I an automatic right to run my neighbour's life, as long as he is in no actual distress? Surely not: for if I have such a right, he surely has a duty to endure it. And how could I have such a right over an animal? If I have a right to command, then they have a duty to obey—and as Thomists are perpetually reminding us, animals have no duties. We therefore have no rights against them at all. If they were beyond all moral consideration—but they are not—we could leave them out of our calculations and say that I have a right, against my fellow men, to be allowed to deal with animals as I please. Once it is admitted that animals have a right not to be caused even Edward Heath's painful sensations in the eyeballs, we have lost all right to exclude animals from the list of creatures of whom we must, morally, take serious notice. And their lack of duties must entail our lack of rights against them.

Let no one doubt the pernicious effect of the sensation doctrine. In popular parlance it is one thing to put a small and sociable dog in a small cubicle on a cold floor and drug her into quietness, and quite another to be 'unkind'. In parliamentary debate it is claimed that the (unnecessary) stress and discomfort involved in transporting cattle to the slaughter over seas (unnecessarily) is no sign of cruelty, nor to be banned. MITCHELL (p. 63) seems to think that a bull-fight with an anaesthetized bull would not be cruel. There are degrees of agony, to be sure, and stages even on the road to hell: what matters on that road is that we should be walking upwards, and not down.

Proper pleasures and 'self-realization'

The concept of natural wants is also relevant to the second device, that animals cannot miss what they never knew. It may be that in some sense they cannot *desire* what they never knew: cannot, that is, put an image to nor, perhaps, even recognize, those things or events which would satisfy the urges and requirements of their nature. But the orthodox readily convince themselves that while there may be a genetically programmed urge to live and breathe and eat there are no limitations on what an organism can be induced to accept as fulfilling his urge to life. A similar judgement has been used to excuse any injustice upon the human poor. If a calf is breathing, and preferably fattening, it can have no wants unsatisfied: the evidence of induced debility, high mortality and common sense, that life is more than eating and drinking even for beasts, is automatically ignored (as it was not by KIPLING (pp. 185 f.) in considering the stables of Indian royalty, and their 'battery horses'). It cannot be too often emphasized that 'life', as Aristotle observed, has many meanings, that a lion's life is not an ox's, that they are differently programmed, that their capacities are differently realized, and that to deprive them of their proper context is to emasculate and corrupt them. Happiness according to their kind is the proper fulfilment of such capacities and wants as constitute their being in that kind.

It is odd that the orthodox so readily forget these things, for they are often eager on the one hand to insist that man differs from the other animals in being so much more flexible, that the animals are held tight to their instinctive tasks. 'The animals' use of their tools (their limbs etc.) is the blossoming of their organic structure. The animal as little needs to learn it as the plant needs to learn to flower.' (POPPELBAUM p. 93.)[1] And in that case to deprive an animal of the proper use of its limbs is as much a mutilation as to lop its legs off; and also vice versa. Though I should in passing add that though some beastly activities are entirely instinctive (as are some of ours— such as smiling), other activities, or the detailed application of the beasts' capacities, are learned: a cat *learns* to use a cat door.

The orthodox on the other hand may well seek to respond to my demonstration that it is unnecessary to be a carnivore that this lack of necessity is predicated upon too narrow a definition of living. It is part of *civilized* living, which we require by unalterable decree, to eat *pâté de foie gras*: so the goose's suffering is a necessity. That is to say: man is superior to the animals because he is more flexible than they, who cannot step aside from their natural programming, and requires that the animals be sacrificed for his sake because he is less flexible than they, who can be content to stand upon wire mesh in darkness and solitude, be fed an iron-free diet and await their only release, a casual death to enlarge the beef mountain. Man is better because more flexible, and so has dominion: he must use dominion as he does, because he is less flexible. It is a paradox and mystery beyond my comprehension.

Aristotle, in his search for the good life for man, employs an argument from the fact of man's distinctive nature as a practical creature with the gift of language (see CLARK ch. 2.1).[2] The argument has often been misunderstood, and ill-criticized with allegations that

---

[1] I quote a Steinerite to emphasize the mystagogic aspects of the notion; but it is entirely orthodox.

[2] *Nicomachean Ethics* 1. 1097b28 f.: man, like organic parts and like professions, has a 'function', i.e. to say what a man *is* is to say what men characteristically *do*, and must do well if they are to be good men. Aristotle concludes that the characterizing feature is simply that man's life is the life of action upon decision: 'man is condemned to be free'. I think it likely that animals do not decide things *on principle*: that they never make decisions seems an unwarranted assumption, unless it means just that.

he makes men out to be but instruments. On the contrary: free men cannot be instruments. Someone who is a natural slave, who must always follow another's will, is effectively an instrument for that other's will: he has no mind of his own. It does not follow that such slaves should be treated without respect, nor that they cannot achieve some sort of good life—though not the excellence of an autonomous career well-performed. Animals are not similarly instruments: perhaps they have no 'wills', never act on principle or with any universal rule in mind, but they are so constituted as not to need such wills—they have wishes, and act willingly or unwillingly (as Aristotle said (*N.E.* 3.1111b8 f.)), and they too have the possibility of achieving a decent life within their kind. Such a decent life is not defined by the absence of painful sensations, nor even the presence of pleasurable ones—it would be no answer to the charge of oppression in a tyrant that his victims were perpetually dosed or electrically stimulated to a pleasure too great for them to rebel. He would still be oppressing them: depriving them, whether they were man or beast, of the proper fulfilment of their genetically programmed potentialities. The arguments invoked, in my opinion mistakenly, against Aristotle's argument in the case of men do not even begin to touch its application in the case of beasts. There is a further point consequent upon the proper understanding of the argument from 'function': those who believe that animals are defined by extrinsic teleology, by their use to man, must imagine, given that fulfilment of one's nature is one's good, that it is to a pig's benefit to be killed and eaten: that is what he is *for*, that fulfils his 'function' (see PORPHYRY (1) III 20). The absurdity of supposing that such treatment can be a direct benefit to the animal itself may weaken the temptation to imagine that such extrinsic functionality is sound.

What I have revived, of course, is Salt's 'right of an animal to its own self-realization' (SALT (1) pp. 11 f., (3)), which RASHDALL (1 pp. 213 f.), amongst others, found so ridiculous. It sounds absurd to say that a beast has its own life to live, and as much right to live it without interference as anything else, but the causes of this seeming absurdity are not wholly respectable. How could any mere beasts' business be more important (to whom?) than what I want to do with them? What would be lost by its delay or prevention? How could a helpless creature like that, a mere lump of flesh, manage its own life at all? Clearly we must, we are morally obliged to direct it to the good ends we see so clearly for it, or rather for ourselves. God preserve us from such ill-meant benevolence. I can no more live my cat's life for her than I can live my son's for him: far less, for I can at least advise my son. Like Chrysippus, we are inclined to believe that animals are so much protoplasmic stuff without species-characteristics or individual personalities. All cats are grey in the dark of our own blindness; all that is not human is mere flesh. But it is not. 'There is very little difference between two healthy jelly-fish; a little more, but still not much, between two monkeys; but the difference between two normal men may easily exceed the difference between a jelly-fish and a monkey.' (HUXLEY p. 141.) SCHOPENHAUER, who similarly over-estimates human variability (1 pp. 131-2), was at least not a biologist: Huxley should know better.

Existence and individuals

The first two devices are designed to minimize the extent of animal distress which we unnecessarily cause; the next two urge that these distresses are the prices paid for certain compensating advantages to the animals, notably existence. I have some difficulty believing that they are seriously intended, for they would, without alteration, justify the vilest imaginable human slavery and oppression. Nor is it generally true nowadays—though once it was—that those who offer such anthropodicies are much impressed by them in their original form, as theodicy.[3] All I will say here of the third device is this: if existence is not an advantage to the individual concerned it cannot recompense him for his manifold distresses. If it *is* an advantage, then the seventh device fails—for to strip a creature of existence is to injure him. I do not think that advocates of the third device are wholly honest with themselves: witness that JOHNSON, who presents it, would not himself admit its application in the case of animals destined for vivisection. He merely underestimated the distress of farm animals: *we have no such excuses now.*

The fourth device allocates the advantage, in the first instance, to the population of which the distressed animals are a part. We are thereby invited to fantasize about the state and size of animal populations in a world whose men, moved at last to feel as troubled

---

[3] Those who have lapsed from the faith of their fathers because of the Problem of Pain are plainly under an obligation, lest they be like the god they hate, to avoid paining animals. Those who have not so lapsed should follow their God's commands and kill *only* for their needs.

by our conduct as we by our ancestors' towards men of another race, have come to behave a little more like DARLING's 'aristocrats' (2). Will we not have domesticated animals at all? Will we use their surplus milk, or eggs? What of lands where men must rely upon the tougher stomachs of their animal brothers to transform scrub into edible protein? I do not deny that it may be a great delight to wander through such gardens of bright images, but in this context such gardens are no more than fantasy withdrawals from realistic responsibility. It is entirely pointless to meditate upon cosy pictures of the self-sufficient household with its family pig, killed in winter that the rest may see another spring. Doubtless such pigs would be enormously happier than they are now; doubtless it is proper that one should die for many—though we do not think highly of such tribes as kill their elderly for similar cause. But all this is irrelevant to our present situation. In that situation perhaps pigs would, as it were, accept the bargain, or perhaps not. I am not myself in danger of starving, nor do I know anyone with a family pig. Nor would I think very highly of a family that found it easy to kill and eat such a pig: on the realities of cottage economy pig-sticking see, amongst many other accounts, UTTLEY pp. 26 f.

In passing, I would add that the orthodox, despite their overestimate of human deserts, are strangely pessimistic about human capabilities. KROPOTKIN ((4) pp. 49 f.) noted that the British tend to blame poor land for their own sloth in cultivation,[4] and Johnson had made a similar remark about the Islanders (JOHNSON AND BOSWELL pp. 112 f.). Much of what is now sheep country could profitably be reforested with nut-trees. We have already replaced many animal products with artificial, and may soon expect apparatus which will transform any vegetable matter into edible form without benefit of sheep. Zoophiles tend, justifiably, to be wary of modern technology, for the ends of our masters are debatable: we need not despair of a sanely directed technology.[5]

[4] 'There are no barren lands; the earth is worth what man is worth' ((3) p. 104). See also the success of Findhorn, a cooperative crofting enterprise in a 'barren' land.

[5] It is worth emphasizing that zoophiles are not, as such, anti-technological: for all its faults the motor-car at least eliminated the hansom-cab (on which see HELPS p. 9 f.). A 1920s vegan remarked that 'the horses earned their quittance in the Napoleonic Wars, and the cattle earned theirs in the Great War, and the time of their deliverance is at hand'. (FIRTH p. 27.) She was too sanguine, but she was right that the evils our technology has brought upon the world may also, in part, be cured or alleviated by technology. This is not a reason not to have a change of heart. On leaf-protein, for example, see PIRIE.

At its simplest, the fourth device proposes that a population of animals, to obtain a guarantee that it would increase and multiply, or that some of its members would be permitted so to multiply (for very few of our animals are allowed to breed), would certainly accept that both the present population and every subsequent generation would live under the conditions of the battery farm. This with such certainty that, as they cannot reveal their preference to us, we are entitled, by what right I know not, to decide the matter for them. I have not heard that any of those human beings who are so certain that this is a fair bargain have offered themselves and their multiplied descendants upon such terms.

The belief that there wouldn't be so many if we didn't breed them to eat is strangely counter-balanced by the obverse claim, that if we didn't eat them they would over-run us. Both fears are futile. In 1973-4 the R.S.P.C.A. alone killed 43,650 dogs (*Guardian* 16 September 1974): there are so many uncared-for because we neglect our responsibilities to them. Left to themselves most animal populations are relatively stable (see WYNNE-EDWARDS): if our interests are deeply threatened by their exceptional increase or decrease we may take steps to counter the threat—though such steps might more decently be contraceptive than military. There is, after all, a human population problem as well: should we argue that we must breed as many as possible (from selected lines) and control the numbers by imprisonment and war?

At its best, however, this fourth device has something to commend it. There are foxes because we hunted them, though the fox population is probably in no present danger of a catastrophic collapse should hunting cease. Because our gentry took to respecting the fox, even if only as an idealized type, foxes ceased to be mere vermin and fair game (VESEY-FITZGERALD (1)). Despite Salt's justified scorn it does seem almost possible that the fox might have accepted the bargain—unlike the hare, otter, stag and badger. Which is as much as to say that zoophiles have better targets for their spleen than fox-hunters. And anyone who does oppose fox-hunting should also oppose chicken-eating.[6]

---

[6] I emphasize that I do *not* support fox-hunting, but merely admit that without that ritualized murder the fox would still be everywhere considered vermin, and treated as such, with poison, traps and guns. The same excuse cannot be made for other sports (on which see MOORE, HUTCHINGS AND CAVER, GODLOVITCH AND HARRIS). And *all* reveal in their rituals their roots in sadistic impulse (see FLUGEL, MENNINGER).

But, as I have already hinted, hard-headed, though unrealistic, talk about populations, genetic lines and so forth, readily changes into less reputable chat. We are amazingly ready to stop considering individuals in preference to species, or types. Indeed we often forget that there is no such thing as 'an animal': there are foxes, ducks and squirrels, ants and bats and bees. Or rather, in the end, there are 'this fox here', 'this duck', Tabitha and Alexander Beetle, Archy and 'this bee'. What, after all, *is* an individual? In logic it is simply an entity to which a singular, rather than a universal term, attaches: there are many instances of being-red, or being-socratic; there is but one Socrates.[7] In this sense any member of an animal-species is an individual: it is a 'this', not a 'such-and-such', uniquely named, not merely described. But this sense is perhaps not intended. Again: individuals are distinct. That is, what is true of one is not necessarily true of another. Only those things, if any, which are true of one individual merely because it is of a certain kind are necessarily true of other members of that kind. In particular, one individual's pain is not necessarily another's, nor can one individual be directly compensated for pain by another's profit. I say nothing here against altruism.[8] A cow *might* be compensated for her distress by the charming thought that there would always, by man's gracious care, be cows: but without such thoughts—and who of the orthodox allows them?—she receives no recompense at all, no matter who gets profit from her pain.

So far, a piece of leaf is logically an individual, though it may not be a *distinct* individual in as full a sense as a cow: that is to say, though all individuals are independent of each other in logic, they may be very similar, and they may be distinguishable only by some more or less arbitrary division. Why divide the leaf thus rather than so? And when it is divided how different are the pieces? The division of plants and some animals—'living democracies' in AGAR's phrase (p. 92)—is varyingly arbitrary (not absolutely so): half a plant is still a plant very much as half a stone is still a stone. A stone

[7] I waive purely philosophical difficulties. It could be argued that the true individuals are momentary *bits* and being-Socrates as much a grouping concept as being-socratic. Conversely, that Red is a single, discontinuous individual just like Socrates. But in common parlance we think people, trees and chairs are individuals, while shades and tunes are not.

[8] Laboratory rats are greatly distressed by electric shocks inflicted, in their presence, on their fellows (CHURCH, see CARRIGHAR pp. 46 f.). They might, I suppose, be correspondingly pleased that another was free: I do not know. The spectacle of their empathetic agony does not seem to have softened the experimenters' hearts.

is a piece of stone; a grass is a piece of grass. Half a cow is not a cow, nor are cows pieces of undifferentiated beef. In some cases logical individuals share so many properties that we can distinguish them only by observing their unique spatio-temporal track: one is here, and one is there. We feel they are so similar as not to be *real* individuals: see one, you've seen them all. But this is very often our ignorance, and when we are dealing with creatures with a point of view, however diffuse and unexpressed, we can never legitimately ignore their individuality: one frog may look much like another, though there is ample scope in its genetic heritage for considerable diversity, but to the *frogs* they are distinct—one's pain is not another's. It is by no means obvious that human beings are so widely diverse for any uninterested eye, but each of us knows well that *he* is not his brother. And 'a cat, though unable to use the pronoun "I" does not mistake itself for someone else' (A. Comte: quoted by HUME (3)). Even if women are 'all alike' they are individuals, and distinct in sentience.

Anyone who has had a close relationship with an individual animal becomes exceedingly aware of that creature's quiddity, of the multiple divergences from any common type despite the convergence of certain basic properties. WILLIAMS has written of woolly monkeys (see (1) pp. 108 f.), GOODALL and others of wild chimpanzees, MAXWELL of otters, HOWARD of birds; even fish, with whom our chances of communion are small, display individual personalities. But even if, which is false, no purposes would be harmed by exchanging one creature for another, no overt difference made, yet it makes a difference to them. Even the vulgar can feel their own pain.

But perhaps yet another meaning attaches to the plaint of 'individuality': to be individual is not to be a mere singular, not merely to have logical independence, a distinct point of view, dissimilar properties. To be individual is to be something more, a source of variety, as a chessmaster is of gambits. It is a property of human language that it is infinite: there is no limit to the number of grammatical sentences that can be formed in any natural language, no limit to the number of true propositions that can be expressed by them. The universe of man's fiction is infinite, even if the physical universe is not. Any language-user is a source of infinite and unrepeated diversity: no mere animal can claim as much.

Once again, this is to exaggerate the *actual* diversity achieved by men: even such skilled language-users as philosophers have hardly, in essence, invented more than three or four philosophies since our records began. And it is perfectly clear, and perfectly permissible, that most people talk in clichés. Our linguistic inventiveness may be infinite in potential, but hardly so in practice. Conversely, animal behaviour is enormously more inventive than the orthodox permit themselves to believe; and I have no doubt that it is more inventive than we are ever likely to discover—many variations are as likely to be as undifferentiable by *us* as, say, 'prophets old' and 'old prophets' are to the non-English-speaker. We simply do not notice.

We do not notice. This is the crux of the matter. We passers-by cannot distinguish, or do not trouble to distinguish one calf from the next, and therefore assume that they are but mass-produced examples of a type, that only the ongoing life of the species is worthy of any respect at all, not this poor clone. We speak of the Cow, the Pig, the Fox, and somehow persuade ourselves thereby that we do no damage when we kill a cow, a pig, a fox. Of animals we are superstitiously Platonic: it is the Idea that is real to us, not the individual, suffering entities. We want there to be pigs, because we want to be able to go on seeing the Pig, or because we think the Pig bizarrely likes to be instantiated.

Most of the orthodox would of course fervently deny that they are Platonists; but our actions and our clichés speak more strongly here than creeds. WILLIS's investigations, as well as those of other anthropologists, suggest very strongly that individual animals are used as quasi-vocables to spell out a society's beliefs about itself and the world. *A* and *A* are different individuals, different tokens, but all that is important about them, all that is noticed about them, is that they are tokens of the single type *A*. Similarly with pigs: all that matters about them, all that we notice, is that they are tokens of the type Pig, and with their aid we can define our doctrines.

As an occasional Neo-Platonist I would not deny that there may be some truth in this, though not a truth that the orthodox should so willingly accept: that the phenomenal universe is in some way the expression of a spiritual reality whose nature is to be discovered by 'remembering' our own psychological archetypes. Such a doctrine at least goes some way to solving the problem of knowledge. But as an occasional Aristotelian I insist that we must not forget the dear particulars in the name of the universal. The idea that one can show love for the Cow by subjecting actual cows to continual pregnancies, taking away their children, rearing them in darkness and solitude, killing and consuming them, is really quite astonishing. There are Dog-lovers who feel it decent to kill a dog before their holiday, and collect a new one from the dogs' home when they return (BROWN p. 52): which, in its infamy, incidentally displays the seventh device for the sophism that it is. When such orthodox as SEYMOUR AND SEYMOUR, therefore, castigate vegans in particular on the grounds that if we were all vegans there would be no pretty cows and sheep in the countryside, we are entitled to ask why it matters, if it is true, that there should be no such poor slaves to be seen. Because we get aesthetic pleasure from the scene, and are therefore entitled to instigate whatever distress be necessary to achieve our satisfaction?[9] Or because the Great Bull will be annoyed if He is not instantiated? Strange worship of the Bull, to sacrifice His bulls to Him.

It may be, of course, that our greed has been the one reason our selfishness could accept for not engaging in a massive pogrom against all other animal life. LEWIS did not *invent* the attitude that 'On the art tree I would have the art birds all singing when you press a switch inside the house. When you are tired of the singing you switch them off. Consider again the improvement. No feathers dropped about, no nests, no eggs, no dirt.' ((1) p. 210.) Indeed, Lewis did not have to invent any of the attitudes displayed in that terrifyingly exact work. Why should we share *our* world (see EISELEY p. 128; H. E. EVANS pp. 276 f.)? Art trees are already preferred in Los Angeles (see TRIBE). From this final desecration of God's world our greed, and our ineptitude, has so far saved us. Sentimentalists may therefore be the zoophile's allies for a while.

---

[9] Those who appreciate such sights might follow Goldsmith's imagined hermit:

> No flocks, that range the valley free,
>   to slaughter I condemn.
> Taught by that power that pities me,
>   I learn to pity them (*Vicar of Wakefield*, ch. 8)

It is of course possible that some indefinite number of sheep or cattle, neither too few nor too many, are necessary to the good health of the land and to successful husbandry (though those who mention this commonly forget that, apart from vegetable-compost, there is no shortage of manure-producing mammals—called people). But it is obvious that the present system is not defended thus (for farm-sewage is a burden on our waterways, not a gift to the land), and far from obvious that the only way of keeping a balanced agricultural ecology, even including cattle and sheep, is by killing and eating the creatures with whom we share the land. It is only our characteristic inattention to animals that so deadens our ingenuity.

But the attitude of mind that thinks it a sign of neurosis to be personally attached to an animal as anything more than an exemplar of the species (as DEWAR pp. 157 f.) has, as Lewis knew, more sinister manifestations. 'The physiologist is a savant, seized and possessed by a scientific idea. He does not hear the cries of animals, nor see the blood which flows. He has nothing before his eyes but his idea, and the organisms, which are hiding the secrets he means to discover.' (BERNARD (1) p. 103.) The words of 'one of the greatest scientists of all time' (GRANDE p. 4), Claude Bernard, whose latter-day disciples still seem blind to what it was that outraged most of educated Europe (as VIRTANEN; see VYVYAN (1)): 'the physiologist is no man of fashion: he is a savant'. By this account he is a psychopath. The love of the Idea of the organism encourages him to torture, to be deaf to the torment of the very organisms whose Idea he loves, and which he sees as 'hiding the secrets he means to discover'. BERNARD's overt philosophy of science, that he investigates only the phenomena of the world machine ((1) p. 67), is betrayed by his language and his practice. He sees only his Idea, not the actual creature he betrays.

'"We must be cruel for the sake of human souls", cried the Inquisitioner. "We must be cruel for the sake of human bodies" echoed the Vivisector. "We get knowledge of God when we burn his image!" cried the Theologian. "We get knowledge of Nature when we crucify her children!" echoed the Scientist.' (POWYS (1) p. 77.)

I have remarked that I think Powys's analysis of the 'unspeakable delight' of such experimentation is faulty, but I agree that the delight is pathological. Science in origin, or in one of its origins, is a love and respect for the workings of nature, yet in the name of the discovery of our beloved's workings we are urged to dissect her living, and in Bernard's day, invariably conscious. Much of his research was done on the properties of curare, which paralyses but does not anaesthetize. There is, regrettably, more to be said on this subject: for the moment I wish only to emphasize that it is not zoo-philes who are the ones to ignore the actuality in the name of their fantasized pictures of the hidden Idea.

Hedonic calculus

With the fifth device we turn from attempts to minimize animal distress or to propose that it is compensated by some animal profit: instead the admitted distress of our more distant kin is to be weighed, in various ways, against our own profit or pleasure. Animal suffering is to be balanced against human suffering in the loss of animal slaves and force-fed geese. The fallacy behind the device needs to be stated: the notion that our desires and pleasures are given, ineluctable facts: that they are, as it were, laws of nature (TRIBE p. 1326). They change from generation to generation, and from year to year within the life of a single individual. Not only do they change: they can be changed. We can want to want some things, and not to want others, and achieve our major wish. We can grow used to states of affairs, or indoctrinate ourselves against them. The carnivore may feel that he would greatly miss his roasted pig: I can assure him that within a month of his turning vegetarian he will find the stench the odour of decay, and realize with some surprise that all cooked meats aspire to the condition of the properly-cooked vegetable. It was a laughable foible of the older vegetarian that he indulged in imitations, poor imitations, of meat-dishes. As a culture we have been purveying meat-dishes to taste like vegetables for many years. Our culinary tastes are so readily re-educable that we have no excuse for taking them as fixed parameters of our calculations. The determination to avoid unnecessary suffering must, as RUSSELL AND BURCH realize, issue in a further determination to make presently 'necessary' suffering unnecessary.

But suppose our tastes were fixed, or not so readily alterable. Our wish for drugs against our various pains, now that the prospect has been held out to us, seems unlikely to be altered. The extent to which we need them to alleviate pains certainly could be, for very many of the pains are consequent upon foolish culinary, or other, practice. The obscenity of offering drugs to remove an expected hangover, or indigestion, or many other conditions which could readily have been avoided, should be most clearly seen, for most such drugs have been tested against laboratory animals, and the demand for them in ever more refined forms must require further laboratory tests (which *could*, to be sure, be made on human tissue cultures or computer simulations: but which won't be). Even ROCHE (1) p. 92 is perturbed that beasts should pay for our irresponsibility. Zoophiles must practise what they preach: those who would save Otmoor from being flooded to make a reservoir must also save water; those who would spare animals must not imagine that science is there to spare us all ill consequences of our irresponsibility.

It is also possible to argue that the whole practice of fighting 'germs' with ever fiercer chemicals, which necessitate yet more tests, is about as foolish as the use of ever-fiercer insecticides: for, in both cases, unless we employ killing agents so ferocious that they kill off the whole population, and us as well, we are merely applying a selective mechanism to breed ever fiercer and less vulnerable germs and insects (see WEIL pp. 140 f.). And as DUBOS ((1) p. 64) has observed, the difficulties that follow antibacterial therapy are similar to such phenomena as the plague of baboons when their leopard predators are dead, or foxes' raids on poultry houses after myxomatosis drastically reduced the rabbit population.[10] It may well be that there are other and better ways of dealing with those diseases which manifest at one level as a pathological state of the whole organism and at another as a population explosion among microbes normally entirely at home in the organism (DUBOS (1) p. 66, 80; WEIL pp. 140 f.; GUIRDHAM). It is interesting that both Bernard and, in the end, Pasteur rejected the germ theory of disease (see FARBER p. 349, SELYE). These possibilities, if real and if accepted, might reduce the toll of animal mortality and distress very considerably, but our desire for health—or rather for a pain-free life (for if we desired *health*, we would already be vegetarians and herbalists and take adequate exercise)—might still be counted (by us) greater than theirs for life and liberty. We might also come to accept that the utterly disease-free life is as foolish an ideal as a bicycle that cannot be upset: 'threats to health are inescapable accompaniments of life' (DUBOS (2) pp. 84 f.), and 'health can be earned only by a disciplined way of life', not by prescription (DUBOS (2) pp. 93 f.).

I do not myself know if these possibilities and probabilities are real, though I think them rather likely to be. I believe it is incumbent on us to seek any way we can of getting out of the vicious circle of animal exploitation. But until, if ever, this is done we are stuck with the present medical situation in which experimentalists hold out to us the cure of our ills and tempt us therefore to countenance what they do to our brothers. Vivisection, as SHAW observed (pp. 32 f.), is tolerated because we imagine we will profit from it.

[10] See also COMMONER p. 13 on a case in Sarawak: insecticides against mosquitoes also kill cockroaches; cats die of eating poisoned roaches; rodents multiply to bring diseases— 'and the last state of that man is worse than the first' (Matthew 12:45).

Whether we have profited is a very uncertain question. 'The tide of infectious and nutritional diseases was rapidly receding when the laboratory scientist moved into action at the end of the past century' (DUBOS (1) p. 28) and the explanation for the ebb and flow of the various disabilities which have plagued us cannot dogmatically be defined as the knowledge won from vivisection. Nor can we be certain that, in cases where some profit has ensued, it could not have been obtained in some other way. It is *possible*, after all, that medical science profited from the Nazis' treatment of Jews. Nor is it easy to balance material profit against spiritual harm to our sensibility.

We have been tempted, and we fell, to the extent that antivivisectionists are commonly regarded as cranks and maniacs: 'Pug-loving sentimentalists who prate about a nature they will not take the trouble to understand—a nature whose genuine students they are ready to persecute.' (RITCHIE p. 110.) Would Ritchie have felt the same if human vivisection had been in question, as long as the humans were from the 'lower races'? Probably not, but the fact that he would not renders the utilitarian form of the device extremely suspect. Antivivisectionists have always raised the rhetorical question 'why do the vivisectors not employ human subjects, plainly so much more relevant to human ailments?' and have always been howled down. Yet we must ask what bar there is to be on such use that will stand against the lust for life that the experimentalist has invoked. If organic transplants ever become a technical success I see no reason to doubt on the declared philosophy of vivisection that 'lower races' and criminal classes will be dunned for their limbs and organs to keep the members of a dominant class alive a little longer (see L. Niven: *A Gift from Earth*). I hope that it will not happen, but there are already ominous signs. 'It is perhaps rather characteristic of the British that they have a law against the use of children in experimentation when it is not for their direct benefit.' (H. K. Beecher: FREUND p. 77.) Beecher goes on to quote G. Edsall to the irritated effect that British laws regulating animal experimentation are intolerably restrictive, adding 'The British have displayed a tendency to be carried away by their emotional reactions in such affairs time and again.' And again: 'Human experimentation is required in order for medical progress to be made...' (L. Lasagna: FREUND p. 273.) Are we to expect courageous and *knowledgeable* volunteers? I fear not. 'Such experiments are never carried out on private patients...' (PAPPWORTH p. 4.) We are to expect that children, mental defectives and the poor—in short, the defence-less—are to serve our experimenters' ends in the name of the well-being of the rest of us. Nor will they be asking *us* whether we wish our well-being to be served in this way. 'Little heed has been paid by the experimenters themselves to the occasional voices raised in protest against these practices.' (PAPPWORTH p. 3.) If Pappworth were an antivivisectionist, instead of wishing animals to be substitute victims in such cases, he would know why experimenters are so complacent: they have had a century or more of adulation by the orthodox. I would be easier in my mind if I were surprised by these developments.

Biomedical experiment is to be justified on the grounds that our current desires count for more than our victims' pains. It will be on grounds like these that experimenters begin—if they have not begun already—to employ aborted, but still living, foetuses as biological material. If we find this thought disgusting—as it surely is to any uncorrupted sensibility—we must ask why we hide our disgust at experimental treatment of animals.

The utilitarian calculus is ambiguous between a comparison of abstract pains and pleasures, and a comparison of the pleased or displeasured entities. In the first case, we are asked to quantify via some common unit the pains and pleasures of distinct entities. This is plainly impossible: there can be no direct comparison of the enjoyments or distresses of different creatures even of the same species: pain and pleasure are not quantifiable stuffs. Even if feelings of pleasure were correlated to the strength of electrical currents passing through the pleasure centre it would still be a grotesque philosophical fallacy to imagine that we could then trade five 'hedones' in Tabitha, a cat, for three hedones in Ricky, a mongoose, and two in Jane, a human child. Pleasure is subjectively assessed, within the whole context of the creature's desires and life-style. It is remotely possible that there *is* some cosmic creature who shares all pleasures and pains of its members, and such a creature might be in a position to reckon how much of pain it will endure to obtain a pleasure: but if there is, *we* are not simply identical with it. We, like the mongoose and the cat, are members of it, and should rather appreciate our secret unity than seize pleasure for ourselves.

If direct comparison of pain and pleasure is practically impossible, we must prefer a grading technique which depends upon a prior grading of the entities concerned: a cat's pleasure is to count for more than a gnat's, because a cat counts for more than a gnat, not because of some impossible calculation about hedones. Such a hierarchy will be the subject of a subsequent chapter. Here I will note only that a straightforward hedonic calculus, though sane as long as it is kept indefinite (e.g. that a burning cat is as anguished as a burning baby), rapidly becomes unworkable if we attempt to quantify it. Nor is there any reason to think such a calculation would give a result satisfactory to the orthodox. If it works at all we must admit that biomedical experiment has created enormously more anti-hedones than it has eliminated. If it does not work—and the orthodox cannot seriously wish that it would—we must revert to a grading of the entities concerned, not of their abstract pleasures. The fifth device then loses its utilitarian form, and becomes a simple declaration that those higher in the hierarchy may do what they like to those lower. Our opinion of this dictum when *we* are the victims is a matter that I will discuss later.

Rights and supererogation

The sixth and seventh devices are those of the liberal zoophile, and have (perhaps) helped to outlaw almost as much distress as they have licensed. But though liberal acceptance of the *status quo* as something to be ameliorated rather than changed may seem decently 'adult' and 'responsible' it is in fact treason. The R.S.P.C.A. may destroy animals on the grounds that their owners, if left to it, would destroy them less competently: but by making this calculation the R.S.P.C.A. makes it *easy* for owners to betray their pets (and see also p. 7). Liberal organizations, by their existence and their agreement with the enemy, have weakened the zoophile cause, with the best of intentions. Because professed zoophiles have been prepared to work with them, experimenters and farmers have been able to dismiss protests as coming from a lunatic fringe. They do not.

The sixth device requires that we ask ourselves whether we would endure such and such distress for the sake of some good end, and thereafter if the answer be positive feel justified in imposing such suffering upon an animal. In origin, this may be sound: 'Is (the experimenter) prepared to submit *himself* to the procedure? ... If he is not, the experiment should not be done.' (PICKERING p. 231.) LILLY has argued similarly—and has avoided self-deception by *actually* submitting himself, not merely professing that he would

((2) 85 f.).[11] But the rule must be applied properly. Perhaps, if I am heroic, I would accept some distress to benefit another: it does not follow that I am justified in imposing that distress upon a third party without the latter's informed consent. We must distinguish between distress inflicted for the victim's sake, and distress inflicted for some other sake entirely (GALSWORTHY pp. 66 f.). I hold myself justified, with many qualms, in ordering a hysterectomy upon my cat because she has an infected womb, or perhaps because there is no other way to prevent her being in continual labour (a state that plainly distresses her): it does not seem obvious that I am *therefore* licensed to order her hysterectomy merely to fit with my convenience, or because I want to see what a feline womb looks like. In 'putting myself in her place' I must not assume a readiness on her part to satisfy my foibles: particularly when I have no readiness on my part to satisfy hers. To claim that because I, in fantasy, *might* be heroic, I am licensed, in fact, to force the hero's part upon another in order to spare *me* distress which, were I actually heroic, I would hardly notice—but this is merely silly. In passing, it is strange that Thomists have not argued from Pius XII's dictum that I have no right to run a serious risk to myself in a medical experiment, that therefore and *a fortiori* I have no right to impose such risks upon an animal: if I should only impose distresses that I would bear, and I should not bear experimental risks, plainly I should not impose them—but coherence is not the Thomists' strong point.

I have remarked ((pp. 55 f.) that we have no rights against animals unless they have duties to us, and I would, in general, agree with the orthodox that they do not. Rights and duties *are* to this extent correlative (though not in the Thomists' sense). But I suspect that guard dogs and the like do have duties, and understand themselves to have such, within the pack-consciousness of which we take advantage. Correspondingly, we have certain limited rights against them (though insofar as it is *we* who have imposed this restriction on their natural ways, these rights *are* extremely limited: a conquered people may feel themselves duty-bound to their new rulers, but the rulers' *rights* are debatable). And they in turn have special rights against us, beyond the normal rights of fair treatment, food, shelter and

---

[11] On the debit side LILLY still insists on trying it out on animals first; on the credit side, he did at least release his dolphins—after several had committed suicide ((2) pp. 69 f.). Given his belief that dolphins are intelligent creatures his assaults upon them (as (1) pp. 46 f.) make particularly distressing reading.

courtesy that other and less communally responsible members of the household have. We, who have taken the place of the dog's pack-leader and doomed it to permanent adolescence, at least owe it kindness. It is for such reasons, amongst other and more openly sentimental or pragmatic ones, that antivivisectionists have often pressed the case for special exemptions at least for *dogs*. The *Daily News* in a *cause célèbre* of 1903 (19 November) spoke against experimentalists with the words 'Does not the overwhelming trust (of the dog) lay upon us some obligation?' (quoted by VYVYAN ((2) p. 57); see DOGS). Even RITCHIE allows that there might be 'quasi-duties' to such 'honorary human beings' as dogs (p. 110). Even KANT urged that to shoot a faithful dog was, at least, to damage one's humanity ((2) p. 240): how much more to torment it. And PATON remarked (p. 323), without naming his target, that 'the attitude of every decent man towards his dog is very different from his attitude to stocks and stones' (see also PLUTARCH ((3) Cato 4.5) on that vile man, Cato the Elder). All this is certainly inadequate from the radical zoophile's viewpoint, but it shows some remaining decency. As GALSWORTHY said, 'if this be sentiment, it is not mere cultured sentiment, but based on a very real and simple sense of what is decent' (pp. 65 f.). Such decencies, however, have not restrained us even in this case. If we have special rights against dogs, they do not include the right to torment and kill.

In general, we have *no* rights against animals: no right of punishment, no expectation of 'good' behaviour, no right to command. Man's dominion, if he has such, is not of that sort. As with babies in our care, so with animals: we may not consent to operations that will benefit only us, but only operations that will benefit the child, or the animal (see PAPPWORTH pp. 31 f.). We may resist attempts to steal the child, or the animal—but not absolutely, for we have no *absolute* lien on either. We may restrain the child, or the cat, from interfering in the other's rightful path. In all these cases it may be said that we have, in some sense, rights *over* the child or the animal: but such rights amount to no more than a general or special responsibility to *defend* the child or the animal. We have no right to do as we please with either; and *a fortiori* have no rights against other creatures that are not even in our care. No-one has a right to experiment on an animal even to the extent of causing such distress as he might endure for his own sake, unless (at most) he imposes it for the *animal*'s own sake. BERNARD admits this

principle in the case of human beings, though with no great conviction, and adds that even operations admitted under it may profit
science ((1) p. 101). No-one has a right to do more: 'of whom could
you purchase such a right? Who could make such a conveyance?'
(LAWRENCE: NICHOLSON p. 92.)

Death

The seventh device is to permit killing, but not hurting. Again,
this does not do what the orthodox would have it do, for present-
day farming methods and any slaughtering technique employed on
a large scale involves great suffering. But, as I have remarked, the
device lessens the orthodox unease. Utilitarian doctrine, of course,
always finds it difficult to isolate what exactly is wrong in 'painless
killing' even of human beings, and C. W. Hume appears to share
this puzzlement. The principle of negative utility—that we should
avoid hurt—seems to require that we take whatever steps seem most
effective to the total elimination of sentient life, for all life involves
some pain. The leading principle of U.F.A.W., as GODLOVITCH
has argued (see also GODLOVITCH AND HARRIS), therefore
requires that we kill every animal we see. If the principle of negative
utility is supplemented by that of positive utility—that we should
endeavour good—it seems that we are committed to creating as
many living beings, human and otherwise, as will give us the highest
proportion of pleasure to pain. This would hardly licence any and
every death we sought to impose, but it might licence particular
deaths, including yours and mine, if the totalizing minimax calculation should so decree. How this calculation is supposed to be carried
out is indeed the fundamental problem of utilitarian theory: I cannot believe that our *present* situation is blessed by it, but I have great
difficulty imagining what exactly would be the end-result of successful action on such a theory. I cannot believe that anyone else is in
much better condition—the one Cosmic Entity might manage it,
and perhaps already does, but we most certainly cannot even begin
to try. It seems appropriate to add at this point that conversation
has convinced me that utilitarianism, whatever its origin, is now
merely a final, and entirely vacuous, pretext for doing whatever the
speaker himself fancies: when it has become obvious, for example,
that foetuses are *not* parts of the mother's body, that *no-one* has a
general right to act as they please to their bodies, that what is *allowed*
to happen in one case cannot therefore be *caused* to happen in

another—and that all the other 'easy speeches that comfort cruel men' are so much wasted breath, *then* there is a sudden appeal to the utilitarian calculus, which is, being strictly incalculable, the dead end of argument. And so we go on burning babies (on foetal sentience see THORPE pp. 215 f.).

But to return to the status of killing. It is possible to believe that the law against murder is not a rule-of-thumb concerning the (usually) poor consequences of killing someone—a rule that may sometimes fail—but a basic, sacred law. If this involves some recognition of a sacred character in the possible victim, it seems difficult to think of any such character in men which would not also, perhaps in less degree, be present in animals—though I shall try to imagine such in a later chapter. But it is also possible to believe that the law is rather the fundamental requirement of any human society: for there to be a society there must be general acceptance of a law forbidding arbitrary killing—though what reasons will licence killing, and so change it from murder, may differ from state to state. If this is the rationale of the law it may seem clear that we need no such law with respect to animals: *their* actions will not be influenced by our ceasing to kill them.

I have already hinted that we cannot be entirely sure of this last, factual point: the records of the saints suggest that a change of attitude in us may sometimes meet a change in the outer world. But I will not argue that point here. Rather consider this: any attempt to relate the moral law to the survival of society must meet the problem that many of our traditional moral laws relate to the stranger, who is by definition apart from our society. Are we to kill him conscienceless? Well, perhaps not: for to kill him, being in so many respects so like our fellow citizens, must gravely weaken our commitment to the avoidance of intra-tribal murder. But if that is so, killing animals, who are so like us, may also weaken our respect for human life. As indeed it does: our mediaeval ancestors were perhaps saved from the slide by positing an absolute metaphysical difference between animals and men—we no longer have such a defence. Those who kill animals for their delight will soon kill men: it will not be long before the N.S.P.C.C. finances 'proper abortions' and 'puts down' battered babies:[12]

---

[12] Lest I be misunderstood: I intend no insult to the N.S.P.C.C. or its sister organizations—I merely draw the parallel with the behaviour of the R.S.P.C.A.

There are enough
born, even too many, and our Earth will be overrun
without these arts.
(William Blake, 'Vala' 7.120 f.)

In fact, I doubt that any moral law, even the law against murder,
is adequately backed by the 'need' to preserve society. There is no
moral law so bizarre, or so immoral, that some society could not
make a tenet of its being. Conversely, it is not obvious that social
gatherings, of the sort that are actually *needed*, need have any *moral*
commitments at all: if we need each other, why should we need
the law to forestall attempts to destroy each other? Do we refrain
from killing our friends and lovers and children merely because
there is a law against it?

When the great Tao declined,
the doctrines of humanity and righteousness arose.
When the six family relationships are not in harmony,
there will be advocacy of filial piety and deep love to children
(Lao Tzu 18: CHAN p. 148.)

It is surely extremely paradoxical that death should not be recognized as the greatest of single hurts, the final pain for fear of which
all other pains are intensified. If death is no hurt, what ill is done
by those who have their cats 'put down' for not matching the new
decorations (BROWN p. 52)? Certainly such behaviour tests, to destruction, the 'person's generosity or meanness of spirit' (LORENZ
(1) p. 29): but that is to admit that *not* all killings are decent. The
fact that it may sometimes be the lesser evil to kill a deeply injured
animal, as Hume insists—and as SALT agreed ((1) pp. 34 f., (4) pp.
35 f.)—does not even begin to show that death is no evil at all. This
is the ancient fallacy that if, for example, it is permitted to kill a
foetus to save a woman's life, it is therefore plainly permitted to
kill a foetus to save her white wedding.

I am less easy in my mind than Salt that we are entitled to kill
those (which?) wild animals that threaten our supremacy. I see in
this a slide towards the muddle which caused Shaler to pass from
a defence of animals' rights, through the assertion that 'we must
continue to burthen, tax and slay; but we may fairly be required
to inflict no *unnecessary* suffering' to the old buffoonery that 'the
only and supreme test of our relations to these subjects is the well-

being of man considered from the higher point of view.' (SHALER pp. 204 f., 210 and 211.) Shaler meant well, but by increasing our self-claimed rights of self-defence from defence of our safety to the ensuring of our advancement he rendered his principles ridiculous (p. 217; as do DUBOS (3) and PASSMORE).

I fear that the seventh device is in the end no better than the first, and the arguments advanced for it lend considerable support to the opponents of human euthanasia—let it be admitted that killing, even as a lesser evil, is allowable, and our human illogic concludes that killing is no wrong at all. This is indeed without reason, but men's hearts are evil from the beginning.

The device, in relation to the Act of 1876, has caused some considerable injustice. I think little of a murderer who comforts his proposed victim with the information that it won't hurt. And even less of a tormenter who consoles us with the promise that we won't be allowed to recover consciousness after his administrations. Yet because killing is thought no evil, in comparison with pains which in other contexts liberals are eager to minimize, laboratory animals are killed in thousands rather than suffer any temporary pain on the road to recovery. Better that such victims *should* recover consciousness, even with some pain, and be delivered into freedom as some honest recompense for their ill-treatment. In this I am in partial agreement with the R.D.S.—though *their* advocacy would urge that the animal be subjected yet again to such tender mercies as experimentalists find in their hearts.

In conclusion, RITCHIE (p. 111) was right where he least intended it: if animals have rights 'we should no more be entitled to put them to death without a fair trial, unless in strict self-defence, than to torture them for our amusement.' Quite so. 'He who tortures a living creature is no worse than he who slaughters it outright.' (PLUTARCH (1) 996a.) Plutarch's passion made him overstate the case—certainly it is worse to kill slowly than quickly: but if the torture be not to death, and not last too long (whatever 'too long' means) would we not prefer it? Men have undergone unanaesthetized operations with such conviction. How then can death not be a hurt? And what right have we to inflict such supreme hurts on our brothers?[13]

---

[13] One last suggestion: is killing men worse than killing animals because it interferes with long-term projects of a sort that animals do not have? Do they not? Do all men? Even if killing men is *worse*, does that mean that killing animals is good? Particularly when breeding animals for slaughter is to connive at the death of starving humanity?

More on utility and population control

Having said so much against utilitarianism, I should in fairness emphasize that the founding fathers of that philosophy reckoned animal pains and pleasures to be morally relevant, and that the utilitarian calculation, when properly performed, clearly outlaws modern farming techniques and most biomedical experimentation. A utilitarian is perhaps more willing for the suffering of the few, or the trivial suffering of the many, to be outweighed by the benefits derived from that suffering. He does not think it out of the question that painful experiments on animals, or on men, could be justified by results. But no decent utilitarian could be satisfied by a mere account of those benefits without any parallel attempt to reckon up the losses. It may be that animal pains are justified by human benefits: but it could also be that human pains are justified by animal benefits.

What is such a decent calculation like? We must not weigh pains directly against pleasures: if we did that any form of animal-torture could be justified by the exquisite pleasure the torturers found in that occupation. Such adventitious pleasures, whose absence involves no serious discomfort (or no discomfort that a decent man should take seriously), cannot outweigh the pains inflicted to obtain those pleasures. Only those pleasures that are 'necessary', whose absence is itself a distress, are relevant to the calculus. We may legitimately pain one creature if the alternative is to pain several; we may legitimately do so (the utilitarian believes) if the alternative is to *let* several suffer pain. But of course if the pain the several would suffer is minor and the pain the one suffers is large, the calculus does not obviously allow this exchange. The pains we seek to avoid or to relieve must be of a strength correspondent to that which we plan to inflict. One should not cause one creature agony even in order to save a hundred from a minor ache.

Again: one must weight the pains we hope to relieve by taking account of the probability of that relief. The pain we inflict is certain: our hopes are almost always uncertain. Perhaps a given act will lead to benefits, but we must not assume their certainty: any imagined benefit, however large, must be diminished by the order of its probability before it is weighed against the certain pain we cause (though I doubt if any exact figure can thereby be assigned to it).

And again: we must prove the counterfactual (or at least render it highly probable) that the benefits could be obtained in no other way. And this is very difficult. Quite apart from the non-vivisective techniques publicized by F.R.A.M.E. (which may of course have their own drawbacks) we already know that many human ills can be avoided or alleviated by the herbal remedies of our ancestors or by changing our diet and way of life. More would be saved from death by cancer by a simple ban on cigarettes than are ever likely to be saved by the millions spent on giving malign tumours to the non-human.

To sum up: any honest vivisectionist who appeals to the utilitarian calculus despite its manifest difficulties of sense and application must surely conclude that he is justified in inflicting pain on the non-human, or in depriving them of their proper pleasures, only where there is a very high probability of thereby relieving substantial pains that could not be relieved in any other way. And in adopting this rationalization as his own he must also admit that humans must be asked to endure some pains in order to save non-humans from their pains. If the calculus works one way, it must also work the other.

Antivivisectionists have recently limited their attack to such atrocities as the testing of cosmetics, allowing (by implication) that certain obviously medical experiments are at least excusable. As a matter of practical politics they did well. But even the 'medical' experiment is open to question, even upon utilitarian grounds. It has been pointed out that cancer affects twenty-two people in a thousand, and costs 1.8 million working days in a year: accident, poison and violence (which is hardly broader a category than the indefinite 'cancer') affect 112 people per thousand and cost 29 million working days in a year (figures for the U.K.: *New Scientist* 69.1976 p. 322). On purely economic grounds it would seem reasonable to divert much of the finance and professional skill involved in cancer research to other areas. If we are prepared to do this for economic reasons, it is surely not too absurd to advise it also for *moral* reasons. Utilitarians allow some experiments upon animals, and upon people: they do not thereby give a blanket defence for all such acts.

One other application for utilitarian theory is in the field of population control. Even zoophiles are likely to be committed to utilitarian argument in this context. For though it would undoubtedly

be *just* that we should release all battery animals from their dun-
geons and provide decent lives for them in return for their sufferings, it is quite certain that we are not going to do that. It may even
be true that we *could* not do that. The most zoophiles hope for is
that the number of such slaves shall be allowed to decline from year
to year as the demand for their flesh decreases. In short, zoophiles
hope that the quantity of animal suffering will be reduced at the
cost of reducing the number of animals. We cannot help the present
inmates of our Belsens and our Bedlams, or at least we (as a nation)
are not going to. There will be less suffering in a vegan world, even
in a near-vegan world.

But it can be said, in a version of the fourth device, that this will
also diminish the amount of animal pleasure. Of course, the
pleasures of our battery beasts could hardly be fewer than they
already are; even the pleasures of more traditionally reared farm-
animals are not as cosy as childrens' literature would have us all
believe. But it is possible, and almost plausible, to argue that some
breeding of animals, to multiply such pleasures, is required on utilitarian principles. And that since animals experience fewer pleasures
as they get older, they should be constantly replaced by young animals in order to keep up the pleasure quota. In other words, beasts
should be reared for a painless slaughter (if such a thing exists) as
soon as they are past their peak of enjoyment. Such a utilitarian
could perhaps avoid the application of similar principles in the field
of human population control by insisting that elderly humans do
not enjoy life less than the young (or that they have different but
equivalent pleasures) and that the prospect of forced death at
fifty(?) would cast a blight on early life.

My answers to this are firstly, that it is plainly irrelevant to our
present situation in which to promote their increase is thereby to
promote their suffering (GOMPERTZ p. 12); secondly, that it is not
clear to me that elderly animals enjoy life less than the young (even
animals have other things to think about than sex); thirdly, that
such a treatment of the elderly in this or any other species is destructive of certain fundamental responses of respect and affection that
are intrinsically valuable and an essential part of any life that can
be considered pleasurable; fourthly, that to deprive the elderly of
a life they think worth living is theft, and the principle which advocates it is treating living creatures purely as a mechanism for multiplying something that the social engineer considers good. Such

a population programme, for men or for the non-human, manages to combine a soaring impracticality with a mean-spirited pseudo-pragmatism: in short, it is 'utilitarian' in about the same way as the terror-bombing of Vietnam.

Necessity and amoralism

The eighth device is to plead necessity: not in the sense that the actual act excused is necessary, but in that so much suffering is un-avoidable, both in human projects that we cannot defer and in the world at large, that there is no point troubling about the pains we unnecessarily cause our kin. This is the line to which such liberals as SMITH AND WILCOX tend, proud of their 'country realism'. 'It's got to be'; 'life is cruel'; 'the world's a mystery' and so forth. The Sherpas similarly, and with more excuse, see that some sin is quite unavoidable, and therefore feel 'no overwhelming incentive to avoid some of the more pleasurable sins.' (FÜRER-HAIMENDORF p. 189.) They at least believe that such minor, inevitable sins, as well as the greater and strictly avoidable must be compensated by the doing of good works. And this is surely a sounder response than the irre-sponsibility of indifference. Few of us are wholly expert in any craft: it does not follow that we should be content to be wholly incom-petent. If we cannot be saints (if we cannot), let us at least not be wholly given over to evil living.

As PATON remarked 'We are what we are by the long struggle of humbler things' (p. 230), and should feel some sentiment of honour as a result to live decently, or with such heroism as we can muster: 'Innocent beasts have had to suffer in cattle-cars and slaughter-pens and lay down their lives that we might grow up, all fattened and clad, to sit together in comfort and carry on this dis-course.' (JAMES (1) p. 50.) Where so much of ill *is* unavoidable, where so much is decreed by our necessities, there is surely good reason to avoid what we can, and ourselves practise some slight degree of the hardiness we expect from others.

Those who invoke the eighth device feel otherwise, and I may perhaps admit that some varieties of zoophily are to blame. The propaganda of pacifism has had the paradoxical effect that, thinking all war is vile, even decent men imagine therefore that all war must be total. If war is vile, and if we find ourselves at war, we can make no careful moral choice nor quibble at whatever means may seem most apt to victory. To wage less than total war seems irresponsible.

The result has not been happy. Similarly, once we are convinced that animals suffer and can be injured, it is bizarrely easy to conclude from 'nature red in tooth and claw' that all paths are evil, and we must not waste emotional energy on making distinctions (see MACIVER). But, as I have remarked, there are stages even on the road to hell. The courtesies of war may seem, and are, irrational: but not to abide by them, even where such treacheries bring some immediate profit, is to weaken the barriers of custom in the world and in our hearts, and to prepare the way for ever greater ill. Just so in our relations with the non-human: if we must kill to live, let us kill cleanly, and let us not forget that sometimes we have no need at all to kill. In short, humane killing is better than careless, but worse than no killing at all; the foreseen, but unintended death (as those of insects on a car's windscreen) weighs less heavily than a deliberate killing; killing for food is one thing, killing for fun another (but see above, p. 52).

Even vegans, in the world's present state, must recognize that animals, from insects up to rabbits, have been killed to save for men the crops on which we live. That even vegans thus require death in no way licences still further death, of cows and sheep and birds. 'But they'd die anyway', the orthodox insist: so die we all, but not all die so young, in slavery, and by the knife. If we must kill 'pests', it does not follow that we may kill creatures that do us no harm (PLUTARCH (1) 964d): and in abandoning the latter practice we may find that fewer things *are* pests than we had thought. 'For the sake of a little flesh we deprive them of sun, of light, of the length of life for which they were born.' (PLUTARCH (1) 994e.)

Doubtless we live, in part, under necessity, but we give that goddess more honour than she deserves. Is it necessary to kill badgers, as carriers of bovine tuberculosis? Perhaps—though less violent methods are commonly employed with human centres of infection particularly where the chances of infection are demonstrably so small—but this necessity is predicated on our keeping cows. Is it necessary to kill 'superfluous' male calves? Perhaps—but only if we require dairy herds of such a size: male calves are not superfluous in the wild. It is *we* that both destroy their function and multiply their numbers—and *we* that owe them courtesy. Is it necessary to kill wild rivals for our food, such as birds and rabbits? Perhaps— but better husbandry of *our* food and less destruction of their natural landscape might leave enough for all. It is *we* that steal their land for cattle, and for roads, and industry, and then complain that they come poaching.

There are stages on the road to hell: what matters is which way we're going. On this road to stand still, to say that here is well enough, is to wake up at some still lower level. If here is well enough, how can a step down matter?

The eighth device, if it is still taken seriously—or taken seriously for the first time, is the rejection of all morality. If we excuse ourselves by prating of a general necessity, a 'realistic' rejection of all dangerous ideals, where shall we appeal to condemn such conduct of man to man as is common in our history? I see no resting point before a complete amoralism. Well, let us be amoral: what follows then?

The true amoralist follows his fortune. He may kill and fight, but he does so without enmity, without indignation: 'The tiger that assails me is in the right, and I who strike him down am also in the right. I defend against him not my *right*, but *myself*.' (STIRNER p. 128.) He may take what he desires, but makes no claim on it beyond that desire. He has no need, nor desire, to 'demonstrate man's superiority' (see p. 19). If he is hungry he eats, but needs no carefully symbolic dish of meat to prove to him he is a *man*. He knows no law but his caprice, and rests in that. His is the state that Walt Whitman, inaccurately, attributed to animals:

They do not sweat and whine about their condition;
they do not lie awake in the dark and weep for their sins;
they do not make me sick discussing their duty to God;
not one is dissatisfied—not one is demented with the mania of
owning things;
not one kneels to another, nor to his kind that lived thousands of
years ago;
not one is respectable or industrious over the whole earth.

('*Song of Myself*')

The total amoralist, in fact, is not in the least like the ordinarily immoral man which the eighth device would have us become. The amoralist, if he wanted to enjoy the flesh rather than the company of man or animal, would set about doing so: but the orthodox must ask themselves why they so readily imagine that he would wish such flesh. Why do they suppose that one outside the law, outside all laws including the honour of a gang, would automatically want to hurt and destroy? It is the moralist who is the sado-masochist at heart, not the amoralist.

In short: the eighth device, if it is serious, marks the end of all morality. Those who think this a bad thing should abandon that device. Those who wonder if it might, after all, be good (in some sense of that term) should wonder what a true amoralist would do: would he really aggrandize himself at the expense of animals? What is there, realistically, to enjoy in that?

There are of course other, seeming amoralists, such as Thrasymachus: who was truly no more a real amoralist than is a thief. Thieves pay tribute to morality, to property, for they claim things valued by society, even to their realistic hurt. The true amoralist makes no claim, nor values property. It is Thrasymachus, however, that such orthodox as Austin have admired: 'might is right'. We are the god-gifted, the powerful, the clever, and none shall take these *our* animals out of our hands for ever.

And may God have mercy on our souls.

V

REASON AND THE IRRATIONAL

Fantasy and the future

I have been trying to rebut some of the many devices with which the orthodox defend their positions. I do not think that any of them, even if they were formally correct, do anything to counter the over-whelming case against meat-eating at the present time. As Anna Kingsford remarked, with characteristic rhetoric, in 1881:

> 'Shew me, O man of prey, for what reason you slit the throat of a living creature and devour its tissues and organs, when you may have nourishment of better value, in purer and stronger condition, without recourse to bloodshed! Shew me why you are not revolted and shocked by all the filthy practices and processes involved in this habit of carnage; how you reconcile the idea of the slaughter-house with ideas of progress, beauty and gentle manners; and when you have made out your case to your satisfaction, it will be time enough for me to begin making out mine!'
> (KINGSFORD AND MAITLAND p. 66.)

It is not the zoophile who should have to apologize for himself, but the carnivore. In considering the last eight devices I have at least attempted to give them what weight I decently can, and hope that I have shown you that they are, at best, somewhat *peculiar* arguments. Ethical disagreements very often depend upon factual error and logical muddle much more than on any inarguable ground of ultimate preference (see MONEY-KYRLE). Those who treat animals so differently plainly *see* animals differently, and the erroneous vision gains power from logical confusions and ill-digested memories of the philosophical fashions of the previous generation. The trouble with most of the orthodox is that they do not listen to what they are saying.

In the end, I suggested, the orthodox must collapse upon the simple claim that this is how we behave, and who shall say us nay? As to that, I know not, though if the gods or extra-terrestrials one day descend I fear that we may *wish* there was some referee. I am disinclined to imagine as some zoophiles do (EVANS (2); SALT (1); HUME (1) (2)) that one day sympathy and justice, already extended to slaves and the poor and women, will be extended to animals. It seems equally possible that sympathy and justice will soon be reverting to the dominant élite. I have little faith in the progress of civilization.

'The development of human personality is the ultimate purpose of civilisation', said CARREL (p. 318), defending with this doctrine the torture and execution of the antisocial and insane, including all those that deceive the public. I do not pin my ethical concerns on fantasies of distant futures that I shall not see: the future is an agreeable domain for fantasy, on a level with the unknown past or that magic land over the hills and far away. It has little more to do with our realistic concerns than any other fable—and may easily be a pretext for the vilest *actual* and present infamy. To be sure, we may influence what is to come—but only you that come after, if you have chanced upon this book, can say what we have influenced. It is yet another flaw of a full-fledged utilitarianism that it demands of us prophetic powers we do not have: 'Germany has long since outgrown the swaddling clout of Pan-teutonism, and no ranting of anti-Semitic agitators and men of that ilk about ur-deutsch and rein-deutsch can permanently affect the public mind or elicit a favourable response in legislative enactments...' (EVANS (2) p. 50.) This in 1897. Who knows what is around the corner? Who, for that matter, can accurately define what good or ill may flow from our actions, or our enemies'? 'From adultery and the violation of prisoners the process of nature will produce fine children, to grow, perhaps, into fine men; and where wicked violence has destroyed cities, other and nobler cities may rise in their place.' (PLOTINUS III.2.18.) Shall we then do evil that good may come? God forbid (see Romans 6:1 ff.).

Our actions need some stronger root than such dull fooling with futurity.

Crisis and hierarchy

But of course I can't be serious. Worried about rabbits? Where will it all end? If it was a choice between human being and animal, I'd save the human being, wouldn't I? I can't really be denouncing farmers and scientists and hunters and planning officers and pest-controllers and fishermen and gardeners spraying insecticide. Can I? It's a matter of proportion, isn't it? I can't be serious. Why should we consider them? They don't consider us.

Once again I ask you, simply, to inquire within if such embarrassed squawks can truly hide the simple truths that *we* do not need meat, that meat-production must involve enormous suffering (and now far more, the more meat is produced), that most of us—until such care is inconvenient to us—desire at any rate to spare our animals such suffering as is avoidable. I do not, dare not, preach perfection—though the Lord Christ did: what could be easier than the step suggested?

Where will it all end? What would I do in a crisis?

The argument from crisis has a familiar ring to it: Thomists in particular should be wary of it. If I had to choose between saving my wife's life and saving my cat's, I would save my wife. I would make the same choice between my wife and a neighbouring human. And most likely I would choose that latter human before I saved the cat. But what if the choice lies between, say, a chimpanzee and an incurably comatose human? Is the choice *so* easy? And how comatose must the human be, or how close to human the animal before we can defend the less racist choice? *Do* we make such choices upon principle? Or do we act, and justify our action afterwards? And what exactly do we gain from harping on such stories, save the covert release of hidden aggression and a gradually diminishing sense of the moral enormity of such crises (see BROPHY)?

There was a fashion for such stories in the 1850s: JAMESON (p. 74) records one such of a girl who asked her lover whom he would save in a fire, his mother or herself. 'My mother', he replied. Doubtless the girl got the answer she deserved, but seeing her chagrin he gallantly added that to save the girl first would be as if he had saved *himself* first. The worse than infantile psychology of the two parties to the discussion should be a warning against such imaginings. But consider further: perhaps the man would as a general principle—though it is to be hoped that it would never come to the test—save his mother rather than his current girl-friend in the event of a fire. And perhaps he would be generally approved for doing so. But would he therefore have the admitted right to *kill* his current girl-friend in order to obtain something that would save his mother's life? Or to save her health, or satisfy an ineradicable desire she felt, or meet a passing whim? Obviously not: what we do, because we must, in no way licences what we may do in the ordinary course of events. Not even to save a life may we kill even such as we would *let die*: Thomists indeed are more committed to that rule than I would be. Still less may we kill for lesser ends. What would we think, as BROPHY asks, of a man who was perpetually having to abandon his girl-friends to the flames? Should we not suspect that he had a rather low opinion of their value? Accidents, the same sort of accidents, do not happen so frequently to one man unless they are not accidents.

So the crisis argument does not entitle me to kill or maim even for the benefit of those whose life I would undoubtedly prefer to save. In the fire Fate, as it were, has preselected my victim: I do not therefore have the right to throw an arbitrary victim on the flames even to save a human life, let alone satisfy a human habit—which is the end for which most murdered animals must die. I might, of course, choose to act unjustly, just as I might choose to commit perjury to save a friend, though even here there would have to be a certain seriousness to the friend's danger. SHAW expressed the hope that he would reject any remedies of his ills based on animal suffering, and Plotinus actually did reject the theriacal remedies of his day (PORPHYRY (2) 2). Such rejection is easier when the proferred draught—as beef-tea to Gandhi's wife—is so plainly a piece of pseudo-medical superstition. Where the remedy is real, and our pain is great, few of us have heroic virtue. But such crises do not legitimate our normal conduct, and only point to those areas of research that must most urgently be supported—to find replacements for all such devil's brews. What if a longevity drug could be distilled from the livers of tortured babies? Who would buy his extra years at such a cost? And how far would his claim of unfortunate necessity be accepted, particularly if he made no attempt to find other sources? What if the drug was but to dye his hair?

The crisis argument, then, has little general force: but it does draw attention to the manifold hierarchies within which we move. So also does that other ancient fatuity that because there are, for example, millions of micro-organisms in a glass of water we may therefore kill cattle with a clear conscience. May we also kill men? To ask the obvious: who is to say that micro-organisms are harmed by being drunk? Is it really supposed that micro-organisms have as developed a point of view as such complex creatures as squids and cows and cats? Are we to commit unnecessary evil merely

because there is some we cannot avoid committing?[1] But the orthodox perennially imagine that all creatures that are non-human are
members of one, homogeneous class—just as the more naïve of
Greeks supposed that all non-Greeks were of a kind. In both cases
this was arrogance: the conviction that the failure to be Greek, or
human, is a property so important as to overshadow any differentiae
between animal species (see Plato, *Statesman* 262 f.). The orthodox
sometimes complain that zoophiles cannot distinguish between men
and beasts (see SALT (3)): *they* plainly cannot distinguish between
cats and cabbages. No serious attack need be expected from the
orthodox on zoophiles who are, like Salt, hierarchically inclined:
zoophiles, unlike the orthodox, neither confuse animals, nor mistake
hierarchic order for a licensed tyranny. There is a possible attack,
with which I will try to deal later, but it comes from the mystic,
not the orthodox.

What hierarchies do we have? First, the personal: there are my
family, household, friends and relatives, colleagues and neighbours
and fellow graduates, fellow-citizens and strangers. The further
away they are, the less I care for them at any personal level—I except
the sudden, momentary flash of sympathy that may occur between
total and continuing strangers—but I thereby make no general
judgement. My strangers may be your friends, my family no more
than fellow-citizens to you. I would save my wife against a stranger,
but I make no judgement on either of them by doing so. I do not
assess how they stand in a hierarchy valid for all·of us, unless, of
course, I am a despot: my personal ties then determine all the
allowed relationships between my subjects, or I intend them to.
Similarly, there is the place I now occupy, and assorted nearby
places, and further towns and lands beyond the sea. Some places
are more distant from me, but I make no judgement on their standing in a map valid for all of us. In neither case are we content with
our personal pyramids of affection and distance: they are real—in
a sense they are the only reality we know. In such a hierarchy I
am fonder of the cat than of most humans, particularly of those that
I have never seen, and daily display my preference by feeding her
rather than sending her halfpennies to Oxfam—as KENNY has
pointed out (p. 117), increased knowledge of what is happening at

---

[1] We cannot avoid being such a cause even by committing suicide, considering the manifold lives embodied in our lives. Death is indeed a part of living, but not all deaths are necessary.

a distance increases our responsibility, and hence our culpability. The fact that the human beings dying of famine are dying a long way away cannot make any *rational* difference to the facts that they are dying, and that we, by withholding our aid and taking their food, are culpable. It makes no rational difference, but of course it makes a personal one. Not that distance alone lends disinterest to the view: 'If Baretti should be hanged, none of his friends will eat a slice of plumb-pudding the less ... You will find these very feeling people are not very ready to do you good. They *pay* you by *feeling*.' (Johnson: BOSWELL p. 417.)[2]

I am fonder of most cats than most dogs; and though I regret the decapitated mice I sometimes find on the stairs I eat my meals with no less relish because of them. Most people find it difficult to feel much sympathy for rats, and whereas snails have a certain charm, slugs are frankly revolting. The uglier the baby, the likelier to be battered. I am not saying that these discriminations are rational: they are, precisely, not. But they are made, both between animals and between men. The orthodox are fond of castigating zoophiles for their habit of playing favourites, and zoophiles as regularly rebut the charge. There is a certain insincerity on both sides, for the orthodox manifestly have a favourite animal, namely man, and zoophiles can no more deny that they have favourites among the non-human than that they have friends and favoured groups among the human. But such nepotism may well be frowned on.

For beyond our personal hierarchy of friendship and attraction, where action is predicated simply on our feelings of love, trust, sympathy and perhaps antipathy, lies a hierarchy that might seem more objective. The personal hierarchy itself leads to this: to have any proper friendship with another entity it is necessary not to wish it well merely because it is cuddly, sings sweetly, adds distinction to one's dining room or has a rich and indulgent father, though all these cues for friendship are entirely proper, and maybe offer more security than more rational grounds.

'The regret we feel when throwing away an old pair of trousers or a faithful old pipe has certain roots in common with our social ties to human friends.' (LORENZ (1) p. 29.)

---

[2] Witness those sentimentalists who cannot bear to see animals suffer—and spare themselves this pain by staying out of sight. Our evolution has not suited us for action at a distance (see p. 156 below).

And PATON, speaking similarly of an old coat, or a house in which we have been happy, adds 'in all this we seem to be imagining—or perhaps discovering—some shadow of human personality in things below the human level' (p. 323). Our natural affections engage our interest in their object, and create in us the hope of some reciprocated affection. The wholly 'rational' man would not feel such movements of the heart where his reason did not affirm that possibility, but the 'rational' man is probably hardly human. James may be right: 'The only experience we concretely have is our own personal life ... and the rigorous belief that in its own essential and innermost nature this is a strictly impersonal world may ... prove to be the very defect that our descendants will be most surprised at in our own boasted science.' (JAMES (1) p. 327.) It *may* be that our fantasy is true, and St. Francis right to pity even a flame (st. FRANCIS p. 292), though it seems more plausible to say that he absurdly classified together animals, fire, water, and the sun as 'creatures without reason'. To feel affection, however, is to anthropomorphize: 'Think of a white cloud as being holy, you cannot love it; but think of a holy man within the cloud, love springs up in your thoughts, for to think of holiness distinct from man is impossible to the affections.' (BLAKE p. 90.) To feel affection is to experience the possibility of considering the object in its own right. It occurs to me to value my friend because of properties he has independently of my love-liking, and perhaps to value him less, or more, on this new scale. I did not need a reason to love him before: now I honour him (or not) for his good or bad *standing* in the world at large. My friends may be your enemies, but good men must be recognized as such by all.

This process is very like that found in the epistemological realm: at first I need no *evidence* that I am typing—what could be more evident to me than that?—but my first, firm conviction, of its own nature, posits an objective fact—that I am typing, really and truly typing—which seems to need backing in an objective world-order. My first, unfounded certainty that what I see is true comes to need confirmation: what I see must be the sort of thing a creature like me could reasonably be expected to be seeing in a world like this, and if it isn't I must reckon my perception but a dream. We seek a scientific world-order that will back most of our firm beliefs, and leave some baseless: reality is the law-governed universe that judges our immediate perception. Similarly in the field of value: my first unreasoned loves seem to need moral backing before they can be affirmed by a 'reasonable' man. I say 'moral' backing, but the rational order that is imagined need not be ordinarily moral: in my first innocence I need no '*reason*' to attempt the seduction of an attractive woman—only when rationality has made itself felt do I need to imagine that my attempt is made 'to obtain pleasure', and only then can I be induced to acts of lustfulness I do not feel, by thoughts of 'being a man' or 'doing what is required'.

This second, rational ordering of entities is still hierarchic: some entities are 'worth more' than others, not in the immediate and subjective sense of the personal hierarchy, but in the world at large. Some societies have rational hierarchies that incorporate the personal, either by being no more than acknowledgements of personal affection (in very loose societies) or by so regulating their members' lives that personal ties are formed only where they match the required 'moral' ties. In such societies friendship and family connections are to ensure that we feel like doing what we, in our particular niche, are supposed to be doing. If I know your standing in society I know who your friends are, and vice versa. In other societies the objective and subjective hierarchies work independently, without too much quarreling: WILLIAMS's monkey colony provides an example of strong personal affection between two monkeys, Liz and Lulu, who are widely separated in the social hierarchy ((2) pp. 85 f.). Similarly Aristotle: master and slave cannot be friends, qua master and slave, but *can* qua men (*Nicomachean Ethics* 8.1161b5 f.). Other societies again may systematically denigrate personal ties, insisting that whatever be done be done for a *reason*, namely that it is the *right* thing for a man to do, not merely (or at all) because you feel like doing it. You should not have special feelings which are not correlated with the generally accepted worth of the entities in question. Indeed, you should not have special feelings: that is to fall into irrationality, away from truth. In the field of value, as in that of knowledge, we deny the only truth we *possess* in the name of an imagined, 'really and truly' Truth. The complex relations between moral and epistemological rationality have been discussed, amongst others, by DOUGLAS (5), in an attempt to discover how a society's moral concerns affect its cosmology, and vice versa. That there *is* some correspondence I do not doubt, though I think her taxonomy is not entirely satisfactory. In the interests of honesty I should add that my strongest temptation is to reckon the rational hierarchy, in both realms, no more than a paranoid fantasy as soon as it takes on a life separate from the heart's affections and the plain evidence of sense (which is *not* to espouse the 'common sense' of current orthodoxy). But more can be said on the other side.

The rational hierarchy of our day is, despite propaganda to the contrary, hierarchic. We profess to believe that all men are equal, but in fact do not: the pleasures of a thief are not weighed equally, or at all, against the pleasures of the respectable; the pains of the censorious are not allowed to count against the pleasures of individual lust. Orthodoxy, both liberal and conservative, may frown on literal nepotism, or the playing of favourites, but only because such orderings interfere with the proper, rational assignment of value. We are equal before the law: but not after it. The detailed examination of our rational hierarchy is probably a matter for sociologists, though we can note certain discriminations: the criminal ranks lower than the honest man, the labourer than the intellectual, the provincial than the Londoner. In short, closeness to the sources of rational law-making is the criterion by which we rank members of our hierarchy. The less 'rational', in symbol or in fact, the individual is, the less (in practice) do we value his desires. I do not deny, indeed I would assert, that other and less respectable motives for the discriminations I have mentioned also exist: including that ancient distaste for the organic—which is unfortunate for farm-workers.

The pariahs in this hierarchy, the lower than the poor whites or the poor blacks, are those defined as animals. In some ways they fill the role of human slaves, sometimes cossetted by greater luxury than the human poor. 'In Britain today', the Thomists sneer, 'animals are sometimes better protected against ill-treatment than children.' (MURRAY p. 98; see also DEWAR p. 115.) Which remark is, of course, a frivolous and disgusting falsehood: *some* animals are sometimes better treated than *some* children, but they are certainly not better *protected* by law or public feeling. Far more often animals are denied the slightest respect: it is still, as SALT remarked ((1) pp. 34 f.), a capital crime to be an unowned animal. *Wild* animals are rarely even protected against 'cruelty' to the minimal extent that the domesticated, that is the more obedient to law, may be. The recent Badger Act, of 1973, seems likely to be a dead letter: for 'necessary cruelty' is to be assessed in accordance with *anything* that can be construed as a human want (see above, p. 5 and pp. 43 f.).

The animals' plight differs from the human slave's in this: however well, by human mercy or by human whim, they are treated, they can never expect freedom within the law. I do not refer to political freedom, whatever that may be, but merely the proper exercise of their autonomy. They are either slaves or outlaws.

Zoophiles have commonly insisted that if rationality *is* the criterion of value, and if even psychopaths and idiots are granted some consideration, as the protection against torture or death, then surely animals, or the 'higher' animals must not be regarded as utterly beyond all rational value. If we respect men because, and insofar as they are rational, surely we must also respect animals, even if we do so less? Alternatively, if we are to respect men in general because they have much the same feelings and nature as those whom we instantly feel as friends, must we not also respect animals? Cartesians may imagine that animals have no feelings, Thomists that they have no souls (whereas even imbeciles *do*), but both positions are too obviously inane to convince most of us. Why then is the zoophile's argument not instantly accepted? Mere greed and stupidity? I fear that there are other reasons: greed may seek efficiency, and stupidity be instructed, but false philosophy is impervious to cure.

Rationality and language

Our moral, or rational, hierarchy (there are other, and to our mind less rational ones) employs the ability or the exercise of rationality itself as its ordering criterion: the capacity to recognize a hierarchic order of morals or cosmology which transcends our personal truth. What is the condition for this capacity, this ability to recognize that two entities of my acquaintance may be directly acquainted with each other rather than indirectly through me? What enables me to know that London is, so to speak, far from Paris even when I am not in Paris? Very often, of course, we do not recognize this, or its moral parallels: there is a certain shock in registering that two of one's friends are each other's friends, that one's parents exist for each other and did so long before they existed for oneself, even (absurdity) that one's wife does things when out of one's sight. That creatures exist in one's absence is, emotionally, a real discovery: call it a revelation. We *can* recognize this, recognize our own entity as an object, certainly peripheral and probably rather comic, in someone else's world. We can even, occasionally, contemplate the glad or dreadful enormity of a world that existed, and will exist, without even a void to mark one's absence. The capacity to think of something, in its absence, as existing in *our* absence is the condition for passing from merely personal hierarchy. And this capacity has, at least since Aristotle, been associated with the possession, or at least the potential possession of a language. And animals, as we are sure, have no proper languages. Animals cannot observe absences or falsehoods, and are therefore absolutely, and not merely relatively, unworthy of the respect owed to the possibly-moral-and-objectivizing. Dumb beasts, as they are in Greek as in Hebraic thought, exist beyond the rational hierarchy. They are not merely less intelligent: they are creatures without reason. It is not surprising that such creatures of the Indefinite Beyond have commonly carried such a weight of symbolic or sentimental meaning (on creatures outside the moral hierarchy see, e.g. REES AND REES).

These are enormous questions. Older zoophiles have commonly suspected that animals did have languages, each species having its own proper tongue. It is not that animals are dumb, but that men are deaf: 'We understand them no more than they us. By the same reason may they as well esteeme us beasts, as we them.' (MONTAIGNE II.12, p. 145.) Not that we are prepared to admit this reasoning: as HEGEL argued of the Chinese, that they do not understand us proves them inferior, and that we do not understand them proves us *superior* (p. 144). In fact, of course, a great many animals plainly do understand us; or at any rate they plainly hear our voices not as mere sounds, but as conveying meaning (PORPHYRY (1) III 15). To understand them, or speak to them as they require, would need sharp eyes and ears and discriminatory voice and posture control that is quite beyond most of us. PORPHYRY ((1) III 3) believed that they truly spoke, according to the laws they received from God and nature (see also CYRANO DE BERGERAC pp. 36 f., 52 f., 94 f.; DEAN p. 113; HILDROP I pp. 20 f.; PRIMATT p. 51; NICHOLSON pp. 27 f.; HELPS pp. 129 f.; EVANS (2) pp. 270 f.).

Gomez Pereira, on the other hand, who advanced the belief that animals were mere automata before Descartes, their voices but the squeakings of ill-oiled machines, insisted that as they had the same organs as men they would be able to communicate with us did they not lack some spiritual gift. He was in fact mistaken about their *physical* competence: even Neanderthal man may not have been able to articulate human speech (LIEBERMAN)—were *his* rights nugatory? Few but the pseudo-psychopath (i.e. one whose behaviour and beliefs are psychopathic not because of early rejection or glandular malfunctioning but because of a particular cultural ideal which I shall consider later)[3] would now be so dismissive at least of vertebrate sentience, but we remain doubtful that animals could be said to have a language. In part, this doubt is a mere device of philosophy: it is not that we have *discovered* them to lack a language but rather that we define, and redefine, what Language is by discovering what beasts do not have. If they should turn out to have the very thing we have hitherto supposed language to be, we will simply conclude that language is something else again. Just so it is taken for granted by many of the orthodox that animals are wholly or largely beyond moral consideration, and the chief philosophical problem lies in isolating some principle of action which will justify decent treatment of the human without demanding decent treatment of animals. We define our own being by opposition to Theirs, and if They turn out to be rather different from our fantasy we will merely invent another and more subtle distinction. I have no doubt that the Gardners' success in teaching American Sign Language to chimpanzees (see GARDNER AND GARDNER; PETERS; THORPE pp. 283 f.) will simply occasion yet more rigorous definitions of what is involved in 'really understanding and speaking a language'. Some of these distinctions will doubtless be real, and really applicable, though I doubt that many will be morally significant (see e.g. BRONOWSKI AND BELLUGI).

Some distinctions, on the other hand, though perhaps real, are only doubtfully applicable. Efforts to show that bees have a complex dance-system which encodes the location of favourable flowers, and therefore a language, have been countered by the denial that this could be enough to show that they have a *proper* language. BENNETT (pp. 8 f.), while admitting that their conduct is language-like, argues that to call it a *language* is to prejudge the question of whether bees have reasons for their actions, reasons which they could in theory recognize as insufficient or invalid or in plain error. Without that assumption we can only say that bees are stimulated to certain dances by certain events, and to certain flight-patterns by certain dances. Ants which advance into a fire, so that their fellows can eventually escape over their burnt bodies, may *look* brave, may behave *as if* they were brave, but really they are not, nor do bees

[3] I have formed this term by analogy with the 'pseudo-homosexuality' of DEVEREUX (2).

really engage in semantic behaviour. Bennett offers some imaginary cases, as of a denial routine when the bees turn out to have been misdirected, or a display of recognizable intelligence in related matters, which might cause him to reassess his judgement (though, as I have suggested, he would be more likely to raise his standards; see also COLLINS).

What infuriates me in such discussion is the rapidity with which it is assumed that a stimulus-reaction description makes no assumptions about imponderables, whereas a language-description does. In fact, both do. Personally I do not know whether ants are brave, or bees talk, and to transmute my ignorance into a *knowledge* of the negative is beyond my powers. As Nelson remarked in a slightly different context, 'To infer, from our ignorance of one thing, that we should know another of which we are actually just as ignorant seems more than questionable.' (NELSON p. 140.) I do not know how far Bennett's tests for rationality would be fair trials—if, that is, they were *really* tests of whether bees were rational, rather than imaginative delimitings of the nature of rationality. Some such tests require that they deal competently with a situation which, for all we know, they simply may not see, or not see quite as we do. Others require that they make imaginative and practical leaps enormously beyond even human powers: how well do *we* deal with the utterly alien or unaccustomed? I do not know, for that matter, how bees react to a notoriously incompetent or perfidious bee, or whether there are such. Nor do I see why bees should waste their time, after discovering that some information was incorrect, in dancing about the place saying, 'Good gracious, Charlie, there aren't any flowers here, after all', and 'No more there are, Reginald, no more there are'.[4] In short, I do not know. Bennett may be right to think that we have insufficient evidence to conclude that bees have, or recognize, reasons for action, and right to require that their having such reasons is a necessary condition for being semantic entities: but *our having enough evidence* is not a necessary condition for their being semantic entities. Nor is our *lack* of evidence bizarrely equivalent to a proof that they do *not* have reasons for action, do not 'behave'. Certainly we must in practice, perhaps, take something for granted:

---

[4] ALTMANN (p. 354) has pointed out that a mechanism for saying 'Not-p' could too easily, by error of transmission or reception, lead to confusion, and therefore is unlikely to develop. As he remarks, our discovery of the negative is a source of our power of intellectual fantasy.

other societies have taken it for granted that animals, and indeed bees in particular, have reasons, and communicate them. Here there are no proofs: only convictions, on either side, and it is dishonest to pretend otherwise.

Neither am I terribly impressed by the information that animals show no consistent application of any one sound or set of sounds to objects of which we think they would have some conception if they were rational beings (BIERENS DE HAAN p. 142). Neither do we, except in the most formal discourse; I see no reason to think that meaning can only be conveyed by sounds (what of grimaces, postures, smells?); it is not obvious to me that our conceptions of things are the only rational ones there are. Rationality at least purports to be content-neutral: if it were not so we should be compelled to admit that most past scientists, however well they calculated and however loyally they abode by the standards of scientific inference (whatever they are), were strictly *irrational*, merely because they were wrong. And by the most obvious of inferences, all present scientists are likewise irrational—which may console the bees. But if rationality *is* content or context-neutral, can we be so sure that we know what world animals actually confront? And if we don't, can we be so sure that their behaviour, however bizarre, is not a perfectly *rational* reaction to the facts as they see them, in the context of their desires and axioms?

Again: although I would agree that Chomsky's work has given us reason to see a difference between human languages and what we know of animal communications—that, for example, animals do not *appear* to recognize different sets of phonemes as semantically equivalent transformations of one-same deep structure— Chomsky's work also raises the probability that we are not properly equipped to internalize the grammar of any other species. For all I know the fables are correct, and the intercommunicating world of animals has been cursing us for deaf adders since the fatal day when our species acquired a distinctive language-learning programme, or lost the universal.[5] In short, I do not know, and I am surprised that so many people seem to know so much about the

[5] According to the book of Jubilees: 'On that day was closed the mouth of all beasts, and of cattle, and of birds, and of whatever walks, and of whatever moves, so that they could no longer speak: for they had all spoken with one another with one lip and one tongue' (CHARLES II p. 17). The idea received a spirited defence from the anti-Cartesian BOUGEANT pp. 59 ff., who also urges that the present language of beasts expresses no more, and no less, than the name of the passions they feel: they lack grammar.

inner life of animals of all sorts, shapes and sizes. 'How knoweth he by the vertue of his undertanding the inward and secret motions of beasts?' (MONTAIGNE II.12, p. 144.)

It seems plausible, however, and no more than that, that BATESON is correct (p. 337) in suggesting that non-human communication is the affirmation of relationships between the communicating individuals: when the cat miaous she is not saying, 'Milk!', nor 'I want milk!' but rather 'Dependency!'. It is up to her human to deduce from his knowledge of her satisfactions what thing-in-the-world it is she wants:

'What was extraordinary—the great new thing—in the evolution of human language was not the discovery of abstraction or generalisation, but the discovery of how to be specific about something other than relationship.'

But as Bateson goes on to say in this extremely illuminating paper (and see also LANCASTER), even human communication is largely, even if subliminally, concerned with patterns of relationship. We have a highly complex tool with which to talk about things, but even in doing so we are aiming to establish or reaffirm direct, personal relationships: to convince, to induce respect, to quieten fear and so forth. Most human vocalization does not even *aspire* to the purely assertoric condition which philosophers are still too inclined to take as the paradigm of rational discourse. Language has many uses, including that of being a *secret* language (see STEINER p. 232); the evolutionary 'purpose' of accents in late learners is to identify the outsider (or the insiders) (HILL p. 313). And as I have remarked before, it is difficult to see how (assertoric) language could have got started, or survived, outside the framework of 'natural' relationship-affirming semantic behaviour. Computers, if they are what we think they are,[6] may speak, but do not understand their speech: for it means nothing to them, nor do they thereby enter into 'meaningful relationships' with their operators. Animals may not speak assertorically about things: it is impossible honestly to doubt that they speak demonstratively about relationships. Impossible, because they speak the very same demonstrative language as us. Of course:

---

[6] It may be of course that the things we call 'computers' aren't computers, but art-born homunculi: but if they are computers (that is, if they have the natures we justifiably think they have), they do not think, any more than cameras see (see THORPE p. 330).

they are our kin. (See further on non-verbal communication. HINDE.)

Some animals, namely some chimpanzees, have learnt to employ, however childishly, a human language, in which mention is made of things and their connections. We cannot say that other animals cannot be or could never be taught such a language by researchers willing to consider the individual species' peculiarities. Many other animals, particularly mammals and birds, engage in the same sort of 'personal' conversation with which we humans define ourselves and our relationships. Many animals have highly complex rituals, so to call them, whereby they effectively guide the subsequent behaviour of other members of their species, or even of less closely related organisms. *Perhaps* they cannot talk of things in their absence, but this is a conclusion which does not seem to be forced on us. We simply do not know.[7] And in our ignorance we might give the benefit of the doubt to creatures who themselves, or whose unchanged descendants, may one day startle us by speech. And what will they say to us?

But suppose that animals do indeed have no language. Instantly to assume that they are only stimulus-response machines seems rather rash, and leads to such inanities as the notion of a 'response *in vacuo*' to describe the play or practice of jackdaws or cats. They may of course be responses to phantasms, mental images: but that is simply to admit that animals can consider things in their absence, because they can have images, pretend-images, of the things. It is very difficult for anyone who has known an animal, particularly (perhaps) a cat, to doubt that animals can consciously *pretend*, that the paper is a mouse, or that they were only intending to wash their tails and not to catch that fly. ... I do not say that it is impossible to doubt this: it is only very difficult, and an exercise I see no good reason to attempt. There are more interesting absurdities on which to practise faith. *We* do not always, though we very frequently, accompany our actions with verbal chatter about what we are doing and why. Unverbalized behaviour is still conscious, deliberate, reasoned and understood as such. It is surprising that *theists* should ever think otherwise: if only those entities with language are

[7] Though the case of Helen (a rhesus monkey blinded by cerebral lesions and treated with unrepentant callousness by her tormenters) demonstrates, by its absence in her case, that monkeys characteristically do possess an awareness of a stable spatial framework within which they can find or recognize things (HUMPHREY).

rational, then God is either unreasoning or has vocal cords (or some equally physical equivalent), for only those with bodies can exercise the gift of language.[8] So: let God be Reason Himself, rather than merely reasoning (a requirement also suggested by the uselessness of reasoning to an omniscient entity). Perhaps He just *sees* and understands, or is Himself that sight. Nothing could be more likely: but in that case it is in our unreasoning intuitions, not our painstaking rationality, that we are most God-like (as Aristotle knew: see CLARK p. 181 f.), and may therefore give some little honour to the beasts, who likewise *see* and do not think things through.

But it seems fair to waive such *ad hominem* argument: God is so difficult a topic that all arguments must be intolerably weak. There is in any case a swifter way to confront the theist with his rationalist twin: if we are to respect only those creatures that can realize the independent and unperceived existence of other entities, we plainly must not respect *God*. For nothing is independent of Him, and nothing exists that He does not continually and unavoidably behold: He therefore cannot conceive of their separate existence, for this would be to conceive a necessarily false and incoherent imagining. Existence separate from us makes sense, and we can conceive it: existence separate from God does not. If animals are as little deserving of respect as God, they still may merit some slight honour.

More generally, it is far from obvious that only creatures with a language and a language like ours can be said to think. Emotion is not wholly without its reasons:

'We need not be put off by the fact that the reasonings of the heart ... are accompanied by sensations of joy or grief. These computations are concerned with matters which are vital to mammals, namely, matters of *relationship*, by which I mean love, hate, respect, dependency, spectatorship, performance, dominance and so on.' (BATESON pp. 438–9.)[9]

[8] I am not confident of this premise, but if the possession of a language does not require its bodily exercise then animals may have languages even if they do not embody their ability.

[9] It may be said that animals cannot feel emotions, precisely because they are unverbal creatures: how can one feel indignation or frustration or spite without some verbalized judgement (see FORTENBAUGH)? I find it entirely obvious, as did David HUME (11.12) that animals, like infants, do feel such emotions. We are not such extraordinary creatures as all that.

Nor is it obvious that our strange intuition of a world beyond our worlds, of the Way Things Are (however they are) is mediated to. us in language—though it may well be the necessary condition of our ability to speak a language. When I examine my own occasional realization that there is a world beyond my seemings, of which my seemings are themselves a part, I find rather that they involve (though they do not consist in) images of myself being looked at, or episodes occurring that I cannot ever see, or the mysterious and non-visible world that springs from neither light nor darkness when I open my eyes. There is indeed a powerful tradition that language is even a barrier to this realization. For all I know cats doze to contemplate, not their ineffable Names, but the appalling and delightful being of the World. Though I doubt it.

One argument that might suggest otherwise, that only the linguistically talented can detect a difference between their seemings and the Way Things Are, is offered by KENNY (p. 48)—though not in a context which would commit him to a denial, outright, of animal rationality: 'A dog may think that his master is at the door: but unless a dog masters a language I cannot see how he can think that he is thinking that his master is at the door,' or, *a fortiori*, that he is *merely* thinking that his master is at the door. Kenny is making the old division between mere sentience and self-consciousness: in my analysis the crucial feature is not so much *self*-consciousness, consciousness that one is acting or behaving in certain ways, as consciousness of the *world* as something not wholly exhausted by our seemings. Consciousness of self seems to me to be inseparable, in a sense, from sentience: to see is to be aware of seeing, not to be so aware is not to have noticed what is before one's eyes. In another sense, one may see remembering that it is Stephen who is seeing, and it may be that animals *are* unable to take the step away from self-forgetfulness. But I am uncertain: firstly, because I cannot detect by introspection that my self-consciousness is verbalized— once again, it is rather a curious sensation as of things giggling out of hearing, or a concomitant perception of kinesthetic factors, such as the position of my head or the pressure of glasses on my nose; secondly, because animals can convey in appearance at any rate an uncertainty about their first impressions. They can rise to a sound, pause to investigate, look questioningly, bark and so on (see further ARMSTRONG pp. 25 f.). And this, if true, is hardly surprising: animals that cannot recognize their errors, and remember them as

errors, would be unlikely to live long. It *may* be that we do not
always find such behaviour convincing evidence that they are self-
conscious as well as sentient, but I do not think that this is always
so (see THORPE p. 363 f.), nor that our *lack* of evidence amounts
to evidence for the opposite.[10]

I cannot help feeling that such philosophical arguments are but
the rationalizations of an attitude to animals also embodied in
poetry:

They do not live in the world,
are not in time and space.
From birth to death hurled
no word do they have, not one
to plant a foot upon,
were never in any place.
For with names the world was called
out of the empty air,
with names was built and walled,
line and circle and square,
dust and emerald;
snatched from deceiving death
by the articulate breath.
But these have never trod
twice the familiar track,
never, never turned back
into the memoried day.
All is new and near
in the unchanging Here
of the fifth great day of God,
that shall remain the same,
never shall pass away.
On the sixth day we came (Edwin Muir, *The Animals*).[11]

[10] Two-month old babies follow their mothers' gaze, as do animals. They thereby display
a very early, preverbal recognition of another creature's point of view (SCAIFE AND
BRUNER).

[11] This error of biblical exegesis (man after all was created on the same day as the beasts:
Genesis 1:24 f.) is perhaps anticipated by BROWNE (p. 15): 'Without (man's study and
contemplation of the world) the world is still as though it has not been, or as it was before
the sixth day, when as yet there was not a creature that could conceive or say there was
a world.' It has long been imagined that other and nobler creatures than man yet preceded
him (as Milton *Paradise Lost* 4.675 f.). But if this is the situation the proper moral would
seem to be that we must complete the world by loving and tending it...

This is indeed an excellent poem, chiefly in drawing our attention to the way in which we build our houses from the factlessness of a world that exists before and independently of any names or interests we may devise for it. But Muir is mistaken in believing that animals, least of all those animals who share our mammalian ancestry, fail to find meaning and memory in the world we and they strangely inhabit. Just as W. H. Auden is entirely wrong to equate 'the eyes of the crow and the eye of the camera' (*Memorial for the City* I. 1). An animal's world is not meaningless to it merely because it does not see *our* meanings: it has its own (see UEXKUELL). It is not even certain that animals do not have a sense of God. HARDY ((1) p. 278, (2) pp. 156 f.) has suggested that a sense of the numinous precedes the birth of language. It is a mere conceit of whoremaster man to be so convinced that it was only with men that meaning, time and death came into the world—though, to be sure, we *may* live for meaning, count the time and fear death more than our unlinguistic, or our unassertoric, kindred do.

But suppose that it is not so. Suppose that animals are indeed irrational, in the most extreme sense of that protean term. Are we to display our rationality in refusing them compassion? 'Nothing irrational is capable of the beatifying friendship with God which is the bond of Christian love of neighbour' (HÄRING II p. 362), and cannot, therefore, deserve our charity. I fear that I think little of a pretended friendship with God which is used to excuse our torture of His creatures (HÄRING III p. 244). Doubtless animals and men cannot, in the present condition of things, exchange much conversation, even if they are not irrational. I cannot see that this fact in any way justifies our failure to do the things we *can* do to assist their being, or our habit of taking from them even what little they have. Here, as so often, careful rationality and 'love of God' are but defences against our inconvenient compassion. Häring purports to believe that the irrational is to be cherished for the Creator's sake, but gives this doctrine little content. Why else, within the theistic system, cherish *any* creature? How dare we stand upon our dignity as 'friends of God' so to oppress His creatures? What is Häring's protest against the 'anti-human sentimentality' of those who oppose experiments on our animal kin but an *égoisme aux hommes*?

'Let this mind be in you, which was also in Christ Jesus, who being in the form of God did not think to snatch at equality with

God ... but humbled himself, and became obedient to death, even the death of the cross.' (Philippians 2:5–8.)

If we are called to be the friends of God, we are called to do as He did, not to employ that dignity as a pretext for deferring *our* obedience to death by the infliction of pain and death on our playmates.

'The beasts will be at peace with us when in the shrine of our souls we tame the clean and unclean animals and lie down with the lions, like Daniel.' (Ps. Jerome Comm. on Mark 1:13; MIGNE 30.595.)

The world will be obedient to us when we are obedient to God: the promise does not license our despotic rule.

'When a man boasts of the dignity of his nature, ... and from thence infers his right of oppression of his inferiors, he exhibits his folly as well as his malice.' (PRIMATT p. 22.)

Lawmakers and moral law

It is, I think, important to remind secular rationalists of their theistic roots. Certainty of truths that were more than personal once came by revelation or tradition: in the absence of such *de fide* certainties those personalities that cannot rest content with the mere confidence of our immediate seemings (that fire is hot, and girls are pretty) seek some security of belief in the laws of reason. In the cosmological field we hope that 'the objective relations between phenomena of the outer world might attain the certainty of subjective truths if they were reduced to a state of simplicity that (our) mind could completely grasp'. (BERNARD (1) p. 29.) Just so in the moral field. We want an objective morality that will bind us as strongly as our personal affection does, or did in the days of our innocence. In cosmology the *ad hoc* explanation is no explanation at all: we must be able to connect the event with all other events, able to deduce its occurrence from our theory without recourse to arbitrary incident. Similarly in rationalized morality, special commandments are anathema. God could give such special instructions, to found a particular temple or to spoil the Egyptians: the new God, or Reason, can give only those commands that can intelligibly be given and obeyed by all. Rules that cannot be universalized cannot be moral rules—a principle that is illogically responsible for the orthodox mention of Eskimos when the question of vegetarianism is raised: if the Eskimos can't be, nobody has to be (which ignores, of course, a highly relevant difference). We should better conclude that no-one should eat meat, for it is quite impossible that everyone should have enough to eat upon such terms.

I have distinguished, because it is fashionable to do so, the cosmological and the moral field, epistemology and ethics. An alternative approach would be to consider the rules that govern scientific acceptance of cosmological theory as embodying an ethics of belief: what evidence ought to be counted as a reason for believing something is as much an ethical matter as what ought to be counted as a reason for doing something. Even if believing itself is not an action, belief involves and perhaps is inseparable from actions: to believe that John is an enemy agent because he stepped on one's toe is as *immoral* as to stab him to death for the same reason, or rather is as much a matter for moral judgement. Standards of evidential rationality vary, as do more ordinarily moral standards, from society to society and generation to generation, but *some* constants are perhaps observable. More importantly, perhaps, they vary from context to context. I entirely agree with MONOD that the principle of scientific objectivity is an *ethical* principle, but I do not think that his attempt to make it the ruling principle of all ethics either has been or can be successful. What is demanded of a man *qua* scientist is not necessarily what is demanded of him as a parent or a citizen. To accept a certain role is to submit oneself to judgement under certain ethical principles of which some are epistemological and some more ordinarily moral. What principles determine, or ought to determine, our choice of rôles within the ongoing enterprise of human life is too hard a matter to be settled here. 'One ought not to contradict oneself' is a principle that currently has some support in intellectual circles, though no-one ever has, or could have, proved that Reality itself is thus consistent. Considered as a thesis about that Reality the principle of non-contradiction is entirely *de fide* (and a thesis which, considering the manifest contradictoriness of the phenomenal world, we can only believe *quia ineptum est*); considered as a moral axiom, a device of thought, a tool of investigation it may be entirely proper, though this is not a reason against trying out some other tool upon occasion.

This demand for rules that can be universalized without contradiction is summed up in the Kantian command to act according to those principles of action which one can suppose a universal law of action for such creatures as can act on principle at all. The true laws of morality are the laws obeyed within the perfect kingdom of all creatures obedient to law. We must do what ought to be done by creatures that can recognize an *ought*: we must act as universal reason decrees to all its subjects, not as our fancy takes us. If I lay claim on something there is no other property in virtue of which I can suppose my claim rightful than the mere ability to lay claims: all other properties, as being pale, or hairy, or six-foot tall, are merely contingent to the essential characteristic of being able to say 'I' and 'mine'. If it *is* in virtue of this that I make my claim I cannot coherently deny the rightful claims of *other* such claim-makers. To say, or to declare in my action, that *I* have such a right requires me to believe that *you* likewise do: the natural rights of men must therefore be pruned into consistency (see GEWIRTH). Our relations with non-claimers are not covered by such laws (see above, p. 22).[12]

Only law-makers can be *ends* of action: all else are merely means. For there to be a moral hierarchy at all there must be creatures who can so discriminate between themselves and the world, standing bizarrely astride the boundary they draw between themselves and the world. Only such creatures are worthy of respect: only such creatures present real barriers to our projects. I fear that I cannot feel much force in these arguments, and therefore struggle in vain to believe them plausible even as rational constructions. The distinction of ends and means does indeed have some immediate force, though not what the Kantian supposes.[13] There was a case recently of a man who broke his four-month old son's arm 'in order to teach his wife a lesson', an act which was surely not wicked merely because of the possible traumatic effects of such an event upon the child's eventual adulthood. We feel that the arm-breaking was, for the baby, the end of the matter: *that* is what the father did, whatever he *said* about his intentions. The flow of purpose is dammed up

[12] A more plausible version of this rationalization would perhaps pin the rightfulness of the claim not upon our ability to *claim* (in whatever technical sense), but simply upon the fact of wishing. If my wishing that X be or not be the case is a good reason (though not necessarily a final one) for X's being or not-being, then I cannot see how any other creature's similar wish is not also a good reason. Babies and non-human creatures have wishes: if mine should be considered, so should theirs.

[13] RAPHAEL has recently suggested extending the notion of *ends* to cover animals, though he rather blurs the proper effect of this worthy notion by insisting that animals only have *desires*, and do not make *decisions*. Nor does he explain why he thinks that it could still be proper to farm, kill and eat such ends.

at such a point. Rather similarly, Bion of Borysthenes commented on some boys' throwing stones at frogs, that the boys did so for fun, but the frogs died in earnest (PLUTARCH (1) 965b). Which truth is more important, ours or theirs?

For what really staggers me about this attempted defence of perfect rationality is its unreason. The characteristic to be valued is a capacity to recognize that things exist in their own right whether we like it or not, whether we are there or not, a capacity to see the sense within the way things are, to recognize that there are other points of view than ours, to let one's impulses be overruled by the demands of a universal reason that must also be the source of the cosmic order. The conclusion is that things exist for us and in our right, that we are the only sense of things, that our interests should automatically override the demands and behaviour patterns of all other things. We are absolutely better than the animals because we are able to give their interests some consideration: so we won't.

Doubtless I have missed some subtlety of the rationalist's endeavour. It is probably evident that I have little sympathy with the claim that we should always and only act as would the generalized One of rationalist myth: I fear that such advice seems no more than an uneasy extrapolation from the demands of social class and professional rôle. It seems to me that there is more to normal ethical concern than such rational obedience: a readiness, for example, to think something worth dying for, as animals at least appear to do. Again, I am not entirely convinced that we should expect *any* absolutely coherent account of the Reality behind(?) the phenomena (whether of 'fact' or value) that we face. It seems to me that much of the charm of the universe lies in its arbitrariness, its just happening to be like this, and some, though maybe not all, divine commands might be like this. I doubt very much if we can easily deduce from any obvious principles just what it is what we ought to do or to believe—though if there are such deductions, the deduction of the vegetarian ethic is one. Those who think otherwise should at least consider whether or not they think it reasonable to argue from our servitude to Reason and the World to our self-claimed mastery of the World, and whether they accept the obvious consequence that the old, the sick, the feeble-minded are variously beyond all law.

If we esteem ourselves because we can intuit the Reality beyond our seemings we do so either because that Reality is worth intuiting—in which case let us by all means serve and succour it—or because this ability, whatever its object, is itself one of the marks of human worth: *one* of them, but there are others, including irrational affection, artistic imagination, loyalty. Whether our God be found outside us or within, our worship surely should and would, were we not liars, involve our care for other living things with whom we share the world. But our true belief, perhaps, is otherwise: it is not that we honour the strange beauty of the World Beyond, nor that we sense the God within. Our hearts are given over to our greed, our passion not to worship, nor to share, nor even to act as stewards of God's bounty, but to turn all living and unliving things into our profit. Man is a rationalizing animal.

Neither affection nor acknowledged duty can be entirely rationalized; that there is reason, and beauty, in both I would not deny. Neither can require us utterly to disregard our fellows in the name of developing a capacity to see cosmic or ethical beauty, still less to create it.

The attempt to transform our various social hierarchies into a single, rationally defensible morality that will license all and only acts of affection and justice to creatures of our species, seems to me to be a failure. The real springs of our action lie elsewhere.

VI

THE IMAGINATION OF WAR

Realism and the natural world

I have contrasted the personal and moral hierarchy, observing that many different relationships were possible between them, and that the moral hierarchy could incorporate many different criteria of value. I have suggested that rationalistic attempts to find an absolute stability in the moral domain, now that God is reckoned dead, are at once implausible in themselves and ineffective to produce any absolute dichotomy between man and beast. They are really no more than desperate and often unintelligible reconstructions of the Stoic ethic.

This last ethic, of course, accepted the parallel which I have drawn between the cosmological and the ethical: the natural was the moral. Latter-day thinkers have thought this a fallacy—facts and values are held to be distinct. Doubtless this is true, that whatever is should not necessarily, merely because it *is*, continue to be, though the orthodox very frequently contend against zoophiles that we ought to eat animals just because we do or because our fathers did. Nicholson records, in a note to his copy of LAWRENCE (1 p. 137), that a lady of his acquaintance refused to help, or to let anyone else help, a cat that was trapped down a grating, on the grounds that 'nature ought to take its course'. Such vile absurdities require us to repeat that what is and what ought to be are not, of themselves, the same. But there is more to be said on the other side. Moralists who drew the cosmic and the ethical together, after all, were not committed to saying that any particular fact was, in the important sense, in accord with nature, nor to denying the title 'natural' to one's own impulses of sympathy.

> 'The law corresponds to the world and the world to the law, and a man who is obedient to the law being by so doing a citizen of the world arranges his action with reference to the intention of nature, in harmony with which the whole universal world is regulated.' (PHILO p. 1.)

It is Nature that provides the ideal, not the mere march of chance phenomena. As I have remarked, our theories of Nature are judged in part by their agreement with our inbuilt standards of beauty and satisfactoriness, so that there are indeed connections between our vision of how Nature is and how things ought to be. William James pointed to the parallel between the cosmic theory of a pluralistic universe of entities sharing space-time and the ethical theory of moral tolerance (JAMES (1) p. 270). More generally the entities we notice as existing and the ones we deem important are much the same: to exist for us, to stand out in the reality we see, is to make some sort of claim upon us. Not to feel that claim is not really to notice the thing's existence, or not to *feel* it—as small children do not really register the proper existence of other beings as beings like themselves:

> 'I had a stick in my hand, so I hit her on the head with it. Her hair was springy, so I hit her again and watched her mouth open up with a yell. To my surprise a commotion broke out around me ... I was intrigued, not alarmed, that by wielding a beech stick I was able to cause such a stir. So I hit her again, without spite or passion, then walked off to try something else.' (Laurie Lee, *Cider with Rosie*.)

In a child this is, perhaps, normal (though the ones I know are certainly distressed by others' pain): such an inability to see beyond one's purposes to the things themselves is pathological in adults. Moral awareness and intellectual vision go hand in hand. And one sometimes misleads the other, so that both may fall into a ditch.

How we believe the world to work and how we believe we ought to act are related matters. So much so that the orthodox, or many of them, plainly find it very important to believe that man is the youngest species on the earth, that other kinds are somehow inferior or failed men, that we constitute a radically new move in evolutionary history. It is in essence a very ancient creed, that man is the standard of animal excellence, and may, in some systems, have something to be said for it (CLARK ch. 2.2). Modern orthodoxy is not one of the systems. Cats are not inferior men. Present-day species are in no way more 'primitive' than men, even if their ancestors achieved their norm many millions of years ago. All present-day animals are our contemporaries, nor is there any reason to think that man is the most recently formed species. Even the famous change from genetic to social evolution (on which see, approvingly, HARDY (2) pp. 44 f.) is implausible: I suspect that it is merely the product of a change of temporal attention. Genetic evolution occurs, if at all, over millions of years; over thousands there is never anything more than change of habit and habitat in any species (on the influence of such changes see HARDY (1) pp. 153 f.). It may be that it is our capacity for preserving and expanding 'tradition' that has given us such power, but (a) we do not know that e.g. mice do not have a tradition,[1] (b) other gambits have given other species great success, and (c) such a gambit is no more a new step in evolution than is the invention of the alphabet—or do the orthodox expect us to believe that literate peoples are automatically superior to the illiterate and licensed to do as they please with them? We sometimes speak of the dinosaurs as failures: there will be time enough for that judgement when we have lasted even for one tenth as long. Within the naturalistically conceived universe of modern orthodoxy the human species is no more than one species amongst billions, whose leading speciality—intellectual fantasy—may yet be its downfall. In the words of Haeckel that so baffled and irritated Wallace:

'Our own human nature sinks to the level of a placental mammal which has no more value for the universe at large than the ant, the fly of a summer's day, the microscopic infusorium or the smallest bacillus.' (quoted in WALLACE p. 374.)

It has more value for *us*, to be sure, but whereas earlier orthodoxies could find an absolute value in our capacity to see, and in seeing transcend, the world, the modern naturalist can do no more than express his own, genetically determined, preference. And in realizing the status of that preference he may come to feel it less strongly.

As Celsus decreed against Christianity, we are worth no more than the butterfly. Origen, to be sure, might have replied that we are also worth no *less*—but that reply would have been as unacceptable to humanist taste then as now. The spokesman of Blake's 'Song

---

[1] Indeed we can be pretty sure that they do: skills are passed on by demonstration and advice. The story of the sea-otter is particularly moving: displaced by man's genocidal activity from their Pacific beaches, the surviving sea-otters have taken up residence in the kelp-beds out at sea, and invented a new, culturally transmitted way of living (CARRIGHAR pp. 66 f.). The macaques studied by Japanese ethologists are similarly inventive (KAWAMURA, KAWAI; on dolphins see LILLY (1) p. 37.

to the Fly' (p. 213) half realizes these alternatives, but falls back into a frivolous unconcern:

> Am not I
> a fly like thee?
> Or art not thou
> a man like me?
> For I dance,
> and drink, & sing,
> till some blind hand
> shall brush my wing.

What may follow from Blake's intuition I shall defer. Here I suggest only that those who profess to find in their own submission to the rationally statable the capacity most to be followed must surely conclude from their acceptance of this egalitarian universe that the proper rôle of man is not to disturb things, to keep his head down where it belongs and to accept his equality with the cheesemite.

'[One] remarked that, whatever I might say, he would never condescend to share immortality with the cheesemite. I replied that, in the first place, it was not likely that he would be consulted on the subject; and that in the second place, as he did condescend to share mortality with a good many cheesemites there could be no great harm in extending his condescension a step further.' (WOOD p. 28:[2] HILDROP (11 pp. 38 ff.) had earlier accepted beasts' immortality.)

We have no extra standing in the world. But the number of those prepared to remember that the land is the mayfly's, and the thrush's, and the fox's as much as it is man's, and that as we crash around, flooding valleys and destroying woods and meadows we are guilty of theft and murder, is very limited. Either we abandon scientific realism—but that route gains us no moral ground—or we abandon any last pretence that we are obedient to a rational hierarchy of an objective sort: and in that case our vaunted morality (including, I suspect, the ethic of scientific objectivity) becomes no more than, at best, rules for pleasuring our friends and, at worst, a psychotic fantasy.

[2] Those who believe in the resurrection of the body must admit that this resurrection involves that of innumerable animalcules, and indeed of the whole terrestrial biosphere of which our bodies are indistinguishable parts. One man's resurrection demands the world's.

In short the only plausible sense in which the natural is the good does not appear to licence our behaviour to our kin. If we are as the fly let us cease to talk of our *rights* and consider how we may best inhabit this strange land we share. Certainly our own necessities and those of our children often require us to compete for food, and we may then be inclined to think ill of our competitors. 'He who cultivates barley cultivates righteousness', according to the Zoroastrian hymn, and such a one is unlikely to have a high opinion of mice and weevils: they are the creatures of the Evil One. Non-human animals after all have rarely distinguished between man's cultivated garden and the free-growing herbs we all once shared: why should they? But though the practice of agriculture has set us apart from our mammalian kin, we might do well to remember the law God gave to Moses: every seventh and every fiftieth year shall be a sabbath for the land, and no crops are to be sown or harvested.

> 'Yet what the land itself produces in the sabbath year shall be food for you, for your male and female slaves, for your hired man, and for the stranger lodging under your roof, for your cattle *and for the wild animals in your country.*' (Leviticus 25 : 6–7, my italics.)

Even when we reap the ordinary harvest we are not to take it all, nor glean the fallen ears: 'You shall leave them for the poor and alien. I am the Lord your God' (Leviticus 23 : 22). We may no longer believe that the land belongs to the Lord, but our very disbelief should lessen the fervour with which *we* lay claim to it: the land is a community to which we belong (see LEOPOLD p. x).

It should do so, but I doubt that it will. For there are other factors than any rational acceptance of the objective order at work, or even than any realistic and utilitarian calculation of our profit—considered 'realistically' after all meat-eating is enormously expensive, and any profit we might gain from exploiting animals might often more readily be gained by exploiting men (the poor, the stranger and the sick).

> 'It is possible that the great intellectualism of the scholastics led to a neglect of the emotions and to an estrangement from the animal world where the intellect is not found.' (RULAND p. 371; see HUME (2) p. 13.)

Such scholastic intellectualism, of course, is only symptomatic of an earlier fault, but there are other faults than rationalism. It is not the scholastics who symptomize the problem, but the bestiaries. Man is a rationalizing animal, to be sure, but before he is that he is a *ritualizing* one.

Nature, culture and art

KLINGENDER (p. xxv) supposed that the reality principle revealed a constant war between man and beast, while the pleasure principle fantasized, partly of Man the mighty hunter, but chiefly of a world where man and beast walked at one. Nature is perhaps more pleasurable than he (and Hobbes) supposed, but that problem I will defer. It is more significant at this point that our fantasy is less harmless, and chiefly displayed in the notion of a war between man and beast.

Anthropologists are by now well aware that dietary rules and other such principles of our relation with the non-human are not straightforwardly utilitarian. Any coincidence between the requirements of custom and hygiene is strictly coincidental, though our images of hygiene may themselves be contaminated by the rulings of folk-taxonomy. The relation of folk-taxonomy to social, particularly marital, custom has often been investigated (see, among others, LÉVI-STRAUSS; TAMBIAH; DOUGLAS), usually in respect of primitive cultures, though E. LEACH has attempted, not very convincingly, to relate our own perception of animals to our sociosexual discriminations (see also DUFFY). It seems likely that it is we that are more limited by such considerations than the more 'primitive' of our kin: it is with the advent of a settled, civilized existence that men can afford to indulge their fantasies. Hunter-gatherers, it might seem, must be glad of what they can get. I do not mean by this that hunter-gatherers live on the brink of starvation: they plainly do not (SAHLINS). Nor that they have no interest in the non-human that transcends their immediate needs: they plainly do (LÉVI-STRAUSS (1) pp. 3 f.). Nor do I mean to denigrate such ritual discriminations: they may often serve the long-term interests both of human and more generally of animal society; and in leading beyond our immediate purposes they encourage a less 'practical' approach to the non-human. But the extent and level of our fantasies is enormously different from that of those cultures who must so frequently confront the naked truth. We do our best to see that our fantasy remains the only truth we know, and it is in the context of that fantasy that we judge animals. To savage your trainer is to be a 'bad lion' (CLARKE p. 184). To be a laboratory animal is to be, all too literally, an 'animal preparation' (DEVEREUX (1) pp. 234 f.). Animals exist for us as objects of fantasy: we make sure that we do not see anything to disillusion us, and if we do see something that does not fit our preconceptions, we blame the beast.

There is a certain grandeur in our capacity for fantasy, and it is likely enough that it neither could nor should be eliminated. To do so, after all, would be to eliminate law, and art, and science:

'Man can't live without delusion, so he creates for himself another form of delusion—the world-at-law, subject to no other law but the will of man, where man juggles with facts to his heart's content, and says "If I choose I shall make a man old enough to be my father my son, and if I choose I shall turn fruit into silk and black into white, for this is the world I have made myself, and here I am master".' (MIRRLEES p. 163.)

Similarly artists create worlds in which there is obvious pattern, where events go as the artist plans them, where there is a beginning, middle and end to stories. And scientists map out a world of mathematical order, where it is man's theorems that rule what may occur, free from the intrusions and accidents that are inevitable in the world we originally inhabit. All these worlds may touch the first reality at times; all may even show in simple some real feature (though only one among so infinitely many) of that reality of encountered fact—where we are not the masters. This gift of organized dreaming may be peculiar to us, and is perhaps the cause of our success—not because it has given us *ideas* for improved technology, but because it has given us the incentive to seek them. Technology, historically, owes very little to science, and advanced technologies may coexist with wildly differing scientific 'explanations' of that technology. What it owes to science, or more generally to the art of fiction, is the incentive to seek to be masters. This may help to explain why, despite our utilitarian professions, we persist in exporting not realistic techniques of medicine, agriculture and child-care but ritualistic incubi in the shape of expensively professional hospitals, large-scale agricultural machines and the murderous insanity of bottle-feeding. We are not simply stupid, nor simply greedy: we are out to replace nature, where we are not masters, by culture, where we are.

LÉVI-STRAUSS (2) has traced this division between nature and culture through many apparently disparate myths, and however debatable some of his interpretations are—particularly as it is very difficult to think of a story which could *not* be analysed by his techniques (which may prove his point)—this fundamental division does seem likely to be very widely accepted by humankind. PORPHYRY, interestingly, records an opinion that it was natural to man to eat *cooked* flesh ((1) 1 13). Once this division is made and we are set to think of ourselves as members of culture rather than of nature, nature itself becomes incorporated into culture as its loathly opposite. We cannot control natural event, so we create rituals and magics whereby what happens is made our own. Either we sanctify whatever happens, in advance, as Stoics would have us do; or we set up a ritual in which success comforts us with a sense of power and failure gives us someone or something to blame. In this context the old theory that ritual and magic was the expression of emotion—a theory that later anthropologists have deservedly abused—may perhaps receive new life. Not that magic is the expression of emotion, but that emotions, in SARTRE's analysis, are attempts at magic: when realistic methods fail we fantasize to cloak the known reality, saying 'the grapes are sour', or fainting, or finding fault with God, our brothers, or ourselves. When we impute our failure to *our* sin we are still seeking meaning, a world where we are masters because it is our rules that are obeyed.

In offering this sketchy account of the genesis at any rate of some rituals I do not mean to prejudge the possibility that some rituals *are* realistically effective. They may affect our own psychological, and hence psychosomatic state; they may even affect the world of encountered facts. Nor do I mean to suggest that it is obviously *wrong* to seek a world that makes sense to us: there may indeed be such a world, despite appearances, and poetic fantasy may indeed be the way to discover it. Shamans and Neo-Platonists alike have believed as much, and those scientists who profess not to believe it at least act as if they did: for they assume that their musings can uncover, when guided by intuited standards of beauty and logical coherence, the principles of being. Which is surely possible only if we are, at some deep level of our imagination, identical with the principles of being, if our archetypes are the prototypes of the visible world. All this may be so, and the visible truly a shadow of the invisible—but the ethics that go along with this cosmology are unlikely to bring much comfort to the orthodox.

But the possible truth of Neo-Platonism is not at issue in the rituals I am discussing: here we do not receive nor join in worship of the Forms—rather we seek to create some. 'The world we are making for ourselves and the creatures who happen to share it with us is one in which man takes upon himself the rôle of an omnipotent power.' (NIALL p. 72.) We have set to work to make our fantasy come true, the fantasy that *we*, the human individuals we are, are masters of the world.

Our effort to make the world our own need not, of course, entirely blind us to the first reality: on the contrary, insofar as we regard the visible world as written for our learning we have a strong incentive to see as much of it as possible: 'The marvels of the creation are revealed only to him who studies its particular manifestations diligently and in detail.' (KLINGENDER p. 152.) Such was the attitude of mediaeval commentators on Genesis, and of the bestiaries (see T. H. WHITE): their information may be scanty or corrupt, but it usually contains some sort of sense. They are also, certainly, charming. The compassion of lions, for example:

> 'They spare the prostrate; they allow such captives as they come across to go back to their own country; they prey on men rather than on women, and they do not kill children except when they are very hungry.' (T. H. WHITE p. 9 after Aristotle, *Hist. An.* 629b8.)

What is strange about the stories is that though they are in origin very often tales, real or imagined, of the intelligence or moral behaviour of animals, and are used precisely to point such morals,[3] the bestiary does not conclude that animals actually are intelligent or moral. They act out moral lessons for our benefit, often obscurely (see T. H. WHITE p. 170).

> 'Perhaps (fish) behave like this so that in them we may see the imperfections of our own customs and be warned by their example—warned that the stronger should never attack the weaker, lest he should, by doing so, offer a precedent in wrongdoing to a Greater than himself ... Take care that while you follow your prey you do not yourself meet with a Stronger...' (T. H. WHITE pp. 207-8.)

---

[3] Chrysippus's story of the syllogizing dog (PLUTARCH (1) 969a), who reasons that his quarry has not gone down *this* path, so must have gone down *that*, passes through the bestiary to reappear in KENNY (p. 147): on its history see BOAS, and DICKERMAN.

But this ruling does not suggest to its author that our dealings with animals might deserve censure, only our dealings with other men. Nature is a grand mirror for humanity.

But because such Nature was still esteemed, interference with it was an offence: 'Before the intervention of men, the great clans of donkeys and horses continued uninterruptedly among themselves. But now, on the contrary, donkeys are crossed with horses, bastardising nature. This is certainly a greater sin than mere fornication, because it is committed contrary to nature: it injures natural affinity, apart from the injury in respect of the person.' (T. H. WHITE p. 205; see also Leviticus 19:19.) In interfering with nature in this way we corrupt the text. Because we despise nature, we castrate and torture men: 'What would good mother water say to all this?' (T. H. WHITE p. 206.)

At this stage, then, Nature is a system parallel to Humanity, from which we can learn moral lessons, and for which we can feel affection and respect even if inadequately. By its standards we condemn ourselves: 'Nature assigns equally to all, that they may have the wherewithall for being born and living ... You ought not to grudge their having in common a thing to which they are common heirs.' (T. H. WHITE p. 143.) What when we cease to esteem Nature, when the world-at-fantasy wholly corrupts the text?

At first we need merely shift the emphasis. For the bestiary that bigger fish eat little fish constitutes a warning to man—a book in the running brook; when the sense that Nature stands in parallel to Culture is lost it becomes only a sour instance of the principle of power politics. Indian textbooks on this latter subject indeed refer to it as the Law of the Fish (ZIMMER p. 36). From the bestiaries we pass to Breughel (see ZIMMER pp. 119 f.).[4] For the bestiary, Nature gives images of moral relationships; for the new man it offers, or his reading of it offers, a picture of that bestiality we alternately abuse and idolise. For the bestiary many animals are chaste and courteous, or at least behave as if they were for our edification. For the new man 'sexuality exposes man to the danger of equality with the beasts' (KANT (2) p. 164), and that would be dreadful.

---

[4] That animals show no justice, but live in a state of mutual war, goes back at least to Hesiod (*Works and Days* 276 f.). The truth is rather that War came into the world with Culture, as the writer of Gilgamesh knew. The Breughel, in its day a popular print, depicts a large dead fish, whose slit belly reveals smaller fish, who in turn are slit open to reveal yet more ...

Similarly AUSTIN's wish to show the beasts who's boss (p. 32) is closely associated with his frantic hatred of that permissiveness 'which besides establishing a Divorce Court and legalising adultery and incest ... under the pretext of giving them education infects girls with ideas and facts of which no modest woman need have any knowledge' (pp. 9 f.).

Like the bestiary, Austin is opposed to the confusion of kinds, fears the breakdown of barriers. Unlike the bestiary he blames not those who interfere with Nature, but those who sink down to her.[5] In the bestiary the opposition of good and evil is represented in the world of Nature by the opposition of the natural and the perverse. For the new man there is only one opposition, between culture and the beast. We distance ourselves from the beast without for fear of the beast within (see MIDGLEY), attributing to them the ferocity and promiscuity we fear in ourselves. Not that we thereby avoid such conduct. '(Sewing up the lips of captured wolves and flaying them alive) may seem cruel, but the wolf is a cruel beast and could scarcely expect to be treated better.' (POLLARD p. 149.) The wolf is a cruel beast, an image of the devil (see WHITE pp. 56 f.): 'They earn their living just like men, without caring for other creatures' sufferings.' (GALSWORTHY p. 7.) But at least the wolf does not flay *us* alive for this. Fear is one thing: there is a certain measure of guiltiness displayed in such hysterical assaults on bewildered and uncomprehending beasts for seeking their food for their necessities.[6]

When Nature is demoted in men's hearts, the fate of different animals is not identical. We discriminate amongst them not for realistic reasons, but for symbolic needs. Those who mourn a dead rabbit are utterly indifferent to a dead mouse; those who would not kick a dog readily support the torture of the equally intelligent pig. These discriminations may sometimes simply reveal a total indifference to animals—as the experimenter who consoles objectors by remarking that he looks on experimental animals and people's pets in utterly different ways, thereby showing that he sees the only

[5] It is not insignificant that one of Austin's favourite pejoratives is 'feminine': MERTON p. 41 remarks that 'to be in the wilderness without fighting it, or at least without killing the animals in it, is regarded as a feminine [and therefore reprehensible] trait'. Nature is *there* to be raped: not to rape 'her' is not to be 'a man'.

[6] It is a further irony that the wolf, like the bestiary lion, *does* spare the prostrate, and kills, when he does kill, only for the needs of himself and his family. We project our own ferocity onto him.

possible evil involved as an offence to the sentimentality of pet-owners. But this indifference feeds upon our fantasy—of cows as placid and incurious hunks of flesh, of dogs as loyal slaves, of birds in general as so much stuffed and twittering fowl. We do not see the individuals; we see the types of our imagination. Our children's books are full of pretty pictures of farmyard beasts defined in terms of an idealized agriculture; the very advertisements in 'Laboratory Animals' rely on such complacent cartoons; the same syndrome is to be seen in the folklore of hunting and fishing—we pretend to ourselves that these creatures somehow cooperate with their would-be killers. PORPHYRY reports an oracle that it was no injustice to kill a willing sheep ((1) 119)—so the would-be sacrificer made quite sure the sheep nodded its head. The practice of the Imperial Court of China similarly made a failure to escape the royal beaters a sign that the animal consented to its death. The guilt that even hunter-gatherers feel, who kill to live, is assuaged by a pretence that the dead beast pardons them—and KLINGENDER may not be entirely wrong to associate this guilt and its appeasement with Oedipal emotions (pp. 11 f.; see also MENNINGER). In killing beasts we kill our ancestors: we proclaim our dominion over them in fact, and fantasize that we are loved for it, and beg their pardon and assume we have it.

The world of fantasy in which we move has such a powerful grip that we have almost forgotten the world beyond, and when we do remember it is as a world devoid of meaning. 'In our life alone does Nature live', according to Coleridge (Ode to Dejection); 'where man is not, nature is barren', said BLAKE aphoristically (p. 152), thereby misleading such humanists as forgot his other opinion that

> each grain of sand,
> every stone on the land,
> each rock and each hill,
> each fountain and rill,
> each herb and each tree,
> mountain, hill, earth and sea,
> cloud, meteor and star,
> are men seen afar (pp. 804 5).

That is, they are spiritual existences currently visible in those forms—they are lives. If we do not discriminate creatures according to our purposes with them, we do not know how to discriminate them. If we do not imagine them firmly set in the reality we fantasize we cannot conceive of their living in any meaningful reality. So pictures of animals rarely avoid treating them as things with certain human values, whether of property or explicit symbolism. Hunting-scenes, which from Lascaux onwards have often been marked by a careful realism in the presentation of the victim, the hounds, the horses (see KLINGENDER pp. 8f., 52f. and 60f.), reinforce my point: that animals are seen most clearly when we have an interest in dominating them, and recording our triumph.

> 'I am Ashurbanipal, king of hosts, king of Assyria. In my abound-ing, princely strength I seized a lion of the desert by his tail, and at the command of Enurta and Nergal, the gods who are my helpers, I smashed his skull with the axe in my hand.' (KLINGENDER p. 61.)

Even when we seek to see them as they are in themselves, we cannot escape the coils of fantasy: what lies beyond our make-believe enters our make-believe as the image of the terrible unknown. We domesti-cate even the burning tiger, by the very act of making it something more than we can know. Moby Dick is not an individual white whale with whom we share the world. He is the thing from over the hori-zon.

Not that such visions are not, occasionally, magnificent and proper evocations of the mystery.

> Can you pull out the whale with a gaff
> or can you slip a noose round his tongue?
> Can you pass a cord through his nose
> or put a hook through his jaw?
> Will he plead with you for mercy
> or beg his life with soft words?
> Will he enter into an agreement with you
> or become your slave for life?
> Will you toy with him as with a bird
> or keep him on a string like a song-bird for your maidens?
> Do trading-partners haggle over him
> or merchants share him out? (Job 41:1 f.)[7]

[7] The translators of the New English Bible, regrettably, employ the pronoun 'it' rather than 'he'. There is no warrant for this in the Hebrew. The whale is a he/she: would the translator care to be called 'it'?

It is a measure of our corruption that the answer to several of these questions would now be 'yes'. And the memory of their asking may help to explain why certain law-abiding men spent days pumping expensive bullets into a stranded, pregnant whale in Newfoundland, while her mate howled upon the horizon (MOWAT). They were killing Leviathan.

The shortage of good poems on animals is not merely a function of the general shortage of good poems. Most poems on the subject are really only about the author's feelings (see SALT (6) pp. vf.): he expresses something about his relation with himself or with his lover or with the world through the medium of a code that employs animals as its symbols. Witness Skelton's sparrow, and Ted Hughes's Crow. It is difficult to identify with animals without diverting one's attention to those features of one's own situation which one thinks one sees in them. Not identifying with them, but seeing them as mere brute facts—a significant phrase—may allow such excellent poems as Edwin Muir's (see above, p. 103) and Auden's:

> The eye of the crow and the eye of the camera open
> onto Homer's world, not ours. First and last
> they magnify earth, the abiding
> mother of gods and men; if they notice either
> it is only in passing: gods behave, men die,
> both feel in their own small way, but She
> does nothing and does not care.
> She alone is seriously there (*Memorial for the City* I 1–8.)

I know very few poems which speak without patronage or self-deceit or self-indulgence from our common heritage, whether as spirits or as animals (there are *some*, not many, in SPEARMAN). Blake and Job come close to it, but are still faced by the basic difficulty of writing poems that recognize our *common* heritage when poetry is a thing, so far as we know, peculiar to man. We need both to exclude from our consciousness, and to employ, our own specific gifts. Good paintings too are scarce.

Our choice then seems to be to regard animals sentimentally, moralistically, or with terror of the unmeaning void. The first is almost the greatest danger: so fixed is our fantasy that it is very difficult to produce convincing photographs of animal suffering—somehow even battery calves and syphilitic apes and rabbits having their eyes dissolved to test cosmetics manage to look rather sweet and innocent. Worshipping animals is not always the most effective way of securing good treatment for them: those who worship animals, after all, tend to sacrifice them (see PLUTARCH (2) 72 f.). We are not the first to have had these problems. DOUGLAS (2) records that the Lele distinguish men and beasts on the point of manners,[8] holding that brute beasts who have no understanding but are fecund and submissive, may be killed at liberty; and it is those animals who step out of line who create emotional problems for their human observers. The Lele react by incorporating the greatest anomaly, the pangolin, into their symbolic system as its lynchpin: 'For Lele ... the world of wild nature, the dark forest beyond the ordered village, is the very foundation of meaning.' (WILLIS p. 121.) Willis's analysis of how the Lele, Nuer and Fipa look on animals, and on themselves, is extremely illuminating. Nuer and Lele discriminate between the wild and tame: for Lele the wild represents the true self of the communal man; for Nuer the tame represents the mystical inner self of the individual man. The Fipa regard all nature, wild and domesticated, as open to progressive control whereby 'the strange and unknown is brought into the light and order of human understanding' (WILLIS p. 124). It seems likely that Nuer do manage some personal relationship with their oxen: pangolin and python are purely symbolic beasts.

WILLIS doubts (p. 136) that such focally symbolic beasts are still to be found in highly differentiated industrial society, and as far as the full weight of semi-conscious meaning goes is doubtless correct. Individuals, of course, may find some animal summing up their attitude to the world and calling forth some strong emotional attachment: cats figure largely in the fantasies of the psychotic, presumably as being unsocialized, self-sufficient, beautiful, pitiless and strong. Even the non-psychotic may sometimes think this not too inappropriate an image of the world. Hebrew and mediaeval western culture could most probably be analysed in terms of the symbolism of the lamb: the innocent, the willing victim, the sought-after stray. But the obvious choice for symbolic animal in present-day Britain is the dog.

Even orthodox philosophers have allowed a certain grudging respect to dogs as 'honorary human beings' (RITCHIE p. 110). LAIRD

---

[8] It is of interest that in the Salamanca debate on the Amerindians they were urged to be *animals* because they countenanced homosexuality and took baths (my thanks to Professor John Metford for this story).

(p. 120) was of the opinion that the dog's fidelity to his master was virtuous and morally good, and folk-lore is full of improving stories to this effect. A dog is a man's best friend, though this has not stopped us employing the creatures in biomedical research and killing them by the thousand when their presence is minimally inconvenient to us. Like JAMES ((1) p. 58: see above p. 9) we like to think that the dog *would* agree if he only knew. We call dogs friends: we mean they are our slaves. When we hear of other cultures that consider dogs to be meat animals, or feral abominations, we are righteously outraged.

So dogs, for us, are loyal, worshipful, affectionate, protective members of the household whom we can pretend to think well-treated. But simultaneously they are filthy, shameless, dung-eating, slavish. Our nausea at the thought of eating dog is perhaps only partly a sign of affection. Cottagers, after all, may often have felt fondness for their pigs.[9] Nor do we avoid dog-meat merely because dogs are carnivores—though our suspicion that the flesh of carnivores is hardly wholesome perhaps marks a certain guiltiness about our own dietary habits. For we are similarly, and unrealistically, averse to horse-meat, and happily eat fish. Dogs embody those traits which we do not wish our children to display: they are dirt, which we, of our kindness, succour.

And finally dogs are dangerous. Indeed, even realistically the domestic dog is an enormously greater danger to farmers and to families than most of the pests we seek to exterminate: or rather, some dogs sometimes are (see VESEY-FITZGERALD (1) pp. 76f.). But our terror of the dog goes beyond realism: 'dog bites man' *is* news. We frighten ourselves with stories of dogs' jealousy of their owners' children, though we thereby admit more 'humanity' in the dog than we customarily allow. Kipling's hideous story of Bertran and Bimi (in *Life's Handicap*) displaces onto the orang-utang the combination of patronizing affection, contempt and fear that we actually feel for the dog. Dirt is dangerous: as DOUGLAS (3) has shown, our standards of hygiene are often matters of ritual more than of realistic medicine.

The dog is the point at which most British encounter Nature.[10]

---

[9] Assuaging their guilt by the fantasy that the pig was 'born to be eaten', as if this were a fact beyond their own control instead of a decision on their part.

[10] Though another, and very interesting case is the *rat*. Our hatred and disdain of rats goes far beyond any realistic injury we may expect from them, or even than any historical

Our relation with the cat is less intricate, though something could perhaps be learnt from its ambivalent character, in fantasy, as friend and witch. The repugnance often felt against cats deserves anthropological attention more than psychological or medical. In the cat, perhaps, we are aware of Nature as an alongside world, without guiltiness or need of us. Cats are serpentine. The common thesis that there are cat-people and dog-people perhaps marks an awareness that there is a way of relating to Nature alternative to the orthodox—but as a cat-person myself I cannot view the human-cat relationship quite so critically (see MENNINGER on more detailed correlations). More work than I know of needs to be done, with more care. The results of such work would probably not be entirely culture-specific: the Thai also make an opposition between cat and dog, in which the dog is dirty, incestuous and the rest—eating dog is symbolically equivalent to incest (TAMBIAH). Equally we should not so readily assume that our society is homogenous (which is the major fault of E. LEACH's analysis). MARANDA's test (pp. 13 f.) for the conditioning effect of myth, in which the relations to be expected between serpent, man and woman vary from society to society, gives insufficient weight to alternatives licensed by cultural tradition, but with that proviso *does* uncover some of our concerns. He points out that *we* generally say 'Serpent deceives woman, and woman cajoles man', whereas a Melanesian of the Eastern Solomon Islands would expect 'Female serpent gives birth to woman, man kills serpent, woman loves and leaves man'. My own answer, just to be awkward, is rather 'Man saves serpent, serpent blesses man, man controls woman'—which I hope says more about my reading of genuinely European myth than about my character.[11]

---

connotations would suggest (our present rats, after all, are not the black plague-carriers—and why, in any case, do we *blame* rats just because they suffer as we do?). We hate them perhaps because they proliferate where we have neglected human welfare; because they swarm (like insects), but are furry (like our pets)—they are anomalous, and therefore (in our culture) loathly; because they present a distorted image of human society—of *our* 'rat-race'. Real rats surely do not deserve to be burnt alive, as one eminent Glaswegian recently urged; nor do they deserve to be tormented in the name of science. KROPOTKIN ((2) p. 54) suggested that it was the sight of rat-granaries that gave our ancestors the notion of cultivating cereals: we have ill-repaid our benefactors. 'Let Boaz, the Builder of Judah, bless with the Rat, which dwelleth in hardship and peril, that they may look to themselves and keep their houses in order' (SMART p. 32).

[11] The story is of a hunter who finds a burning bush, and in the bush a snake. Moved by compassion he lets the snake crawl out across his gun. The snake thanks him, and gives him understanding of the talk of beasts, on condition that he never speaks of his encounter. If he does, he will die. Thus talented, the hunter returns home and refutes, by his knowledge

With these caveats and precautions, however, it does seem possible to take our curious relationship with the dog as indicative and symbolic of our attitude to Nature. Crudely, we despise Nature, the uncultural, and react by taming it and making believe that it is our willing slave. Yet still we fear it and suspect its unreason will knock down our flimsy barricades. We are kind to animals, all too often, because it makes *us* feel superior. We are unkind, indifferent or hysterically restrictive because the world beyond our worlds still pains us. Witness the irrelevant campaign to enforce licensing laws and keep dogs off the streets that follows on a (licensed) terrier's assault upon a baby (in her grandparents' home). We do not wish to descend to Nature, to bestiality, but keep the chief and shameless image of that bestiality enslaved to us. We dislike Natural living, but have made the Law of the Fish our own. And because of that familiar quirk whereby we feel increasingly inimical to those we have injured we increasingly surpass our piscine exemplars (see also CARRIGHAR p. 182).

A new mythology

We have accepted the Law of the Fish, that the greater eat the lesser. So much so that zoophiles who query our greater iniquities are greeted with such patronizing glop as 'the question is one of priorities. If the lives of animals have priority over the needs and lives of mankind ... experiments on animals should all be prohibited. Yet it is well to remember how domestic animals have gained, side by side with men, from living experiments' (C. L. Evans: R.D.S. p. 9). To which one can only reply that one does not give priority to a human slave if one merely insists that his needs and life should not be sacrificed at his master's will. Are slave-owners *injured* by being forbidden to dominate their fellows? Is it my need that is met by dissolving rabbits' eyes to test a cosmetic? My life that is preserved, or enhanced—and why should it be enhanced at such a cost?—by inflicting electric shocks on rats, swapping gonads from animal to animal, cutting their nerves, stimulating their brains with electrodes, injecting them with strychnine (see particularly RYDER)? Are we to say that if a few tame Jews accidentally benefited

---

of dog-speech, his wife's claim to have treated the dog well. His wife nags him continuously for an explanation of his knowledge of her doings, and he is on the point of telling all, and dying, when he overhears a cock's acid remarks about humans who cannot manage even one wife. He accordingly asserts his authority, and all live happily thereafter. I leave the sexual interpretation to Freudians—in this context I invoke the story to suggest that kindness may lead more quickly to a knowledge of nature's ways than does random curiosity.

by Nazi experiments on their brothers then everything was all right, and you're a fool if you object?

Apparently we are. We have declared war on Nature, and this war knows no chivalry. Let us beware the Stronger. I do not see that the barriers which moralists and preachers have erected against the exploitation of whatever sub-species and pseudo-species of humanity the social engineers come to see as expendable are exactly secure. Certainly they have not, historically, been secure. If the values of Culture license tyranny, where will it end? 'It is a question of priorities. If the lives of the stupid, the irresponsible, the old, the sick have priority over the needs and lives of normal humanity . . .' We began by killing pests, progressed to the harmless, and then to the labouring ox and sheep and cock, and concluded our career with war and murder even against our species (PLU-TARCH (1) 998). 'The danger of accepting any form of life as cheap is that each successive generation might accept slightly lower standards.' (HARRISON p. 3.) I am not arguing that though there is nothing wrong in torturing animals, still we shouldn't do it because we might end up torturing Me (horrors). My contention is that our attitude to Nature is already so unrealistic, so irresponsible, so contaminated by fantasy that no coherent grounds will be available to outlaw attitudes even the orthodox consider vile. Particularly as our technicians are carefully shielded by education and the law from any suspicion that their behaviour is or ought to be subject to moral sanction. We are already being prepared for experimentation on the aborted 'products of conception', with the vague promise that so we may be saved a few more inconveniences.

Nor am I suggesting that all ritual fantasy should be abandoned. In the present state of man's character such an abandonment is likely to be half-hearted, and result in practice in such fatuities as the (pseudo-) scientific world-view, for which everything is mere material for our purposes. If we lose ritual discriminations, we are likely enough to be told that it makes no real difference where our food or profit comes from—perhaps from the human poor. In the name of abandoning unrealistic principles we shall devote yet more energy to defending and building up the psychotic fantasy of our present culture without even the last few ancestral repugnances to save us from ourselves. Ritual, fantasy discrimination gives us felt reasons for action or inaction that assist or surpass such immediate incentives as hunger and affection. Such extra reasons include honour, wealth, power, purity: truly to abandon such ritualized goods would be to abandon war—to abandon merely such ritual as is inconvenient to the greater fantasy is merely to make war inhuman (see PORTMANN p. 217). What we need, as Portmann says, are better rituals, not none. Though true amoralism, as I have remarked, might be the paradisal solution.

Let us keep ritual, for our sanity's sake perhaps, and discriminate between animal kinds, and feel unrealistic repugnances. But let us at least abandon war. In the early tradition of the Christian church the return of paradise involved the promised reconciliation with the animal kingdom—a tradition only slowly ousted by the converse view that salvation required the conquest and suppression of the beasts. The earlier view is still evident in the Celtic saints, and on the Rothwell Cross (SCHAPIRO), and reappears, in part, among the early Franciscans (see KLINGENDER pp. 441 f.) It seems to me a better vision, both of the beast without and of the beast within, than that offered by orthodoxy.

The bestiary believed that the Law of the Fish was a warning to beware. The orthodox have made it an example to imitate: 'if you [fish] eat one another, I don't see why we may not eat you' (Benjamin Franklin: quoted by SALT (4) pp. 9 f.).[12] The bestiary believed Nature to be a mirror for Humanity: the orthodox have made it a thing to be feared and changed. But whether we like it or not we are part of Nature: '*We* are food', as the Taittiriya Upanishad exults. And if we are food, and subject to the same laws as the beasts we oppress, should we not fear the Stronger?

'If we look downwards, we see innumerable species of inferior beings whose happiness and life are dependent on man's will; we see him cloathed by their spoils, and fed by their miseries and destruction, inslaving some, tormenting others, and murdering millions for his luxury or diversion; is it not therefore analogous and highly probable, that the happiness and life of man should be equally dependent on the will of his superiors? As we receive great part of our pleasures, and even subsistence, from the sufferings and deaths of lower animals, may not these superior Beings do the same from ours?' (JENYNS p. 66.)

[12] Thereby forgetting that 'fish' is a very general concept: pike are not cannibals for eating trout, nor are all fish fish-eaters. Some fish, like stickleback, are fond parents and clever problem solvers. We should not assume that, just because our ancestors once were fish, the life of the sea is unchanged since that date.

Or as Johnson continued the fable:

'As we drown whelps and kittens, they amuse themselves now and then with sinking a ship, and stand around the fields of Blenheim or the walls of Prague, as we encircle a cockpit. As we shoot a bird flying, they take a man in the midst of his business and pleasure, and knock him down with an apoplexy. Some of them, perhaps, are virtuosi, and delight in the operations of an asthma as a human philosopher in the effects of the air pump. To swell a man with a tympany is as good sport as to blow a frog. Many a merry bout have these frolick beings at the vicissitudes of an ague, and good sport it is to see a man tumble with an epilepsy, and revive and tumble again, and all this he knows not why....'
(JOHNSON (2) X p. 249.)

Do such frolick beings truly deserve our or any respect? Do we?

'What would you think of gods who shot women with babies in arms for the sake of obtaining their white skins or their crop of hair to wear on their heads, eh?' (GALSWORTHY p. 15.)

Even this world, the world of Generation, is perhaps not so entirely cruel as our fantasy suggests.[13] If we abandon magic and accept the world, we shall live according to the heart's affections with our strange fellows. If we retain that curious magic called scientific reason, whereby we posit a stable world where our laws are the masters, still we must find, on present theory, that we men are not supreme nor readily distinguishable among the entities of earth—even our vaunted ritual is matched by other kinds. If we take our magics seriously, and say that here, in the exercise of the imagination lies the higher truth—why, then we should perhaps attend to the claims of those who have espoused that truth:

'(The tradition) that Man contained in his Limbs all Animals is True and they were separated from him by cruel Sacrifices.' (Blake, 'Jerusalem', 27.)

[13] JAMES's ((2) p. 169) evocation of melancholia is partly valid—'our civilization *is* founded on the shambles'—but he grotesquely exaggerates, for example, the probable agonies of the age of the dinosaurs. This aspect of mythological thought is still with us— we like to imagine that 'we' (which for mythological purposes is how we think of the struggling insectivores of that age) somehow survived the terrible ferocity of the great reptiles. Sadly for such phantoms: most dinosaurs were vegetarian, and the predators amongst them were doubtless as unferocious as modern carnivores. They killed to live, and quickly.

We fell, the Greeks supposed, by murder (PLUTARCH (1) 996c; and see RHYS DAVIDS IV 82 f.). And may hope to rise:

> 'The beasts will be at peace with us when in the shrine of our souls we tame the clean and unclean animals and lie down with the lions, like Daniel.' (Ps-Jerome on Mark 1:13: MIGNE 30.595.)

When we tame them, or when we forgive them:

> And I heard Jehovah speak
> Terrific from his Holy Place, and saw the Words of the Mutual
> Covenant Divine
> on Chariots of gold and jewels with Living Creatures, starry
> and flaming
> with every Colour. Lion, Tyger, Horse, Elephant, Eagle, Dove,
> Fly, Worm,
> and the all wondrous Serpent clothed in gems & rich array,
> Humanise
> in the Forgiveness of Sins according to thy Covenant,
> Jehovah (Blake, 'Jerusalem', 98.)

It may be that Blake's magic is but one more phantom, but there is no fantasy with stronger claims to truth that can defend our treatment of our kin.

> 'Whatever is under the coape of heaven ... runneth one law, and followeth one fortune...' (MONTAIGNE II.12, p. 153.)

Let us not be afraid of treason to the phantom of Man's kingdom upon earth, nor fear to corrupt justice by extending it to animals (PORPHYRY (1) III 26), nor boast that we are sons of Adam—the Lord may yet raise up new sons for him from the dead stone (see Luke 3:8). In short, let us stop day-dreaming, and face our friends.

> The world is charged with the grandeur of God.
>   It will flame out, like shining from shook foil;
>   it gathers to a greatness, like the ooze of oil
> crushed. Why do men then now not reck his rod?
> Generations have trod, have trod, have trod;
>   and all is seared with trade; bleared, smeared with toil;
>   and wears man's smudge and shares man's smell: the soil
> is bare now, nor can foot feel, being shod.

And for all this, nature is never spent;
    there lives the dearest freshness deep down things;
and though the last lights off the black West went
    oh, morning, at the brown brink eastward springs—
because the Holy Ghost over the bent
    world broods with warm breast and with ah! bright wings.
                    Gerard Manley Hopkins, 'God's Grandeur'.

VII

THE DREAM OF REASON

Psychoanalytic realism and the values of humanity

In my last chapter I suggested that much of our behaviour to animals stems from our readiness to see them as symbols of our own potentialities, particularly of those potentialities we wish to suppress. We treat them as creatures without individuality or purposes of their own, and attempt to conceal or to destroy any features which do not fit our preconceptions. We consider ourselves the only sources of meaning, and think our animal kin are brute, or bestial. The full investigation of the ways we think of animals would be an investigation of all human thought and culture, and far beyond my powers. My suggestion, which stems from a prolonged and conscious attention to what people in our present society think about animals, is that we wish to create a world where we are masters, and where such sad reminders of our real defencelessness as wild nature are kept firmly in their place. In constructing this phantom, as I shall argue, we are compelled to deny and denigrate our own immediate, emotional experience.

My point is really a very simple one. In human relationships the ability to live happily in love and charity with our neighbours, working at tasks to which we can seriously devote ourselves, is often weakened or destroyed by fantasies about one's own status or the character of a would-be friend. It is difficult, if not impossible, to give any formal account of the difference between a realistic outlook and a fantasy: I am myself quite prepared to believe that even the most carefully realistic picture of the world is essentially a fantasy, and it certainly may *operate* as one, cutting off the possibility of love and work as effectively as any more obvious psychosis. But we are nonetheless convinced that people are better off when they can love and work, when the heart's affections are not stifled. I am merely extending this principle to our relations with the non-human. A world-picture which permits the recognition of other living creatures as affectionate, curious, appetitive and the like and allows us to live together in friendship is plainly, pragmatically, better than one which pretends to license a total separation of man and beast. Such a pragmatically preferable world-picture may be spiritualistic, like Blake's, or naturalistic, like Haeckel's: in either case, it has better claims to truth than the common fantasy of the non-human as wickedly or passively materialistic, as devils (literally so, according to BOUGEANT's sardonic fantasy (see ROSENFIELD pp. 36 ff.)) or as dummies. A man, whether he is Thomist or Darwinian, who thinks of non-human animals as stones, devoid of any value till men give it them, is, quite technically, an idiot: he lives in a world of private fantasy. He is also a dangerous idiot.

But our ancestral pride is such that we will continue to insist on an absolute division between men and animals, even if we nominally espouse philosophies and theories which outlaw such a division. What can any materialist have to say for it? Yet Marxist and liberal humanists alike will sneer at any who proclaim animals as worthy of respect alongside men. The search for pretexts for the division grows ever more desperate: 'Forty or more years ago ... it was said (1) animals cannot learn; (2) animals cannot plan ahead; (3) animals cannot conceptualise; (4) animals cannot use, much less make, tools. (5) It was said they have no language; (6) they cannot count; (7) they lack artistic sense; (8) they lack all ethical sense.' (THORPE p. 271.) Every one of these disparities has lapsed, to be replaced by metaphysical assertions that animals cannot conceive of themselves as objects, or cannot conceive of general laws. Insofar as these claims have any actual meaning, I doubt that they will endure for forty years. It is true, as far as I know, that no non-human animal would have an interest or an ability to write this book, so there (perhaps) I surpass them. But the same may be said of most members of my own species: academic writers tend to forget that the high-flown disparities they sometimes mention as of the essence of man are of enormously little concern to most non-academic men. If animals, on these criteria, are less than human, so are men.

But suppose that it is not so. Suppose that the human species is unique in the possession of various highly-thought-of faculties (highly thought of by us, that is). In the first place, any species is similarly unique. It is probably true that data on laboratory rats tell us little about human behaviour. They also tell us little about rabbit behaviour. Indeed they tell us little about the behaviour of rats, except under certain conditions of extreme stress. The fear that some humanists feel at the adoption of a rat-model for human society should be assuaged by the realization that even rats, even laboratory rats, are sources of novelty, social affection and constructiveness. Instead of shrieking that men and rats are quite, quite different, anti-behaviourists should insist that behaviourism is inadequate at all levels, and that all species are at once unique and variously similar to other species. We are no exception.

In the second place, what if we were significantly unique? What if the human species does enshrine possibilities which for better or worse must affect every other species on earth, possibilities which are to some extent under our (whose?) control? Well, in that case 'man (should) accept his position in nature as the species granted the privilege of fulfilling the aristocratic ideal of noblesse oblige, of being the servant of his people.' (DARLING (1) p. 82.)

In the real world of encountered fact we are not the masters. We are as subject now as we ever were, or as any species is, to the changes and chances of this mortal life. All our culture is designed to conceal this from us, or to reconcile ourselves to our own contingency by postulating a wider and so far imaginary world where our culture, our species marches to yet higher, and still unmeaning, heights. Perhaps there is a world where everything makes sense, and all is reconciled in God: if there is we shall meet our victims there. But perhaps, also, there is not, and we shall forever be beneath the threat of sudden death and cataclysm, however much we seek to postpone or conceal it from ourselves. And in that case we might allow ourselves a certain solidarity with creatures of another shape who also take things as they come.

The question really comes down to this: I am a provincial Englishman by birth, a Briton, a Caucasian, a human being, a primate, a mammal, a warm-blooded creature, a vertebrate, an animal; in mentioning each of these categories I variously associate myself with other creatures of the various kinds, and could, in principle, connect my more obvious individual characteristics to one or other category. Why must I think of myself as a *man*, to the exclusion of all other categories? Many of my features are better explained by remembering my Britishness, or my mammalian ancestry; in writing this I employ abilities shared by all or most men, but also ones shared only by, say, English-speakers or else by all primates— why should my humanity be thought all-important?

One obvious answer is that my species-membership determines

far more of my nature than my membership of a particular sexual, racial, national or linguistic group. Some isolated human populations might eventually turn into new species: there is no evidence that any has yet done so. Even if, as seems very likely, my immediate ancestry (which is to say, my race) gives me some of my properties (we inherit more than physiognomy), yet every human population most probably contains the genetic potential for everything that has ever been realized as a human activity. My infant son, if transported to an alien culture, would doubtless (leaving aside the problem of self-fulfilling prophecy) grow up to be an indistinguishable member of that culture. Racial and cultural difference does exist, but no human population has yet sold its birthright of human flexibility. These are the sort of considerations which are commonly used to draw our attention to the brotherhood of man, and they depend in the end upon its being and continuing to be the case that we are one species, one potentially interbreeding population. We have a sexual and parental interest in each other. In this we are like any other species. We are, in general, sexually indifferent to other species—though the bestiary, and also the experience of zoo-keepers, is there to remind us that individuals may mate outside their kind, or wish to.

In short, the usual (though not absolute, nor universal) interchangeability of human beings depends upon the continuation of a mutual sexual responsiveness. Racial groups that feel antagonistic to the alien tend to define intermarriage as bestiality, and such sexual antagonism, triggered by colour, smell or body hair may eventually generate new species, or may even be (though this seems enormously less likely) the relic of ancestral differences between hominid species that have gradually interbred. These sexual, and parental, and in general 'humane' responses to creatures felt to be of our kin adequately explain why 'man' is a more crucially important category than any lesser division, and also why it is not an absolute imperative. There may be several hominid species in the future; there were several hominid species in the past. We have no real explanation of the victory of 'true man', nor any reason to think that that victory was entirely complete. We are one species, to be sure, but species do not have rigid boundaries, nor any absolute cohesiveness.

In the non-human, sexual indifference leads to territorial tolerance (see HEDIGER pp. 17f., CARRIGHAR pp. 168f.); other species are not sexual rivals. Even prey and predator can co-exist in harmony, or indifference, save when the predator is hunting. In man sexual indifference, whether to animal or to man, seems to lead to intolerance. We have sufficient wit to notice that other creatures may compete with or be a danger to our children, and insufficient intelligence to realize that our children will be dependent on the whole health of the biosphere, a health that requires a multiplicity of living species that are not all attractive to us. Even our sexual responsiveness too easily becomes, under the influence of prudential reason, a search for sexual satisfaction at the expense even of our fellow humans. We are not alone in this: rhesus monkeys and baboons, or so it seems, have similar confusions—they, and man, are the only creatures that are truly bestial at times (see CARRIGHAR pp. 113 f.). We take more than we need, more even than we want, because the serpent-voice still whispers 'you will be the masters, then'.

Sexual responsiveness makes me man, and ensures that I am 'on the side' of the human species, but it does not do so absolutely. Our species is one of many related kinds, and our sexuality is not so readily distinguished from that of those other kinds. Our species may yet dissolve (again?) into many different species, and such species *could* be mutually tolerant and affectionate. Doubtless they would have different styles, different habits and habitats, maybe even different predispositions in the field of language learning. Do we not prefer to imagine, at any rate, that such differing hominid kinds would treat each other decently, if only for their common ancestry? Would we think well of one kind that seized the chance to enslave, torture and kill its kin?

And how does this imagined situation differ from our own? We torment our fellow primates, our fellow mammals, our fellow animals, because we have the power to do so. *We* do this, but not we *men*, for many lines of man are relatively guiltless (though none wholly so).[1] We *civilised* men do this, and are as contemptuous of 'primitives' as we are of the beasts we think to rise above.

---

[1] The legend among zoophiles (as J. WYNNE-TYSON) is that men were once vegetarians, like the other primates, and were tempted from the right path: there may be some truth in this. But it is likely that most animals eat some meat, when they can get it, and almost certain that our proto-hominid ancestors ate at least as much as modern hunter-gatherers. Other primates also grab and sometimes hunt small creatures they consider game (GOODALL pp. 180 ff.; DEVORE AND WASHBURN; TELEKI). But certainly we men do more damage, and can hardly excuse ourselves by observing that our 'inferiors' do some. But I have no doubt that some critic of this book will seek to justify his habits by pointing to pictures of chimpanzees gnawing at the skulls of young baboons.

Man, as such, is one natural species amongst many, and to recognize one's identity as a man is to find oneself inside a complex of attractions and family resemblances that allow for comfort and affection and tolerance even between species. Man as a cultural ideal, the god of civilisation, is another matter.

Sensibility and science

'If you think you are naturally built to eat flesh,' said PLUTARCH dryly ((1) 995a: and see SHELLEY p. 329), 'kill for yourself with your bare hands.' It is commonly said that there would be few carnivores if we had to do just that, and as commonly remarked that such squeamishness would not outface our hunger (ROCHE (1) p. 63). It surely would if we had other food-sources—as we do. But it is not an argument from squeamishness. Castaneda is led by his Amerindian guru, Don Juan, to the point where he must himself kill a rabbit caught in his trap (CASTANEDA pp. 113 f.). He finds, he who had killed hundreds with a gun, that he cannot in the peculiar intensity of that moment regard the creature as 'nothing but a rabbit'. He is forced to the realization that the rabbit is a living and now despairing creature with whom he can entirely identify himself. If you must kill, do so knowing what you do: that most of us would not willingly and with open eyes kill a living creature unless autistically blinded to the realities of what we do is not a function merely of squeamishness at dirt, and blood, and the decaying flesh.

Though if it were, we would perhaps attend to this sensibility. I have no doubt that slaughtermen are quite indifferent to the nature of their task, as are public executioners (though see BERGER AND MOHR pp. 132 f.): 'He feels much the same regarding the slaughter of a beast as a bricklayer feels about laying the next brick: it is another job to be done before knocking-off time.' (SMITH AND WILCOX p. 134.) Is it absurd to think that his humanity is diminished thereby? Why are we so repelled by the story of the butcher who bribed his young son to learn his catechism with the promise of being allowed to kill a lamb next day? 'If the slaughter of lambs be a virtuous and humanising business, why should not the child be initiated into his father's craft as early and as innocently as any other?' (KINGSFORD AND MAITLAND p. 66.) Is it not entirely proper that we shrink from slaughter? Even the true carnivores kill only, and quickly, what they must. If innate revulsion is so easily dismissed as mere sentiment what power is there so strong as will prevent our killing of even human beings? What power has there been?

Claude Bernard's chief recorded arguments in his self-defence are as follows (BERNARD (1) pp. 99 f.): firstly, that famous men have vivisected in the past—and also, though he does not mention this, burnt witches and staged gladiatorial contests;[2] secondly, that if we have a right to kill for food or diversion we may surely do so for mankind's instruction—though as ROCHE remarks in another context ((1) p. 38) our right to hang a murderer, if we have one, gives us no right to turn him out on the moors and hunt him to death;[3] and thirdly, that the man of science has no time for squeamishness. 'The science of life is a superb and dazzlingly lighted hall which may be reached only by passing through a long and ghastly kitchen.' (BERNARD (1) p. 15.) Bernard clearly feels that the only motive of 'men of fashion' who found his behaviour vile must be a gentlemanly distate for noise and stench. The physiologist is a man of science, deaf to screams and blind to blood.

'Similarly no surgeon is stopped by the most moving cries and sobs because he sees only his idea and the purpose of his operation ... no anatomist feels himself in a horrible slaughterhouse; under the influence of a scientific idea, he delightedly follows a nervous filament through stinking, livid flesh which to any other man would be an object of disgust and horror.' ((1) p. 103.)

BERNARD's inability to comprehend that even condemned criminals might have some claim in decency to be granted proper burial ((1) pp. 101 f.), his blindness to the horror engendered in the poor and defenceless by body-snatchers, may serve to remind us that even such irrational squeamishness is part of our human heritage. One of the few features in which our species does seem to differ from most, though not all, others is our care even for our dead. We are repelled by the thought of eating human flesh, unless we can

[2] They have also been condemned for vivisection in the past—Xenocrates, for example was heavily fined for skinning a ram alive (PLUTARCH (1) 996a).

[3] All those who disapprove of fox-hunting or vivisection, bear-baiting et al., should indeed abandon flesh-eating in their own defence. Witness Johnson's tormented realization that he cannot consistently condemn the slaughter of one's old horses when they have laboured their lives away in one's service (BOSWELL p. 1256 f.)—the same dialectic might have led him to deny even his honest horror of vivisection. But at least he wished to spare his victims pain—even if he did not count it injury to take away their proper pleasures.

regard it as a sacrament. A corpse is an object of horror to us, but also of an agonized tenderness. Simian mothers remain devoted to their dead, even their decomposing, children (THORPE p. 281): not because they 'do not realize the child is dead'—what is it to realize, or not to realize, such a thing?—but because the child, their child, is there. Socrates may have been right, for his own reasons, to think the disposal of his body irrelevant to him (Plato, *Phaedo* 115c5 f.), but the common sense of mankind, indeed of primate-kind, and particularly the cultural tradition of the Christian West are against him. We are not ready to think of our dear bodies as soon to be delivered up to mere material law (and perhaps now prefer cremation precisely to avoid that fate); we are not prepared to be sure that our dead are entirely 'not there'—in one sense they are precisely *gone*, but in another, there they are, silent and dissolving. They are our dead: we will be our dead. This may all be absurd, though it has been the conviction of the Christian Church that what is sown in corruption will be raised in incorruption, but even if it is absurd, yet still people feel it so. By what right do trendy intellectuals, Bernard, or the state deny the validity of such concern? It is not they who own our bodies (JONAS).

I labour this point, though it is not directly relevant to our treatment of non-human animals, because it is symptomatic of three frequent corruptions of our ethical sense. The first, our readiness to discount all such 'emotional' reactions as cannot, we think, be backed by any general principle; usually indeed the only admitted principles are those determined by a naïve calculation of immediate utility. The progressive weakening of our sensibility is a danger far more real than over-squeamishness. The second, our readiness to believe ourselves the masters: perhaps we should not be so concerned about what may happen to our dead, once they are dead; perhaps, indeed, no man owns his body (though liberals think otherwise); but does it follow that *we* own the dead, that *we* have a right to determine what shall happen to those that cannot defend themselves? Who made *us* guardians of the law? Let us beware: there yet may come a day when those in power believe, quite sincerely, that it is absurd to worry about what may happen to our living bodies, so only that our souls be safe. And so perhaps it is: but will we relish being treated on those terms? The third, our readiness to think that those unlike ourselves, the poor, the weak, the stupid, have no title to their lives: it is not only beasts Bernard despised.

And what restrained him and his epigoni from assaults on such human wreckage? Nothing at all, except (in him) a dying flicker of moral sense.

His remarks about the kitchen are derived from Aristotle:

'We must avoid a childish distaste for examining the less valued animals. For in all natural things there is something wonderful. And just as Heraclitus is said to have spoken to the visitors who were wanting to see him but stopped when they saw him 'warming himself at the oven'—he kept telling them to come in and not worry, 'for there are gods here too'—so we should approach the inquiry about each animal without aversion, knowing that in all of them there is something natural and beautiful.' (Aristotle, *De Partibus Animalium* I, 645a15 f.: D. M. Balme.)

The beauty which Aristotle hoped to see was that of 'fittingness' and organic unity, the delight of seeing how living organisms, amongst others, make sense in terms of their environment and way of life. The scientific idea which Bernard pursued, not by the techniques of natural history, but by exploring the connections of the animal machine with scalpel and poison, was rather (precisely) the idea of a mechanical contrivance whose shrieks were no more than the scraping of gears. Later experimenters have often believed to judge from their actions—much the same, or have done their best to transform the creature into an 'animal preparation'. Aristotle conquered squeamishness by recognizing beauty, the perfection of nature: Bernard simply did not *see* the beast—it was for him only a mechanical puzzle.

At the name of Science every knee shall bow. Bernard at least was not hypocritical in his devotion: he neither concealed it, nor used it as a cloak for personal ambition. Later experimentalists have pretended that they act for the good of 'humanity', or concealed even from themselves that they act so as to have publications to their name. It is in the name of science, and with the specious bribe of release from all our ills, that we have been cajoled and threatened and insulted into permitting the continued torture of our kindred and the continued blunting of the sensibilities of those who come to work in our laboratories. Let no-one rely on common decency in such a situation: the pressure of one's professional peer-group, the atmosphere of dismissive tolerance of all outside the clan, the calm assumption that this is what we do, are all far too strong for most of us to resist.

> 'Does a man ever mean to be cruel? He merely makes or keeps his living; but to make or keep his living he will do anything that does not absolutely prick to his heart through the skin of his indolence or his obtuseness.' (GALSWORTHY p. 6.)

The terrifying thing about Nazi Germany is that its agents were often ordinarily decent husbands, fathers, citizens (see e.g. SERENY): as Plato knew long ago, the 'honest citizen' would often be a tyrant if he had the chance (*Republic* 10.619). MILGRAM's experiments merely confirm our fear: decent men will readily torture other men if that is what they think is expected of them, even without any greater threat than the experimenter's disapproval to be braved (see also SHERIDAN AND KING). When we can pretend that it is for Science, not merely for our personal curiosity, but to increase the body of 'objective knowledge' stored in libraries for the benefit of some future investigator equally an 'egoist who seek(s) (his) own pleasure and satisfaction but find(s) it in solving the puzzles of nature' (SZENT-GYORGI; see PAPPWORTH p. 11)—why, then anything is permitted. It is not for myself, but for Science.

I can see no good grounds for assuming that 'it would be interesting to know' is any more final a reason for action than 'it would be pleasant to possess', unless it is seriously suggested that a man's whims are always adequate excuse for his subsequent action—in which case such men might please stop professing a professional untouchability: my whims are sometimes distinctly homicidal. It would be very interesting to know how Claude Bernard, let alone his epigoni, would react to the treatment they gave and give our fellows.[4] 'I was curious' is no better excuse for a long-term policy of animal torture than 'I was lustful' or 'I was greedy'. CAMPBELL (p. 278) thought it a sophism not worth discussing to contend that any increase in knowledge could excuse the smallest moral turpitude: I fear it is used to defend more than that.

How can it be? 'As it would be an indication of great injustice, and inexhaustible avidity, to destroy those of our own species for the sake of divination, thus also it is unjust for the sake of this to slay an irrational creature.' (PORPHYRY (1) 11 51.) Yet still we do

---

[4] The orthodox should not assume that I thereby display my misanthropy (as HÄRING III 244): it is not zoophiles who hate humanity.

it, and worse than that. Why? I have said (above, pp. 43 and 76) that Powys was probably wrong to think that even the worst experimentalists are actively sadists. Possibly they take some pleasure in exercising their power over their victims, which might be a sadistic perversion, but I suspect that it is indeed often 'only a job'. Where I do not think that Powys was wrong was in suggesting an analogy between science and religion. I think we should take very seriously the tendency of devoted religious and scientists to commit enormous evil. 'Man is apt to think that he has reached the heights when he has only touched the lowest depths of his spiritual nature.' (MARETT p. 90.) 'We never tempt so successfully as on the very steps of the altar', said Screwtape (LEWIS (2) p. 27.)

Much of this evil is, of course, merely the stupidity and greed of small minds, of all of us, given a chance to step beyond the law, beyond normal justice and affection, by the false title of a more metaphysical, a grander concern. But Bernard, whatever he was, was not ordinarily stupid, nor was his a small mind. While I agree with MÉNARD's comment (p. 211), much derided by Bernard's followers (as VIRTANEN (1) p. 119), that 'Bernard's widow has opened a home for dogs ... On Judgment Day this offering will weigh more in the awesome balance than all the discoveries of her husband', I would not deny that he had great gifts. He was aided in his disregard of his victims by the influence of Cartesian philosophy, and by the acclaim of Thomists. But there is more to the phenomenon than that. He speaks, disapprovingly, of 'the Aristotelian entelechy. Every being works for itself. It makes itself the centre of everything. It utilises everything for itself that it can from the external world. From this results the law of the strongest which dominates and subordinates to its profit all that is below it. Christianity reacts against this law. Charity is anti-entelechic. All the virtues are anti-entelechic' (BERNARD (2) p. 84). Yet the effect of this rejection of the Law of the Fish seems rather to be hostile to the entelechies of his victims than to his own purposes, very much as it has often been in the history of mankind's more obviously religious traditions. Bernard plainly believes that the purposes *he* has are those of the whole: *he* is not working for himself, but for science, which is the knowledge of the whole. By being made to serve him, rather than their entelechies, all other creatures likewise pay their dues to the one God. It is easier for him, indeed, than for other devotees: since his vision is of the world-machine, it is a condition of his own felt identity with it that he edit from his consciousness all emotional responses that might suggest that there is more to life than mechanism. His disciples might consider what sort of life his wife and daughters had before expressing their contempt for their 'disloyalty'. (VIRTANEN (2) pp. 18 f.)

We are adept at turning laws of love into our profit:

'The principle of vicarious suffering pervades history, some suffering and dying for the good of others ... Is it not in accord with this great principle that animals should play their part by sometimes suffering and dying to help in keeping Britons, hardy, healthy and brave, by providing healthful recreation for so many, in providing the means of livelihood for many thousands?' (Rev. J. Price: BATEMAN p. 42; see also WESTERMARK p. 388.)

The editors of 'This England' (in the *New Statesman*) found this funny, though they also found any expression of concern for the non-human quite riotously eccentric. The Reverend Price was honest, if absurd. They, the non-human, are doing what they ought to do in suffering for us, and we must therefore make sure that they suffer. The principle of vicarious suffering, which might be thought to imply a readiness in those who accept it to endure a little discomfort for other's sake, happily turns out to be the Law of the Fish. Bernard's anti-entelechic charity is only another name for greed.

What is Science, after all? It is an activity of men, of some men in a particular historical tradition, which some men take as the chief meaning of their lives, while others follow after them like jackals. It constitutes an ideal picture of Man—not of men as they are, placental mammals with a gift for rhetoric, but of men as they might be, impersonal masters, who know and act upon the Law. Such scientists are fanatics for their god: they have ceased to be men, for they will not admit to being mammals. Even though scientific realism assures them that men *are* mammals, that we are one species amongst uncounted millions, their own appreciation of this vision somehow becomes a reason for forgetting it. It is a vision we have made ourselves, and by making it we cheat the gods. By pretending to submit to the one Law, we make our whims the law. By pretending to be purged of all personal emotion, we act as perfect egoists. By torturing His creatures we pretend that we do God service.

It was not *wicked* men that betrayed and condemned the Christ: it was the elect. Bernard, unlike Castaneda, did not *see* the creature he was killing: he saw only the motions of universal law. Or rather he saw only his own purposes, and named them God.

Nihilism and the Tao

The tale of religious science can be carried further. Consider Jacques MONOD's ethic of objective knowledge. He has attempted to argue that science is dependent on the insistent elimination of all self-identification, all evaluative concepts, from the bare scientific facts; that this insistence on self-limitation has, amazingly, enabled us to see the main outlines, at least, of a true account of the universe; that the universe thus revealed is utterly indifferent to our evaluations and purposes, leaving us with no external arbiter or standard of value; and that we should, accordingly, admit that the original insistence on self-limitation is an arbitrary, self-chosen ethical axiom which must stand at the head of a properly scientific ethic for modern man. Every thesis, and every inference, in this argument seems to me to be enormously suspect. In particular, I would note the naïve surprise with which we are urged to contemplate the fact that a universe, from whose description all terms of value have of set purpose been eliminated, has been described as lacking values. We might as well decide not to mention the *colour* of anything we describe, and subsequently announce that the world is colourless. I would also deny that the theses describing even Monod's world have been selected without any eye to such values as beauty, logical rigour or general 'satisfactoriness'. Nor do I know what he means by 'true', nor why he is so certain that historical development will not at last reveal even our greatest certainties as false. But the arguments and counter-arguments on this issue would take me too far afield. What is of concern to me now is that Monod's ethic has the merit of clarifying the dogma of 'c'est pour la science'. (See VYVYAN (1) p. 147.)

The scientific enterprise as here defined is a consistent effort to eliminate oneself and one's purposes from one's picture of reality. The real world as here defined is that of matter in motion, wherein life, terrestrial life, is a single complex event of rather low probability. The realization of our oneness with the entire biosphere, and of that biosphere's contingency, might be expected to induce a feeling of solidarity with all life—but that is what we must not allow. Exactly what Monod has in mind, I do not know, but in practice his ethic of scientific objectivity precisely exalts non-solidarity, non-participation as our highest ethical stance. We are not to feel any solidarity with the doings of nature, not to read our purposes into nature, nor to suppose that purposeful entities are anything but a chance transformation of matter in motion. The only values are ours, including the values of objectivity, logical rigour and the rest. The world itself cares nothing for these things—which might raise, but does not for Monod, the question whether we can reasonably rely upon such chance-found values to reveal the visage of nature to us. The end-result of such uncompromising naturalism seems, to me at any rate, to require a total scepticism about our ability to know the world.

Perhaps that is what Monod intends. Whether it is or not, his reaction is perhaps intelligible: to continue his absurd commitment to scientific objectivity, to look upon the world as his world looks (as it were) upon itself. In taking the objectivizing attitude, rather than any form of participatory one, we construct a model of a world that disallows all participation, for which all entities, all processes are merely objective. There are no preferred end-states in nature, no allowances for good intentions, no different treatment, in the end, for prince, or peasant, man or bird or stone. The appearance of a radical disjunction between animate and inanimate entities is illusory: all alike are more or less complicated transformations of matter. Without warning, without any fairy godmother to bless or curse us, we have appeared, value-creating entities in a world without value. What value shall we create? The value of seeing things as they are, valueless. Shall we create others, when this numbing vision has been fully realized? Shall we, for example, create a world-at-fantasy where stories have a beginning, middle and end, where certain end-states are preferred, where good intentions count? Doubtless that is what we do, and call it culture, and the law, and art, and science: I have already discussed our current, and psychotic, fantasy, and urged that a little ordinary participation in the lives of our fellow mammals, vertebrates and the rest might be better advised. The fantasies, if such they are, of St. Francis, and of Blake, are not obviously less realistic or soundly utilitarian than our current absurdities. If all value stems from us, let us allow some weight to our untutored sensibilities and remember who *we* are: namely, placental mammals.

But the creation of such a world is not licensed by Monod's principle. We are to live in the unmeaning void, and precisely *not* invent excuses, fairy-stories and the like to save us from that vision. I do not know how aware Monod is that science itself thus loses much of its psychological impetus: the world we face will never make our sort of sense. Of everything we can only say, in the end, that it just happened: our only advance to be able to describe the 'it' a little more compendiously. But let it be that we can train ourselves to serve science only in the hope of seeing ever more clearly how all event is utterly indifferent.

'Perfection or imperfection of unconscious beings has no meaning as referred to themselves ... There is no evil but must inhere in a conscious being, or be referred to it; that is, Evil must be felt before it is evil.' (JOHNSON (2) x p. 224.)[5]

And in what is in fact the Stoic tradition this fact (if it is one) is a reason for adopting the attitude that nothing is evil, for finding nothing evil. We must accept the indifference of things, and recognize that error only enters the world with the strange illusion of conscious beings that some states are to be preferred to others. Seriously to make Monod's ethic of objectivity our leading principle is to live naked in the void, thinking nothing either good or ill.

Once again, I do not know how much of this Monod intends, nor how far he realizes that this response is yet another, not unexampled, effort to make an endurable sense of felt reality. Seriously to attempt the belief that whatever our immediate responses of anguish, fear and rage, yet still the world is, and *we ought to be*, uncomplainingly continuous is to resolve our alienation in the world by making ourselves alien. Have not students of the Way that is no way heard this somewhere once before? Why did not Chuang Tzu weep for his wife?

'In the limbo of existence and non-existence, there was transformation and the material force was evolved. The material force was transformed to be form, form was transformed to become life, and now birth has transformed to become death. This is like the rotation of the four seasons ... Now she lies asleep in the great house. For me to go about weeping and wailing would be

[5] The consciousness required is merely that of having desires and a point of view: evil came into the world with the first appetitive creature.

to show my ignorance of destiny. Therefore I desist.' (Chung Tzu
18: CHAN p. 209.)[6]

The feeling that there is something a little inhuman in this, that
other values, after all, than objectivity are perhaps to be maintained,
is not entirely unexpected. If thinking of my wife as so much matter
is the price I pay for objectivity, why should I not decide, with equal
absurdity, to be a participant, and feel for her—as also for all other
living, in such degree as I can manage? Because the universe
demands otherwise? But what is that to say, especially for Monod,
but that I have decided to view the world thus? If the ethic of objectivity is an arbitrary decision it is one I am disinclined to make;
and I am inclined to suspect the good faith of those who do make
it, or their good sense.

But suppose I do make it, and from thenceforward see the world,
and all things in the world, as utterly devoid of sacral significance:
all is utterly alienated from me, and I see all things alien. Science
requires me not to feel personal attraction or personal repulsion;
nothing is valuable till we make it so, and we ought not to make
it so. 'The physiologist is a man of science....' (see above, p. 66).
All that matters is that we should come to see the unmeaning truth—
and that only matters because we have decided so. 'C'est pour la
science': the final and only justification for anything we may do to
animals, with whom it is mere superstition to identify, *or to men*.
'A human life is nothing compared with a new fact...' (see above,
p. 36). 'The development of human personality is the ultimate purpose of civilization' (see above, p. 86)—a personality and civilization
that seems frankly psychopathic. And it is a very familiar madness.
'The transcendent significance they ascribed to the act (of sacrificing men or animals) paralysed their power of recognising its revolting nature.' (MARTINENGO-CESARESCO p. 32.) She was speaking
of religious sacrifice: but what else is this? It is not a coincidence
that experimentalists speak of 'sacrificing' animals. And it should
by now be clear to Whom they sacrifice.

But there is more to be said. I greatly fear that Monod's ethic,
in practice, merely confirms the casual habit of our laboratories,
merely formalizes the abandonment of deeply rooted repugnances
and sympathies which is urged on us as the proper 'scientific' atti-

---

[6] This does not *seem* to offer the Christian, and Socratic, hope of a spring awakening:
the point is not that she will come again, but that she never was.

tude. A cat being whirled in a centrifuge and occasionally extracted to permit a sample of spinal fluid to be taken (see BROWN pp. 152 f., after Ryder) is but an unmeaning physical event—a proper demonstration of the laws of matter (see RULAND p. 372).[7] But such pretended worshippers of the unmeaning void do not go far enough for consistency. Not that they have so far been restrained by law and the threat of violence from extending their kindly attentions to humankind—that moment may not be so far off, may yet be here (see FREUND, PAPPWORTH). Rather they neglect to consider their own flesh and purposes with the same indifference they extend to the *rest* of the world.

Objectivity requires that we strip our vision of all emotive difference, all 'participation mystique'; but objectivity itself reveals that our bodies, our dear selves are entirely part of the world. We must not participate even in our own bodies' demands: how could we, indeed, without thereby admitting an emotive significance in the world external to our bodies? Where literally all is seen as flat, indifferent, so must our bodies be. We cannot be permitted to notice which state of the world allows for our continuance and which does not—or rather, we may notice this, but must not care. It is not only the cat from whom I stand aloof, nor only my wife: it is my self. And once again, students of the Way that is no way may notice a certain parallel. We may begin by seeking our own enlightenment, our own escape from Maya, the web of illusion: but the greatest of Maya's illusions is precisely that opposition between the world and self. 'The universe has no opposite.'

The most obvious immediate result of this change of attitude is that we can no longer be moved by thoughts of 'our' continuance, still less by thoughts of professional approval or a healthy list of publications to our name. If animals, and the world, are no longer to be held sacred, neither are we nor any of our former aims. One who has espoused the unmeaning void, like the true amoralist (see above, pp. 83 f.), has no incentive to seek his own profit or that of his immediate kin. Unlike the amoralist, he does not even do what pleases him: for nothing does. Doubtless the seeds of karma sown in days gone by continue to sprout and issue in new acts, but the sowing is over at last. Or put it otherwise: one day this body I call

---

[7] KEITH similarly sneers at those sentimentalists who are perturbed by what is done to matter 'in that state known as living', commenting that there are no societies to protect atoms against physicists.

mine will be the victim, the example, of material law—falling and dissolving like any other thing. Then will be obvious what is true now, that even now my body's motions, my behaviour, are but the working out of universal event. The realization of this enjoined by objectivity will issue in a new mode of behaviour, but not one that is *more* in accord with nature than before. Enlightenment is the discovery that everything already is. Nirvana *is* samsara: the objective universe and the web of Maya are not, never have been, two, but one. The Buddha is he that is wholly identified with the workings of the world-machine (WOODS): what else could we ever have been identical with?

A further, and perhaps even less palatable conclusion of absolute objectivity is this: that so far from revealing the 'real facts' it can only reveal the factlessness of Being. Once I have eliminated from my field of vision all discriminations based on sacred significance, emotional attachment and the like, what reason do I have to notice one thing rather than another? Specks of dust and Emperors are alike indifferent to me. More, after-images and mountains are as much, or as little to be noticed. What reason can we have for discriminating any particular entities out of the sheer suchness of cosmic event? More, how can any one variety of consciousness—as the sane, waking state—be paramount over the indefinitely many ways of feeling open to us? In our ordinary practicality we notice such things as are relevant to our survival—the bus, and not the butterfly; aesthetically, or with sympathy for life, or with collector's zeal we may observe the butterfly. But now all things are to be seen indifferently, without any preference for any one way of considering them, without any impulse to classify some appearances as illusory. True indifference makes all things of an equal weight; true indifference prevents our seeing particular things, any particular things, against a partially noticed background. Everything is background, or foreground, indifferently. 'The void is full' (HUI NENG p. 146).

As to what action may spring from this enlightenment, we can only say that those who have professed it have not been inclined to pursue their own phenomenal interests at the expense of animals. It seems unlikely that the experimentalists who rely upon the ethic of objectivity are fully conversant with the dialectical thrust of true indifferentism. Unacknowledged and pernicious, that last of illusions lurks still in their hearts: that *they* are not part of the world.

The purely material nature of things means merely that all other things are mere material for *them*. And who are *they*? They have denied such sympathies as might identify them with the world at large, or with their animal victims, or indeed with *any* creature, save those few who share their own presupposition, their own supposed objectivity. What they do to animals, they also do to men, if they have the chance: what can prevent them? Sympathy? They know it not. Moral decorum? Such transgresses objectivity. Respect for human powers? They only respect objectivity, which is to say *pure* selfishness, and that is a capacity which not all human creatures have or wish. Fear of the law? But antivivisectionists have long been so insulted and despised that few men indeed will wish to act against the arrogance of science.

In short, a certain cultural ideal, that of the objective scientist, is effectively responsible for corrupting and denying certain human sensibilities. True objectivity, applied also to the self and to its professional context, drives remorselessly towards the mysteries of Buddhist enlightenment. False objectivity, which is merely a pretext for discounting such interests as are not one's own, is one source for the creation of pseudo-psychopaths. Who is it but the psychopath, after all, who sees the world without emotional affect, and can see nothing wrong in injuring others for his own purposes? Experimentalists do not have the excuse of glandular disturbance or parental rejection: they are what they are because they feel they must live up to a certain professional ideal, because that is how things are done. Let us be afraid of them: for it must be an axiom of much research that animals are very much like men, that there is no absolute divide between our kind and those poor beasts.

'The dream of reason produces monsters': it is one of the gravest charges against modern moral philosophers that they have permitted this to pass, without qualms or comment.

Love and knowledge

All men by nature desire to know, according to Aristotle (*Metaphysics* 1.980a22). If it is true of men, it is also true of monkeys, who can be bribed to solve puzzles with the mere promise of having another puzzle to solve. Indeed, it is true of cows, as anyone who has walked down a country lane must know. That we have greater power than they can license our conduct only in the eyes of a moral barbarian.

We desire to know because the object of our knowledge or would-be knowledge interests us, in its beauty or complexity or general attractiveness. Also because it touches on our practical and emotional life in some way: why does Monod study *living* creatures, or their roots, rather than the behaviour of more recondite entities? Such a desire to know is predicated on a love of the object: some things, we know well, are not worth knowing—though it may be that some more sympathetic mind will discover interest even there. But the very fact that we desire to know, and enjoy coming to know, creates the possibility that we may turn our attention and desire to the exercise of our own skills and away from the purported object. Just so in the sexual field, our wish to 'know' another can easily become a wish to achieve a private satisfaction that is independent of our interest in the creature 'known'. It is this shift of attention that creates the possibility of brutalized sexuality, of rape, of inattentive lust, of mutual masturbation. Our attentive care for the other is lost in our enjoyment of our own prowess. [8]

Science originates in this love of Being: a love that transcends the dictates of immediate, practical profit. As long as it is this, no scientist could even think of tormenting the creature he loves, nor think that *any* item of knowledge could be worth obtaining at such a price. But our emotional interest is readily diverted from the *thing* to our own activity, and then it no longer matters to us what the thing may be, or how it fares at our hands. Science ceases to be the love and worship of created Being, and becomes the pursuit of personal satisfaction. This psychological quirk is assisted by the philosophical dogma that we can only enjoy, or desire, our own activities. By ceasing to care for and enjoy the thing itself, we transform the quality of the activity. We cease to esteem the thing we paint, and come to admire our own brush-strokes: it is a familiar fallacy, and its results in art, and social life, and science speak for themselves.

In short, those who offer 'science' as a pretext for the way they treat our kin, and who have done their little best by propaganda and by their control over techniques of teaching and research in our schools and universities to destroy and corrupt and denigrate

---

[8] As Aristotle also remarked, the intemperate man desires not food but eating (*Nicomachean Ethics* 3.1118a29 f.): he is willing to vomit up his food so that he can start again. This perhaps casts a new light on the occasional philosophical allegation that it is not knowing the answer that matters, but the process of getting there. . . .

the ordinary sensibilities of our young[9]—these men are not even *scientists*. They do not accept the conclusion of honest science, that *we* are part of the world; they do not feel that love of created Being which is the origin and meaning of their profession; they do not submerge their own personal interests in admiration of the Way. They seek their own satisfactions, and have been encouraged to abandon all such ties of fellow-feeling or of squeamishness as might interfere with their egoism.

In the name of science, they serve Satan.

'If God were your father, you would love me ... Your father is the devil, and you choose to carry out your father's desires, who was a murderer from the beginning and is not rooted in the truth.' (John 8:42 f.)

[9] It is not unknown for the lower forms of schools to care for mice as 'pets': which pets are killed and dissected by the upper forms. In America they may be dissected alive, or starved to death upon deficiency diets. What state of character is induced in a child constrained to dissect a pregnant female mouse in order to learn the mechanics of reproduction? The casual brutality of such an institutionalized dismissal of normal affection, normal sympathies is a symptom of how far the rot has gone. It isn't even as if the demonstration were—pitiful pretext—*necessary*. At this rate of corruption female teachers will be being bribed to conceive and abort a foetus for the fifth form's biology lesson.

VIII

THE NATURAL ORDER

Reality and the sacred

I have argued that the religion of science has helped to create the cultural ideal which I have christened the pseudo-psychopath, to deaden or to render unrespectable the normal affections and sympathies which we feel as mammals, warm-blooded creatures, vertebrates. Because it is for 'science', apparently sane men calmly recount actions which even they would normally regard with horror if performed by a nasty little boy. I hold no especial brief for cockroaches, and am prepared to believe that their sentience is of another order than mine, or than a monkey's, but I cannot regard such experiments as are devised to see whether decapitated roaches can run mazes as being at any higher level than a child's pulling the wings off flies (see H. E. EVANS p. 52). But it's done to satisfy our curiosity? And maybe someday some human being will get some more sensual profit from the information gained? I cannot see that these excuses raise the level of moral argument. Do they apply also to our treatment of our closer relatives, of whose experience we can be enormously more certain? To syphilitic apes, and rats being given electric shocks under the experimenter's 'delighted gaze' (LECOMTE p. 100), and pigeons having electrodes inserted slowly into their skulls—after a time they begin to 'vocalize'? Who can imagine that all this is quite all right?

> 'Vivisection ... contradicts and cancels the one single advantage that our race has got from what is called evolution, namely the development of our sense of right and wrong ... Certain forms of sickening and unthinkable cruelty that hitherto, when perpetrated by individuals, have been stopped at once, condemned by both moral opinion and law, are now—as long as we *vaguely* assume it is done for the advantage of science—tolerated as an unfortunate but inescapable necessity.' (POWYS (2) pp. 638 f.)

Doubtless the fanatics of this vile religion will continue to profess their own untouchability. I hope only that their hangers-on, their public audience will hesitate, and ask themselves whether they truly think that all things done for science are well, and whether they believe the claim to absolute objectivity when the claimants are so plainly egoists.

We are animals: we are not merely rather *like* them, we *are* animals (MIDGELEY p. 114) and we need not be ashamed of our status. It is because we are animals, warm-blooded and mammalian, that we display parental and familial care, pity the weak and give our lives up for our friends.[1] That our sense of justice arises from such family and clan relationships was the opinion of Aristotle (*Nicomachean Ethics* 8.1159b25 f.; and see PORPHYRY (1) III 22) as well as of the Confucians. Doubtless true justice lies beyond such cares, but they serve well enough for most of us. Maybe only a few rare men are *truly* moral beings, autonomously choosing by the standards of intuited right: we and our kin live as we find ourselves.

In postulating proper moral standards beyond the immediate attachments of our personal being, we should not hypothesize such standards as require us to deny our personal being. No more should we postulate accounts of the real world as require us to deny the general truthfulness or the existence of our immediate perceptions. If we are not right most of the time how shall we even begin to find more rational order? What could such orders have to do with *us*, the really experienced and experiencing persons? My charge against science, or rather scientism, is that it would destroy our personal lives in the name of a god whom only the pseudo-psychopath could love. Does 'science' say that all the world is an unmeaning mechanism?[2] Then let us mock the world, and our pretensions in it, by making a world of meaning where *all* flesh may find enjoyment. Let us forget the unmeaning void: what could it have to say to us? Let us instead appreciate our kin, the whole absurd event of which we are a vocal part, and cease to torture them in service of such an irrelevant deity. If the world is as dull as Monod says, is it worth a moment's suffering to find it out?

---

[1] These features must of course be cued by social experience. Parental deprivation, as HARLOW AND HARLOW have shown (see THORPE pp. 230 f.), has a devastating effect on the proper development of monkeys. These experiments, incidentally, also show the effects of the pseudo-psychopathic ideal on the experimenter.

[2] Obviously not: for if the whole world is unmeaning, so are these printed symbols and the whole of science (see ROSEN p. 70).

Suppose it is, or that we find it so: then our appreciation of such wholly indifferent being, our true service of that perfect objectivity, likewise requires that we leave off our moralistic preference for our own species, our own purposes. To be truly objective we must *have* no purposes: and such a strange enlightenment, again, provides no pretext for the scientist's pride. ROSZAK rightly fears (p. 271) what men may do, what men are doing, when the barriers of the sacred fall. But the real problem is caused not by the desacralization of the world, but by the incompleteness of that dread event. Where nothing is sacred, neither one's own body nor one's professional rôle nor any purpose founded on a preference for one state over another, there is no reason to expect that such a one will act to animals or men as would-be objectivists do. 'If the fool would persist in his folly he would become wise.' (BLAKE p. 151.)

The reality we know, the one which our current theories tell us we have evolved to see, is one of living entities who form a living whole. Some entities are plainly of our kind, all such as feed their young and talk to one another. 'There is no motion, nor jesture that doth not speake, and speakes in a language very easie, and without any teaching to be understood. Nay, which is more, it is a language common and publicke to all; whereby it follows ... that this must rather be deemed the proper and peculiar speech of human nature.' (MONTAIGNE II.12, p. 147.)

Other sorts of entity are more opaque to us, as the great tribes of insects, or, still more, the plants. The tree of evolution has no single crown (ALLEE p. 60). Here, it may be, there is some scope for reason: to discover those realities that are not obvious to our untutored sense, to show us what the worlds of insects may be like. Further, it may give us grace to see what our imagination hardly grasps at all, that creatures out of sight of us, and happenings far away, may be much like the ones we know. '(Man's) horizons are not the very limited home territories of most animals, but the limits of the universe itself.' (H. E. EVANS p. 29.) I greatly fear that this is quite untrue: our imagination stops much more abruptly. What are small earthquakes in Chile to us? What are the distresses of our kin in farm and laboratory, so long as we do not see them? Very much the same as if we did. If reason has an office, it is this: that we give some slight attention to what is more distant from us, whether that distance be spatial or emotional. Cosmological reason must depict a world where our immediate sensings have their place;

ethical reason likewise must allow, and strengthen all our personal attachments. A rationality that tells us not to cherish those we love, not to believe our senses, is surely self-refuted. What such reasoning should do is to remind us that there are creatures out of sight of us, and sentient beings whom we do not like who suffer nonetheless. Let us cherish our immediate friends, whatever their ancestry, and let us also remember that there are other things who might have been our friends and whom it is our weakness to ignore.

We may feel that human beings are sacred, in a way that natural things are not. If this sacredness is in virtue of some empirical feature of actually existing human beings, then all other creatures who share that feature are, in their degree, possessed of the same sacredness—and there are *no* such features that are entirely peculiar to man (except perhaps his *power*). If the sacredness is in virtue of some metaphysical feature of human beings, as that they will one day awaken to a new life in God (or maybe not), then let us give the benefit of that same doubt to all our other kin: there is certainly no reason, in science or revelation, to deny to them what we arrogate to ourselves (see DEAN, HILDROP, WOOD). If the sacredness is a derived, a granted thing, as was the mark of Cain (Genesis 4:15), then let us see that that same mark is on all living things. And finally, if human sacredness is but the last remnant of the glory that our ancestors saw in all life, all nature, let us ask ourselves why we have ceased to see the sacred save in our own shape.

If *nothing* is sacred, on the other hand, then neither are human beings, nor scientists, and all our action must arise either from our immediate loves or from the mystery of Buddha. I would trust either to be more 'humane' than is moralistic humanism. What is *Man* or *Science* but the last ghost of religion (STIRNER pp. 56 f.)? We torment beasts as once we tortured heretics, and think to do God service.

'I will take no bullock out of thy house, nor he-goats out of thy folds. For every beast of the forest is mine, and the cattle upon a thousand hills. I know all the fowls of the mountains: and the wild beasts of the field are mine. If I were hungry, I would not tell thee: for the world is mine, and the fulness thereof.' (Psalm 50:9–12.)

Those who base their defence upon the Bible, as well as those who castigate the Hebraic tradition for 'making believe that all nature is made just for man' (as L. WHITE (though he is far less guilty than his imitators); see PASSMORE pp. 4 f.), have plainly never read the Bible (see WELLBOURN). 'When ye spread forth your hands, I will hide mine eyes from you: yea, when ye make many prayers, I will not hear: your hands are full of blood.' (Isaiah 1:15.) What answer shall we make to Him for all our doings with His world?

Nature and civilization

I have attacked philosophers, and aesthetes, and scientists, and doubtless offended many more than them. Philosophers are often better than their principles, and many that 'keep pets' may treat them well. I do not deny it, any more than I deny, so far, the worth of science. I am sure there will be readers who conclude, as Passmore does of Roszak (PASSMORE p. 176) and with as little reason, that I am an enemy of science. I must ask them to enquire of themselves what 'science' is. My belief is that there is a constant impulse in at least some men to construct models, or more compendious descriptions of event which may license certain predictions or draw event a little closer to the intrinsically intelligible. Such men wish physical event to be as obvious, as self-explanatory as the theorems of mathematics. Whether such an end is possible I do not know, but I say nothing against the effort. Such 'science' dispels mysteries only in the sense that it subsumes them in larger mysteries. In the end we are still faced by the brute fact, the pure glory of what *is*, even supposing that we have carried our model-making, our successively more exact descriptions all the way up to the first cause. And that we certainly have not done. I see no great harm in such activity and much to admire, but its innocence does not excuse the things done in its name. Nor is it absurd to think that our current techniques of education in this craft have ill effects. 'We are training, in the name of experimental science, a race of young exterminators.' (MUMFORD p. 720.) Those who have been systematically trained to think that everything is but material for their purposes, and their purposes the only *sacred* things, are unlikely to give much consideration to the well-being of Nature, or of natural things. Attempts to revive a traditional respect for natural being, a disinclination to do just anything that may bring immediate profit, will not destroy true science. On the contrary: a science of the unsacred merely totters on from habit and professional esteem—its sources are burnt out. What is not worth respecting is not worth understanding either.

Except, of course, as a means to power. Science is the handmaid of plutocracy.

There are those who will resent the implied sneer. It is not merely the rich who benefit from greater understanding of the causes and conditions of material event. The rich in any age may have their slaves, and food, and warmth, and clothing. It is only our capacity to invent new ways of dealing with 'Nature', taking advantage of newly understood processes, that gives us any hope of delivering the great mass of mankind—and maybe animals will benefit as well—from their agelong adversity. Those who think otherwise, from the comfort of their studies, warmed and clothed and lit and fed by the efforts of men who took from Nature what she did not give—those preachers of thrift to the poor, and of spiritual values to the starving, *they* can afford the luxury of admiring Nature. Other men must suffer under her unlovely sway, until science comes as saviour.

> Jubal sang of the cliffs that bar
>   and the peaks that none may crown—
> But Tubal clambered by jut and scar
>   and there he builded a town.
> High—high as the snowsheds lie,
>   low as the culverts drain—
> wherever they be they can never agree—
>   Jubal and Tubal Cain
>   (Rudyard Kipling *Jubal and Tubal Cain*,
>   ll. 25–32.)

Jubal and Tubal see the world through different eyes: William JAMES ((3) pp. 215 f.) sees a forest made ulcerous by a squatter's hut, 'without a single element of artificial grace to make up for the loss of Nature's beauty'. But the squatters see a personal victory, a living torn from the wilderness (not that such farming practices are even economic: DARLING (3) p. 207). If Jubal had had his way mankind would still be singing in whatever corner of the world our weakness permitted, and since we, with our particular genetic and cultural heritage, would not then exist, we are bound to suppose that all was for the best. Jubal builds no towns: equally of course Tubal dreams no dreams, and it is the mirage seen by Jubal that we have followed to our present state. Jubal sees a possibility that Tubal seeks to realize, and so we advance to remake the wilderness.

This enterprise requires that we take over responsibility for running such parts of the natural world as we have remade. Before the remaking there are mere events, some agreeable and some not, and (there being nothing to be done) we can only hope that the tides of death and life will leave us some security. It has even been hypothesized that the biosphere itself behaves to some extent as if it were a living, homeostatic organism (LOVELOCK AND EPTON), avoiding disaster in the several crises that have afflicted the world not by mere chance, but in the way that organisms do. It is this overarching entity, our sister and our mother, that we are seeking to remodel or replace. More and more natural events, we hope, will become domesticated, something to be turned on and off by us for our purposes. We are slowly beginning to realize that it is a heavy burden: things no longer happen—they are done, or not done, by us. And our science is not yet compendious enough to predict with certainty what the consequences of our action will be. Some very minor greediness may yet unravel all the earth: if it is not Concorde, it may be something else. Our species, like every other species, has always played a part in the great game, has always altered pieces of the earth for good or ill. But the beavers have not sought to seize all water for their own, nor chopped down every tree. If they did, they would find their environment an increasingly hostile one. We *are* attempting the equivalent, and have only recently noticed that our chances of replacing the multi-millionfold life-support system that is the terrestrial biosphere are vanishingly small. Might it not be better not to seek quite so much of our own way? Our knowledge is limited, and always will be: some actions we know to be foolhardy even from our own immediate interest—as wasting fossil fuels; others we suspect may damage the flimsy safeguards that, once down, cannot be replaced. To judge from our behaviour, we do not merely believe that the biosphere is our living mother: we believe that she is invulnerable. We sometimes even persuade ourselves that we are her agents:

'We are natural creatures, and who is to judge whether or not our destructiveness, however we may deplore it, is not an ordained path in nature's road of terrestrial development?' (M. R. Zavon: cited by GRAHAM p. 45.)

As Graham comments, it is odd that men who can envisage *this* should attack Rachel Carson for 'unscientific mysticism'. It is not in the least odd that men who have been trained to think that only transformed nature is of value, that nature exists to be transformed, should so grotesquely overweight our standing in the scheme of things.

Let us agree that humankind seeks food, and warmth, and security, and the chance to develop those imaginings known as art and science and religion. In the past we have been prevented by lack of strength, and by the threat of natural disaster from seeking these things so successfully as to destroy our own environment. In the present day we have the power, or some men have the power to do just that. Predators who are too successful, in the short term, decree their own extinction. That is what we are doing: we are living off our future, and must quickly learn some self-control before we perish utterly or are, by nature's resurgent strength expressed in war and plague and famine, brought to a more realistic sense of our capabilities. We must learn to leave what we do not need alone, to recognize that there are other powers and entities within the world than ours, and that our continued being is dependent on that of our neighbours'.

In short, we must somehow come to recognize that other lives have lives to live, that there are other sacred presences than man. That we think them sacred does not mean (*pace* PASSMORE p. 176) that we do not recognize their fragility. On the contrary, it is the fragile that is most precious: if men were invulnerable they would need no protection, of law or sacred mystery. It is their fragility, their weakness, that calls forth the agonized tenderness of our mammalian heritage. It is time that we recognized that same weakness in creatures not of our own shape: for if we do not we shall soon have proved our total inefficiency as a parasite, by killing our host. There is no other earth to which we can leap, as fleas from a dying man: if this earth dies, so do we; if this earth merely undergoes another of its crises, and finds some new homeostasis (whether by chance or purpose), we are unlikely to remain the same.

It is, of course, insufficient to say that we *must* feel a tenderness that we do not in fact feel. If we do not feel it, self-interest will be insufficient to restrain us. We can probably believe, though the task is growing harder, that the last days will not come in our time. Our care for our posterity is nebulous at best, and can readily be cooled, as by false philosophy (see above, p. 16). Our long term interests, as a species, will be best served by a present tenderness to other life—a tenderness that we do in fact feel, though it is over-laid and ridiculed by our philosophies. In acknowledging this ten-derness, this fellow feeling, we may come to see our earth as a cooperative endeavour of many million creatures, each with some contribution to the commonwealth.

What PASSMORE scathingly, and inaccurately, describes as 'mystical contemplation' (p. 194) will not, he says, 'clean our streams or feed our peoples'. Doubtless this is so, though there are precedents. But the tenderness and care I have sketched might not have fouled the streams, and might not have snatched so much of the earth's harvest as to starve the weak. And it is more likely that the earth will be healed by our released tenderness than by any more technology of the modern kind. The Green Revolution, as was pre-dicted of it, has aided the *rich*, briefly; oil bonanzas will run dry; nuclear power will add still greater dangers to our long-suffering earth.

There is a place for craft. Kipling forgot one brother: we should remember also Jabal, the father of such as dwell in tents, and of such as have cattle (Genesis 4:20). There are crafts that do not aim to clutter every uncrowned peak, and relations with our animal brothers (even, perhaps, carnivorous relations) that do not deny our tenderness. There are tribes that know their own dependence on the living world, and feel for their brothers. These are they for whom Passmore has no enthusiasm, preferring such explosions of artistry as Venice, Salzburg, and Bath. When he admits to being a human chauvinist he is too generous to himself (p. 187): it is civil-ization to which his heart is given, at whatever cost to the victims, human and otherwise, that supported it. 'What god would not be proud of having created eighteenth-century Bath?' (p. 179).[3]

What will such tenderness cost us in terms of comfort, or of civil-ization? The first steps will cost us nothing at all, for it is manifestly cheaper to eat plants rather than animals. Later steps are less eco-nomic, on a short term and a narrow view. KLUCKHOHN AND LEIGHTON comment disapprovingly on the Navahos' 'unreasoning sentiments' for their livestock, which clutter the range with un-productive stock that should (of course) simply be killed (pp. 70 and 75). Doubtless we should simply kill all elderly and unproduc-

[3] 'It requires a special innocence to delight in the monumental accomplishments of the Renaissance cities ... without appreciating that the generating impulses were more authori-tarian than humanitarian—authoritarian towards nature and man.' (MCHARG p. 28.)

tive humans too. It seems to escape the anthropologists' attention in this case that soil erosion in this area sprang not from overtenderness to livestock, but from treating the animals as livestock, and multiplying them unduly, on the advice of white administrators.[4] But we may admit that an increased recognition of our solidarity with other living things is likely to prevent our seizing the main chance of any profit that we think we see: of course—that is the point. We should *want* to be restrained, for if we are not we shall eat up the world.

Will our restraint—and it must be *our* restraint, not that of some careful scapegoat—destroy our chances of a human life? Will it cause hunger, for example? The question is ironical.

> '*This* is the era of hunger unprecedented. Now, in the time of the greatest technical power, starvation is an institution. Reverse . . . a venerable formula: the amount of hunger increases relatively and absolutely with the evolution of culture.' (SAHLINS p. 36.)

Will it stand in the way of human satisfactions? But what *are* human satisfactions, if not those of sharing the life of loved entities, and working at tasks recognized as worthwhile by oneself and by one's society? How many men *now* have that chance? Most men do not even have the specious pleasures with which we have hoped to fill our days, and for whose sake we have subjected living creatures of our species as well as of others to unrecompensed suffering. Will a newly recognized tenderness prevent great art? I see no reason why it should, though it may prevent some manifestations of it. And, once more, how many men *now* can admire or practise such arts?

In short, those who threaten us with the collapse of human life and civilization if we should acknowledge the lives and feelings of creatures not of our species, are guilty of an unintended irony. It may seem reasonable that life will be improved if we continue to grab at everything we can get, continue to encourage ever increasing aspirations. But the fact is that such aspirations cannot be satisfied for more than a tiny minority (who will, of course, then demand still more: on this problem, of 'hedonic relativism', see APPLEY). And a further fact is that our satisfaction increasingly implies not merely other men's dissatisfaction, but our own doom. This is no

---

[4] PFANNER AND INGERSOLL are similarly delighted at any signs of corruption or doublethink amongst Thai and Burmese villagers that might permit more intensive animal husbandry: they fail to ask whether such husbandry is even economically desirable.

new thing, though our time has given us greater power. It always seems reasonable to get what you can, and fight anyone who tries to get what he can. This reasonable doctrine has brought us as a species to the edge of destruction, whether by war or by the unintended products of our greed. Phylogeny recapitulates ontogeny: the doctrine brings each one of us to the edge of the pit. Is it not time that we recognized our own stupidity?

'All ethics so far evolved rest upon a single premise: that the individual is a member of a community of interdependent parts. His instincts prompt him to compete for his place in that community, but his ethics prompt him also to cooperate (perhaps in order that there may be a place to compete for). The land ethic simply enlarges the boundaries of the community to include soils, waters, plants and animals, or, collectively, the land.' (LEOPOLD p. 219.)

Whether we like it or not, we are part of what Leopold calls the land. If we recognize the claims of other creatures in this community, we may still perish—we have no security on that—but if we do not respect them, we shall perish the sooner. So long as we *civilized men* imagine ourselves to be apart from the land, and from our fellow creatures, we shall attempt to exploit them for our private gain, and the attempt will kill us.

Tradition and objective value

In all this I have said nothing new. My betters have said it all before, and will say it again. What precise steps the new way—or rather the very old way—requires in the scientific and political enterprises, I cannot say, at any rate in the present context. The details of such endeavour must as always be left to honest practitioners. I, like BATESON (p. 437), can only urge that no-one be trusted to make decisions on our behalf who does not, to some small extent, recognize reality—that nothing is purely material for our purposes, that we are indistinguishably part of the living world. My present purposes, however, are the more limited ones of isolating some last few corruptions of our moral sense, visible even here, and of answering from within this new perspective the ancient Stoic hypocrisy 'what about the plants?'

Long before the word 'ecology' was known, there were preservationists. First of all there were the rich who wished their game preserved, whether as food supply or a source of 'healthful recreation'. It was doubtless they who saved the fox from extinction in Britain, or at least from radical control of its numbers. And after them there were the not-quite-so-rich who wished animals, and plants, and land-scape preserved so that they could have interesting country walks, or imbibe a spirit of freedom from the woods. This seems to have been the philosophy behind many nature sanctuaries. One of the many problems of this approach is simply that any enjoyment of such rural pleasures must be limited to a few: firstly because it is likely that the majority have other pleasures, and secondly because any attempt to make such sanctuaries accessible to all must destroy the very character that is found pleasant. On these terms, therefore, such sanctuaries are devices whereby the relatively poor pay for the pleasures of the relatively rich, without any real hope of being allowed to share in them.

Ecology has given the preservationists another card, that wild life, trees and plants and beasts and insects and birds, must all be pre-served in order to maintain the biosphere intact. Doubtless this is true, but it is not always entirely and specifically true. One species more or less can hardly matter. And one animal, or plant, more or less certainly does not matter in such a utilitarian calculation. In-deed, such preservationists often encourage the 'cropping' (con-venient euphemism) of stocks, the critical assessment of each species' right to live upon *our* earth. Such an attitude shows very little tenderness or care to living things, and in making such wild life into one more human asset, whether of recreation or of biological necessity, licenses our weighing such an asset against others. Water, even water for wasting, is more important *to us* than is a rare but-terfly or orchid or the homes of the wild beasts. Certainly the few will lose their pleasures, of walking admiringly over that soil, but the many will keep theirs. If our criterion is human pleasure, there can be no doubt of our choice.

Again, as KRIEGER and TRIBE have variously argued, such an argument leaves us no objection to the systematic replacement of trees by plastic trees. Our oxygen needs can be supplied by soya beans, instead (and maybe better had be if the sea is likely to go the way of Lake Erie, which it might). There will be no mess, no unsightly branches and the like if we choose the art-tree ... Yet certainly most of us, or many of us, *do* feel some desecration in such a 'utilitarian' attitude. There seems no argument against it, save to say that such a world is not one we would choose to inhabit. Such a psychology is not one we would choose to have. 'By articulating environmental goals wholly in terms of human needs and preferences (the environmentalist) may be helping to legitimate a system of discourse which so structures human thought and feeling as to erode over the long run the very sense of obligation which provided the initial impetus for his very protective efforts.' (TRIBE p. 1330.) Tribe argues that we should rather admit that animals, and plants, and in general the land have *rights*, and he seems to have a decision of an American court on his side (SAGOFF p. 219 n.): even a valley can have rights, and hikers can plead on its behalf.

SAGOFF himself observes that such a system need not give the answer which the environmentalist would like. If hikers can plead for a valley, so can a developer. Man, after all, was created to admire and care for the cosmos, and his arts are needed to *complete* the world (ASCLEPIUS 8). Who is to say that a valley, being wilderness, is not benefited by being turned into a place of culture? Sagoff is surely correct that these things *could* be said: slaves too were supposed to be benefited by being incorporated into Christian civilization. And it may be that some of them *were*, but the trade was no less abominable for that. Sagoff further comments that it might certainly be true that animals and plants should benefit by being made into a park. No-one really likes to struggle for life, and if the wilderness were wholly tamed they would be spared that struggle. So returns Paradise.

I do not myself find the vision quite so distasteful as Sagoff does. If it were true that everyone would be better off in this situation, and if we really did have the power to bring it about equitably, making due allowance for the right of the animals, at least, bloody-mindedly to prefer what was not to their profit, why then perhaps we should transform the earth into a pleasure garden. My doubts are practical, and historical. Most generally, it seems quite likely that all animal organisms are so constructed as to *require* a struggle, and problems surmounted in a worthy purpose (LORENZ (1) pp. 22 f.)—that is why we falsely suppose that heaven itself will be boring. Again, the fate of our domestic beasts and such park animals as now exist does not encourage any optimism about the way we would treat them. And how precisely, once we have taken on the role of arbiter and lord shall we decide their disputes? 'One law

for the lion and ox is oppression.' (BLAKE p. 158.) And what will
happen when our civilization falls—as fall it will—to such poor
creatures as have been stripped of their ability to find their own
way in the world? Even genetic patterns of behaviour might well
lapse, and culturally transmitted patterns very probably would. I
could continue, but I trust that the point is made. God save us even
from well-meant benevolence. It is possible to be sure, in individual
cases, what is or is not to an entity's profit or harm. It seems entirely
obvious that we should not wantonly do harm, but only (at the most)
for our necessities. That we should do good is a much more dangerous thesis: it is not one I could conscientiously deny, but equally
I cannot wholly affirm it, whether for beasts or birds or men.
Very often, when we think to do good we are only enlarging
our self-esteem. I have no doubt at all that that would be the
chief motive in any attempt on our part to turn the wilderness to
paradise, and we would therefore fail. It is better to do small
works within the wilderness than one large work to change the
whole.

Sagoff's defence of the wilderness, however, is a matter for interest. He suggests that we desire to retain it, if we do, because it
represents to us certain cultural values to which we are deeply
attached. Our landscape is part of our cultural heritage, our very
morality, and to lose that landscape is to diminish ourselves. Once
again, I am sure that he is right about some of the motives for preser-
vationism. We do not seek to preserve old buildings, old lands
because they are beautiful—such beauty is in the eye of the
beholder, and beholders often are rare. We do not willingly see them
go because they are the land of our ancestors, the signs of our covenant, the reminder of who we are, or take ourselves to be. This is
a strong, and not despicable motive for wishing there always to be
a badger in Binsey lane, orchids on Otmoor, stags in the Highlands.
Of itself it shows no tenderness to the creatures concerned, though
it may awaken that. We preserve our material as we preserve our
moral heritage, because this is the land and nation to which we were
born, and we will not have it otherwise. If animals should have to
suffer to make it so, so be it. If men must suffer to make it so, so
be it. This is the thing which makes all suffering worthwhile, and
even the animals' pain is so transmuted into artistry. 'Far from me
and my friends be such frigid philosophy as may conduct us indifferent and unmoved over any ground which has been dignified

by wisdom, bravery or virtue. That man is little to be envied, whose patriotism would not gain force upon the plain of Marathon, or whose piety would not grow warmer among the ruins of Iona!' (JOHNSON AND BOSWELL pp. 134 f.) One who would destroy such places is not offending against beauty, but against our past. He is turning the spiritual landscape we really inhabit into material for his own purposes.

But though I have great sympathy for this approach, and think it one more flaw of far too much 'frigid philosophy' that this awareness has not been thought worthy of more philosophical comment, I must still ask whether such a culture is in the end worth remembering. If its preservation is bought at the price of present suffering in men or beasts, I have my doubts. Wordsworth's Leech-gatherer represented something enduring, but is it entirely obvious that someone should be appointed to that task—'employment hazardous and wearisome'—merely to preserve our heritage? And if this is not obvious—as it is not to me—why is it obvious that non-human animals should be kept in suffering for the same reason?

In short, we should recognize or remember what Sagoff seems to think a platitude, that animals and plants and all the creatures and ecologies that variously inhabit the earth have, in a sense, some *right* to our consideration.[5] Our ethical system should not, and cannot hope to eliminate such personal attachments as friend to friend, parent to family and even man to conspecific. But such natural preferences must not become prejudices, whereby every case is settled, in advance, to the profit of ourselves and our immediate kin. Other species rarely have the power to bend the world to their own purposes, and we think very disapprovingly of those that, partly, do (such as rats, or locusts). We have, temporarily, that power: if we succeed in using it we shall have destroyed ourselves. If we do not limit our own demands, the world will limit them for us.

In saying this I am not offering an egoistic justification of ethical decency. I am pointing out that the rationality of immediate self-interest that has brought us to the edge of disaster is thereby

[5] Features of the landscape, river banks and valleys are not merely geological features, as PASSMORE and SAGOFF suppose. Valleys and pools and all such living places are biocoenoses, harmonious systems that maintain themselves in the constant interchange of material, *living places*. Not all our actions are destructive of such things: sometimes we have even created them, as when the Parliamentary Commissioners ordered the planting of hedgerows (VESEY-FITZGERALD (2) p. 96). A hedgerow is more than a hawthorn.

revealed as a failure. If success is the proper criterion of value for theories and techniques, then the 'rational' exaltation of men above their environment is a proven fraud. Let us then at last consider acting according to the principles to which we have paid lip-service. If we cannot create paradise, let us at least stop fouling the wilderness. Other creatures than we human beings have an interest in that wilderness: they have as much right to its benefits, and considerably more need (see above, p. 20).

Plants, individuals and violence

How much am I saying in saying this? In urging respect for all life, including that of plants, am I not laid open to the Stoic reductio, that since I cannot avoid eating plants it is only sentiment that stops me eating animals? My first response might simply be that the Stoic himself declines to eat human animals, and our mammalian kin display the same agony and fear of death that puts him off anthropophagy. Whether, if starving, I would eat a rabbit, or a Stoic (who surely should not object), has little relevance to our present situation.[6] Even if my life is of more value (to me if not to the world at large) than that of a rabbit, or of a Stoic, yet their lives are worth something, and should not be lost to satisfy a whim. Such an acceptance of hierarchical order in the natural world can hardly be faulted by the Stoic, whether it claims simply that I feel more for rabbits than for trout, for vertebrates than arthropods, for animals than plants, for men of my kind than for men of yours, or whether I attempt some rational ordering, as that rabbits feel more than tomatoes, or that cows have a more complex and individual reality than jellyfish. And why, in the second place, 'only' sentiment?

Such hierarchies, whether of personal attachment or objective value, admit the existence of priorities, and characteristically place men on top. Obviously so: the hierarchalist is human. Such a system is doubtless most congenial to our present common sense, and such a system does not license our present treatment of animals. All those who believe that animals are not utterly beyond moral consideration, that they should be spared all avoidable pain are duty-bound

[6] Some people do not eat the strictly edible, even when in need: RENNER (pp. 129 f.) sneers a little at Saint-Exupéry for not seeing that snails were *food*—but would not Renner have honoured a man to whom it simply did not occur that *babies* were edible? Is it quite absurd to die rather than eat the forbidden thing? Such virtue may be saintly or heroic: fortunately we are not called upon to exercise it.

to abstain from meat, and to campaign against vivisection. But I will now go further.

Plants too, and every clod of earth are animate: not mystically so, but in straightforwardly biological terms. The earth itself, the biosphere itself is made up of living things and their products in a single, interconnected whole. We are all members one of another, and the lowliest organism may be as vital to the whole as any Nobel prize-winner. More so, indeed. For the very fact which can immediately be adduced to mark the difference between men and plants, or men and micro-organisms, reveals that the latter are strictly very much more important than any one of us.

For consider: whereas in speaking of 'the fox' we falsely forget that there are foxes, with individual interests and points of view, and that even if there be the Fox we have no dealings with Him, when we turn to the Grass or to the Yellow-fever organism it is very much more plausible to doubt that there are individual grass-plants or individual bacilli in any sense not covered by saying there are bits of grass, or the like. It is of course true that not just any dissection of a stretch of living grass would leave us living grass: but there are many more such grass-conserving dissections than there are in the case of the 'higher animals'. In the case of micro-organisms we can note that there are, say, seven bacilli at one time, but those seven pass into and out of each other to maintain a single bacillus-population that does not require the survival of any one momentarily separate individual. In such cases it is not inappropriate to concentrate our scientific, and our ethical attention on the population, and not on any one individual cell. After all, we too are composed of individual cells, though of a heterogeneous sort. Similarly, in the case of ant-colonies it is not wholly implausible to believe that we are dealing with one, 'multi-individual' individual, the colony. In this case, our acquaintance with free-living insects is there to remind us that even ants, even bees are not entirely 'pieces of a colony'. And the colonies themselves are discrete, compact individuals in a way that stretches of grass, or populations of bacilli are not.

This line of approach—and I make no apologies for the fact that it reveals a continuum, not a discrete taxonomy—implies two things. Firstly, that to cut a blade of grass, or pluck a leaf of spinach, or cut down the corn need do no injury to Grass, or Spinach, or Corn. It may in fact encourage all of them. Some plants are benefited precisely by being eaten (as are some intestinal worms), for that is how the species spreads.[7] Secondly, that such ethically relevant individuals as Grass, and Spinach (or even all-the-spinach-in-Britain), and the Nitrogen-fixing Bacterium are enormously more important to the world at large than any human individual.

'Mankind is the highest form of life and so incomparably more valuable than a mouse or an ape.' (DEWAR p. 88.)

By the same argument, and very much more realistically, Dewar himself could be sacrificed to the Nitrogen-fixing Bacterium, that single fluid population which upholds the world. What do men do for the world?[8]

In saying all this I am of course speaking from a human perspective. It may be that moments to us are millenia to bacilli, that they see themselves as individuals in an ongoing civilization, just as we do. It may be that grass-blades are more individualist than I suppose, and it is very likely true that not *all* plants are as I have suggested. Some plants may be individuals, as trees most probably are; some plants may have points of view. Some plants may feel. I say nothing against such research as has been done on the point, except that the interpretation of galvanic twitches as *distress*-signals seems much more dubious than the experimenters allow (whom are the plants signalling to? why are they not thought joy-signals? or merely material consequences of the experimenter's actions?), and that the speed with which normally conventional thinkers refer to these experiments when faced by a zoophile strongly suggests hypocrisy. Even if a plant does not feel its own destruction I would

[7] We do not need to kill plants in order to eat fruit or grain or leaf or even root, and do them little injury thereby (PORPHYRY (1) 111.18). If killing and eating animals were as inescapable a necessity of our lives as eating plant-matter, drinking water, breathing air we might, as he says, accept that 'that is how things are'. But as such use is not essential, but the product of greed and indifference, it must be counted as iniquitous. It does not need asceticism to teach us this, as PASSMORE supposes (p. 178): do the orthodox think themselves ascetic because they do not eat men? Finally, even if plants were sentient, and injured by our attentions, carnivores do far more harm even to plants.

[8] 'Civilisation', replies PASSMORE (p. 179), but give no better reason that I can see for his answer than that he experiences aesthetic thrills at some of the products of human labour, and perhaps that some nations allow their citizens some measure of the liberty that pre-political man enjoys. Even if I too am addicted to 'civilization' is that a nobler addiction than an alcoholic's? Why? Only when human society finds a goal beyond its own continuance, in glorifying God or tending the earth, will it begin to seem a worthwhile endeavour. Or does Passmore really mean that the thrills of the international jet-set are sufficient justification for the agonies of sentient existence imposed by the 'need' to maintain such a 'civilization'?

certainly admit that some plants are 'ethical individuals' and that their wanton destruction is murder, of a sort. Our distress at the destruction of a living tree is not merely at our loss of pleasure in its beauty—there is likewise pleasure in a roaring fire, or in a clear view. We recognize trees as long-growing individuals, not merely pieces of oak. What motives we are prepared to admit as licensing arboricide will vary from generation to generation, but it may well be that we already think of some arboricide as culpable and may in time think more. But until we have put earth's household, or our household in some order, I cannot help feeling that those who mourn a tree, but take 'unspeakable delight' in murdering ducks (as LEOPOLD pp. 6f., and 120) display a certain lack of proportion.

Plants can be respected, and also eaten, for they can spare their surplus. 'Man's vegetable nourishment is not the destruction of vegetation but a sensible use of its superfluity.' (BARTH III.4, p. 351.) Left to itself any plant would swamp the world, to its own destruction. All kinds 'wish' to do this, but none dare succeed. We may therefore garden them, and live with them, allowing even noxious plants some place. I am encouraged in this by noting that those few extremists who most talk to plants, and think them conscious beings, still crop their food. And once again, our 'reasonable' treatment of plants as mere stuff for our profit has led us so close to disastrous failure, that we might reasonably turn to consider such successes upon other principles as the settlement of Findhorn (see TOMPKINS AND BIRD pp. 310f.).

A similar point may be made about bacilli. Our 'rationality' in this decrees that we must oppose all such bacilli as threaten us with danger, and our efforts have bought us a few years of disease-free life—or rather life free of such diseases as we can equate with the action of bacilli, or of those bacilli we have noticed. I have already said something on this point, and here sum up by remarking that our use of DDT is a convenient symbol of our practice. Certainly, we have saved lives with it, but at the price of fouling the whole biosphere and polluting even human mothers' milk. Certainly we have saved lives with it, but at the price of strengthening our 'foe'. Bacillus populations react to threats, even if only by the automatism of natural selection. Our chemists will never be able to eliminate such threats, and must always be involved in an arms race in which our 'foes' are always winning. Is it not time we altered our approach? Utilitarians should surely think so.

'You think your laws of violence correct evil; they only increase it. You have tried for thousands of years to destroy evil by evil, but instead of destroying it you have increased it.' (TOLSTOY p. 345.)

I say nothing, in this context, of Tolstoy's application of the principle of non-resistance. I only suggest, with complete seriousness, that our reasonable antagonisms have only made things worse. We are encouraging other kinds, both microscopic and arthropodal, to seek to absorb the world, because we are threatening them with ever fiercer weapons. Is it not time, past time, to see what other attitudes there might be to the living world? For this brief period we have had the power and will to save our weak, our children from such distresses as have in the past contained our species from a catastrophic expansion. If we do not change our ways we shall have saved them only that they might suffer worse things when we do collapse.

What am I advocating? A quietism that would not oppose the evils that threaten us, perhaps in the hope that the world itself will change if only our hearts change? There are precedents. But there is a further possibility. Instead of seeking to destroy our 'foe' let us see if we can live with it. It is notorious that only occasionally do we suffer the catastrophic bacterial expansions that manifest as disease. Let us devote our research funds to learning why this is so, and how we may contain such populations. It is surely not beyond the powers of intellectual man to devise such systems: what has been lacking is the incentive. Our medical ideal should not be the anti-septic, anti-human hospital—which is in any case unexportable to many areas of the world—but the man who *can* use all things to his profit because he knows, and his body knows how to cooperate with the other lives of the world.

In Bateson's terminology, such a man would know that he exists only as a part of the total organism-plus-environment, and that to save himself distress or gain himself profit by shifting distress onto his *environment* is, in the end, self-destructive (BATESON pp. 454 ff.). We *cannot* unendingly exploit our kin, or fight our 'foes'. Let us learn to live otherwise: for, in truth, we have no choice in the matter. Either we do so, and maybe live; or we do not do so, and our few descendants will live entirely as hunter-gatherers once more.

Nature and choice

Suppose, then, that we do recognize ourselves as one species amongst many in a natural order which we cannot hope wholly to control or to remake. What shall our life be like? Some men, and not the worst of us, may choose to go to the extreme of Taoistic quietism, and *take* as little as they can. What life will be like for such men in their old age, I do not know; nor do I know how far our despotically liberal society will permit them to lead their own lives, or those of their children. The rest of us may perhaps achieve enough of grace to leave them alone, and grant that not all men require settled townships, that those who take as little as may be from the land are no great burden on society. Some of us may refrain from fighting even such creatures as the main line of zoophily has reckoned fair game, namely those who threaten us. Such a life, though it does not fill me with the quivering distaste that PASSMORE feels (p. 181), is at the moment too heroic to contemplate—though the survivors may be forced to it. That such an option should be there is perhaps important even for those of us who do not take it—as a constant reminder that 'natural event' is perhaps not wholly unendurable.[9] We need such reminders to restrain us from an automatic action in defence of what we imagine to be our immediate interests, action which has been disastrous in the past. 'The distribution of tse-tse can be linked quite often with human mismanagement of land, for example, bush encroachment following an inept fire regime; and removal of tse-tse may lead to serious soil erosion and habitat deterioration if grazing of domesticated animals is thereafter not very carefully controlled.' (DARLING (2) p. 134.) The more we interfere with, the more we must, so that we lurch from crisis into crisis with accelerating speed.

Such a quietism, however, is not on for most of us—or we refuse that it should be. Most of us will continue to make every effort to

---

[9] The orthodox are always attacking Jains, and zoophiles as often are apologizing for them. The spleen and the apology are signs of a bad conscience. If Jains go enormously further than most zoophiles in the avoidance of killing, and yet lead happy and useful lives, what excuse have we? Perhaps, if all were Jains, we could not 'civilize the world' (PASSMORE p. 126): could we not? Does it matter? Yet even 'if we could not, and it matters, yet still such Jains constitute a standing reminder and rebuke against all wanton killing (as BARTH III.4, p. 355 says of vegetarians): most of our killing is entirely so. Jains incidentally are neither so callous nor so naive as the orthodox commonly suppose (see KALGHATGI pp. 161 f.). It was probably the challenge of Jainism and Buddhism that led to the general Hindu acceptance of vegetarianism as the superior form of life (DUMONT 25.6).

prevent our own dear flesh, our own dear kin, from being merely material swept in the world's tides. I certainly do not say that we are wholly wrong to attempt the protection of our weak, our old, our sick, our young, our incompetents—though I wonder at times if *we* think we are wrong, and have wantonly created the perils of a mechanical world to do the job for us. Having escaped from natural selection, perhaps we are subconsciously imposing the car, and chemicals, and faulty diet, and sectarian war to select a new breed of men. This may be so: our rationalizations of these things may well conceal the inner causes of our acts. But if it is so, we should recognize that consciously we might not wish such a method, or such an end. Our subconscious is not always the best of guides.

How then shall we live? If we are creatures in the natural order may we not feed on other creatures? Death will come to all, including us, and creatures in the wild die young in any case. LEOPOLD's land ethic appears to allow as much: he opposes wasteful killing, as 'a training for ethical depravity elsewhere' (p. 197), but offers the sportsmanlike hunter as a decent life. The hunter is an appreciative artist (p. 212). Doubtless, in some degree, this is so. Some hunting tribes beg pardon of their prey, and it has always been true that hunters appreciate 'speaking likenesses' of their victims.

> 'We offered our respects and gratitude to the fish and the Sea Gods daily, and ate them with real love, admiring their extraordinarily beautiful, perfect little bodies.' (SNYDER p. 139.)

I am uncertain what it means to *love* the thing you are destroying, and feel doubts about admiring 'perfect little bodies' that are no more perfect than are butterflies on pins. Nor am I convinced that eating grubs with enjoyment itself constitutes 'paying nature her due respects as the universal provider' (WILLIAMS (2) p. 149). Even if the terrestrial biosphere is a single organism, it is hardly appropriate for us to feel gratitude to It when we eat living creatures who, realistically, would rather not be eaten. *Our* relations are with other individual creatures who seek and suffer and enjoy, very much like us. Maybe we sometimes live under necessity, and when we do it is not inappropriate to pay respects to the creatures we kill, if only to remind ourselves of what we owe them and their kin. But let us not pretend that we are now in such necessities, or that the creatures we eat are much gladdened (so far as we know) by our gratitude—a gratitude that never seeks to repay its debt.

'Distant' creatures vanish into 'Nature', just as distant places vanish over the horizon into 'elsewhere' and periods before some arbitrary date (which varies with our education) are vaguely thought of as contemporaneous. We owe Reason more respect than that.

The trouble with such pictures is that they are excuses. True carnivores kill as they must, and very often live on berries or on carrion; when they kill, they kill quickly, and their prey is often old or weak with (maybe) little life worth living still to live. As species, prey and predator are symbiotic, and the deadly game they play is overarched by as-it-were rules of war that allow the individuals to live together peaceably, save when the hunter actually hunts. Predators do not kill in the centre of their territories, for example (HEDIGER pp. 14 f.; VESEY-FITZGERALD (1) p. 53): whether from cunning, instinct or neighbourly feeling—which explanations are not necessarily exclusive. I do not think it impossible that something like moral corruption can be found amongst the non-human, that much of the present way of the world is consequent upon the past choices (or 'choices') of living creatures; but certainly it seems likely that non-human carnivores can now do little to change their habits. We have no biological excuse for taking part in this game, good or evil, least of all when we break all the rules.

We have no biological excuse. By this I do not mean to beg the question of man's origins, only to emphasize that we *can* live well without meat and that *we* are not entirely custom-bound, even if the non-human carnivores are. The point at which our ancestors turned from the largely frugivorous diet of those ancestors we share with the apes is in dispute. It may be that the proto-hominids turned, or took more systematically, to scavenging across the veldt (SZALAY). It may be that Homo erectus detected a useful source of protein in his cousins, Paranthropus and Gigantopithecus (HOWELLS p. 130). In the palaeolithic period, it may be, our hunting ancestors were responsible for the extinction of the megafauna of the northern hemisphere (MARTIN AND WRIGHT; see V. L. SMITH): though present-day hunter-gatherers get most of their food from plant sources. Whenever it was we turned to meat, it is clear that we are by now reasonably well-adapted to its consumption. It does not follow that we are well-adapted to its consumption in the quantities that habit has made second-nature in the developed west (see PLUTARCH (1) 132a). It does not follow that we *need* meat, or are not healthier without it: vegetarians and vegans suffer less from cancers of the bowel; vegans very likely suffer less from heart disease. It does not follow, finally, that it is somehow obligatory, because 'natural', to eat flesh. Nor do zoophiles need to claim that it is, contrariwise, 'unnatural' to do so. Our ancestors made a choice, for whatever reason or upon whatever impulse of desire: we are not bound to imitate their errors. *Nature is not static*: our natures and the natures of our offspring follow upon our choices, and no choices are final save those of the First Cause.

The First Cause, if It chose anything, chose that the members of the world It made should be mutually dependent. Those members, over millions of years, have as it were directed their own evolution by 'choosing' ways of life, by seizing opportunities, by advancing into ecological niches created by yet other creatures' 'choices'. We are all committed by our ancestors' choices in that those choices have made the world we inhabit, have made us: but we are not always compelled to abide by them. The vegetarian panda is a member of the order of Carnivora: even rabbits can be induced to eat flesh (BERNARD (1) p. 153; and lambs, according to SHELLEY p. 330). What has been is not what must be, nor is it necessarily what ought to be. We can change our ways, and ought to do so if our ways are evil.

We do not need meat, nor do we have any general, psychological need to hunt down animals and kill them if we are to satisfy our atavistic urges (what, in any case, if we did?). Those who say otherwise are seeking pretexts for their own preferences. My own suspicion, indeed, is that meat-eating always was what it is now: a corrupt application of symbolic processes, as PORPHYRY ((1) 115 f.) suggests (also TRYON p. 94). Even in Paul's day the available meat was mostly that from temple sacrifices, and he has to pick his way through the casuistry that allows Christians to partake of this rite (I Corinthians 8; though see Revelation 2:14, 20). Perhaps in the beginning flesh-eating was only a metaphor, and then a sacrament, and at last a secular feast. It has similarly been suggested, I do not know with what plausibility, that the Aztecs' practice of flaying or performing cardectomies upon their victims was a materialistic reading of Mayan psychological and spiritual exercises (SEJOURNE). We eat flesh in origin because we thereby share in the immanent life of the god of our tribe's devotion, we share in the life of our tribe. All those who have turned vegetarian soon realize that such social reasonings are often still the strongest—not to eat with people is to deny their consanguinity.[10]

It is open to the Christian in particular to say that all such sacrifices, all such flesh-sharings were ended with the one perfect and sufficient sacrifice, and the institution of the eucharist—a return to the bloodless sacrifices of ancient times. We being many are one bread, one body, for we all partake of the one bread (I Corinthians 10:17). The content of our secular meals is governed by ritual needs, whereby we define our class and kin and degree of shared life (DOUGLAS (4)). Christians, after all, should perhaps not share in them. It is perhaps worth noting that KINGSFORD AND MAITLAND ((2) pp. 98 f.) held that flesh-eating did service to astral beings: I do not know whether they were right in fact—I am sure they were right in ritual.

Unfortunately, a Gnostic tendency in the Christian tradition has suggested otherwise. Christ's promise that his followers would not be hurt by poisons nor by serpents (Mark 16:18) was twisted from its proper reference (which is more or less the medical and personal ideal I have already mentioned) to a declaration that the Christian could share in anything.[11]

'We are not defiled by food, as neither is the sea by the filth of rivers. For we have dominion over all eatables ... If we were afraid of food, we should be enslaved by the conception of fear. But it is requisite that all things should be obedient to us.' (POR-PHYRY (1) I 42.)

Porphyry here quotes a standard Gnosticism that reappears in Häring (111 p. 230), and adds 'instead of obtaining liberty, being precipitated into an abyss of infelicity, they are suffocated'.

Our food is chosen for symbolic needs, in this case to prove that we are the masters. That absurdity we can perhaps forget. But even those who have forgotten it sometimes commit a like absurdity—

[10] Peter's vision (Acts 10:9 f.), in which he is commanded to forget the division between clean and unclean beasts is certainly not an injunction to eat everything, but rather to accept gentiles into the faith. But it is not quite so irrelevant to the case for flesh-eating as zoophiles sometimes say: eating patterns define societies (see Leviticus 20:24 f.), and it was important that the early church should not be exclusive brethren. It is not insignificant that one question which vegetarians are always being asked is 'but what do you eat for Christmas?'.

[11] Christ's dictum, that it is what comes out of a man and not what goes into him that defiles him (Mark 7:15 f.) was invoked: and this really is irrelevant, or works the other way. Food should not be chosen for its ritual significance, and nourishment spurned because it is somehow 'unmanly'. What matters is what we do.

that of defending their actions, or even beginning their actions on the basis of what 'nature' does.

'I had lost sight of the fact that life and death are a cycle, endless, continual, everlasting. I would eat the lamb, enjoy its meat, have its fine curly skin cured, washed, brushed and combed to make a rug for my bedroom. Unless I did this I would never convince myself that I was a realist, capable of seeing that the world was as it was and not as I dreamed.' (NIALL p. 68.)

Niall came to have a different attitude, but here he chooses to act as he imagines 'nature' acts, chooses to believe that he ought to act as if he incarnated the basic principle of 'nature', chooses to kill to prove the hardness of his heart. The same 'realist' ethic would license all acts of murder. Such unrealistic 'realism' is the thief of pity. Perhaps we pay for living by our perpetual tithes, our more than tithes, to the ongoing process that is nature. Must we therefore be forbidden pity? Perhaps in nature the lamb might die, by wolf or weather or sickness, before its prime. And all die in the end. Is that a reason for our not helping it to live? Or for killing it? We have chosen to take control, to some extent, of fate insofar as it touches our kin: why should we not extend that carefulness, remembering always that we cannot wholly control the earth, that there are other creatures than the ones we immediately love who have a claim on 'nature'? Acceptance of the tides of life and death is better shown in bearing *our* death than in drowning others.

How then shall we live? Doubtless in practice we shall live much as before, allowing only a gradual change to move us from our present patterns—I hope that the change is not too gradual, for time is short. But let us at least acknowledge as an ideal a community not merely of many races, many cultures, but one of many species. Let us begin to learn how we can live—we mammals, warm-blooded creatures, animals and living things—in an acknowledged and mutual dependence. We have examples, on a small scale, in 'primitive tribes' and communes of the ecomystical—in whom, despite their manifold absurdities, I see the only hope that has yet been lit. In the end, only a sound ontology, a sound epistemology can guide us right, but in the meantime our unacknowledged sympathies are there to urge us in a less wasteful and immoral path, and the laboriously gathered information of ecologists and natural historians is there to demonstrate how necessary even to our own survival such a change must be.

Change will come gradually. Let us pray we have time to learn.

He sendeth the springs into the valleys, which run among the hills.

They give drink to every beast of the field: the wild asses quench their thirst.

By them shall the fowls of the heaven have their habitation, which sing among the branches.

He watereth the hills from his chambers: the earth is satisfied with the fruit of thy works.

He causeth the grass to grow for the cattle, and herb for the service of man: that he may bring forth food out of the earth;

and wine that maketh glad the heart of men, and oil to make his face to shine, and bread which strengtheneth man's heart.

The trees of the Lord are full of sap; the cedars of Lebanon, which he hath planted;

where the birds make their nests: as for the stork, the fir trees are her house.

The high hills are a refuge for the wild goats; and the rocks for the conies.

He appointeth the moon for seasons: the sun knoweth his going down.

Thou makest darkness, and it is night: wherein all the beasts of the forest do creep forth.

The young lions roar after their prey, and seek their food from God.

The sun ariseth, they gather themselves together, and lay them down in their dens.

Man goeth forth into his works and to labour until the evening.

O Lord, how manifold are thy works! In wisdom hast thou made them all: the earth is full of thy riches.

So is this great and wide sea, wherein are things creeping innumerable, both small and great beasts.

There go the ships: there is that leviathan, whom thou hast made to play therein.

These wait all upon thee; that thou mayest give them their food in due season.

That thou givest them they gather: thou openest thine hand, they
    are filled with good.

Thou hidest thy face, they are troubled: thou takest away their
    breath, they die, and return to their dust.

Thou sendest forth thy spirit, they are created: and thou renewest
    the face of the earth.

The glory of the Lord shall endure for ever: the Lord shall rejoice
    in his works.

Psalm 104.10–31

IX

CONCLUSION

Aristotelian ethics

Of the making of many arguments there is no end. If I choose to finish here it is not because I believe that there is no more to say, but only that I am sure that enough has been said to demonstrate the desperate need for a practical and philosophical reappraisal of our standing in the world. It is no longer enough to fantasize, for example, that dolphins may prove our intellectual equals and be admitted into a new, terrestrial society; it is not enough to tell ourselves stories about those other intelligences who may inhabit other worlds of this galaxy, and speculate on how we may treat each other. There are other sentient creatures all about us, who may lack our verbalizing gifts but who have their lives to live and their own visions of reality to worship. We are not separate from them, and owe them honour. To imagine that their lesser 'intelligence' (whatever that may be) licenses our tyranny is to leave the way open for any human intellectual élite to treat the rest of us as trash. Intelligence is a great gift, certainly, but it is of value only in its service of the multi-millionfold enterprise that is the biosphere, and beyond that, the world. 'There is not a beast upon the earth, nor a bird that flies, but is a nation like to you.' (Koran 6; see KHAN.) Let us try the experiment, you and I, of meaning, when we say 'we', not merely 'we men', but 'we mammals' or 'we animals'. Maybe very few mammals or animals will ever join with you and me in any fully and mutually conscious enterprise: but the same is true even of human beings. And in remembering our solidarity and common ancestry with creatures not of our immediate kind we may come to be kinder to such creatures of our species as are not to our taste. Humanists sought to purchase the welfare of their fellow men by denigrating 'beasts': such antagonisms are counterproductive.

In pursuing the various self-deceptions endemic to man, particularly but not exclusively to civilized man, through the labyrinth of orthodox thought and of my imagination, I have not committed myself to any particular view of the 'facts' or of the nature of 'moral enquiry'. I do not believe that there is any credible account of either which could excuse our present depredations. I am inclined, perhaps unfairly, to think that no-one has any standing in such a discussion who has not taken the simple, minimal step of abandoning flesh-foods. Honourable men may honourably disagree about some details of human treatment of the non-human, but vegetarianism is now as necessary a pledge of moral devotion as was the refusal of emperor-worship in the early Church. Those who have not made that pledge have no authority to speak against the most inanely conceived experiments, nor against hunting, nor against fur-trapping, nor bear-baiting, nor bull-fights, nor pulling the wings off flies. Flesh-eating in our present circumstances is as empty a gluttony as any of these things. Those who still eat flesh when they could do otherwise have no claim to be serious moralists.

This judgement is perhaps unfair: though those who say so should remember that I make it also against my own past self. Nor do I forget that there is no end to human hypocrisy, and that at any stage of our progress we are cosily engaged in practices which at a later date we will consider grievous wrongs—often for their *silliness* as much as for the harm they did. In short, none of us, save some saints or Bodhissattvas, is a decent moral authority. The most that we do is *try*, remembering some of the time to wonder what a decent man *would* do. Such decency is not ours: a decent man would hardly need to think of what to do—he'd act as if the decent thing was the only option, and that an enjoyable one. We struggle to correct our biases, our blindnesses, our secret fears and fantasies, and work out rules that more or less define the sort of life we think we see as proper. But the decent man, the sound man, the reasonable man does what he knows he must.

This ideal was Aristotle's. The good man is he that acts well, from a stable state of character which brings to an integrated whole such emotional and intellectual capacities as are open to creatures of humankind. He relates realistically to things in the world, living and unliving, and finds the meaning of his life in natural friendships and the shared worship of natural beauty. He does well in doing, as we say, what he *ought*: in Aristotle's terms he does rather what he *must*, what he is *bound* to do. So do we not all? No: for it is the mark of wickedness that we tell lies about our motives, about the springs of our actions (*Nicomachean Ethics* 6.1144a34 f.). We pretend that we simply *must* do this or that, well knowing that we need not. Only the sound man is in accord with nature: the wicked are unnatural. Sometimes, perhaps, we can say that a man's *nature* is itself to blame: but such men are precisely *not* wicked—though Aristotle was wrong to think them bestial (see *Nicomachean Ethics* 7.1148b15 f.). Again, it may sometimes be that events overpower *us* which would not have overpowered a truly good man, and yet we are forgiven, the compulsion reckoned too great (see *Nicomachean Ethics* 3.1110a23 f.). Perhaps so: and at such points the virtue of the truly good man becomes something more than human. But such compulsions are, in truth, a rarity for most of us. We act from greed, and jealousy, and spleen, pretending to ourselves that so we must. The good man does what he must, is drawn to act not so much by the desire of *having* goods, as of sharing them. Aristotelian decency depends crucially on *sharing*: what good is prosperity when you have no-one to share it with (*Nicomachean Ethics* 8.1155a7 f.)? The good life, the life that the decent man would lead and which we, in following that ideal, should lead, is one of sharing open-heartedly in the life of friends and family and city and the celestial spheres themselves. We should share, as far as we are able, in the life of the world, finding it our joy to guard and to make manifest the glories of that life.

We may no longer believe in the celestial spheres, though the belief that the whole world is itself a sort of living system is by no means dead, nor need it die. And Aristotle himself gave little attention to the life we share with animals—though he gave enough to know that animals were often loving and intelligent within their kind (*Nicomachean Ethics* 8.1155a17 f.). As MAIMONIDES remarked, in considering the (then) humane techniques of kosher slaughtering, 'the love and tenderness of a mother for her young ones is not produced by reasoning, but by imagination, and this faculty exists not only in man but in most living beings.' (3.48: p. 371.)

The Aristotelian ideal can readily be extended to embrace all sorts of lives, some more easily than others. In founding our lives upon such a passion of sharing, we may learn to give and receive with gratitude (see *Nicomachean Ethics* 5.1133a3 f.), and to recognize with our emotions as well as with our intellect that living worlds are more secure the more different *kinds* of creature that they house. The more different sorts of creature that an area houses, the more it *can* house, and the less subject it is to catastrophic failure. Once again: to seize all for ourselves is self-destructive. This principle, of necessary diversity in unity, was a metaphysical before it was an ecological discovery, and it is badly misunderstood by PASSMORE (p. 119). It is not a plea for aesthetic variety, but a recognition that the life of the whole is increased and improved by the diversity of parts. Love shared is love doubled. Nor are Passmore's ironical queries about universes that contain only human beings and a cobra (is that better than one containing only human beings?) very relevant. No such universe is strictly conceivable:[1] for there to be a man there must be uncounted millions of other lives on whom he depends, and who, to some extent, depend on him. To separate ourselves from that shared existence, or to imagine its replacement by an automated wilderness are equal absurdities. Even to deprive the prey of its predator may be a mistake (see DARLING (3) p. 333 on the wolf's 'shepherding' of deer).[2]

This much for the Aristotelian mood: the good life, which the good man naturally and easily lives, is one of shared enjoyments, free of all psychotic fantasies, in a world whose beauty and companionship can only be maintained and improved by generously deploying our several and diverse gifts in the service of all. We must learn to share our wealth not only with our immediate kin but with the land from which we take. In doing so we may at last begin to repay the debts we owe to other life. And when at last our hearts are sound, and our motives pure, we may begin to make the desert blossom. Until that moment, we should perhaps hold our hands: until our hearts are sound, such enterprises will be merely efforts at self-aggrandizement, whether merely economic or with the added thrills of aesthetic appreciation. The wholly decent man, in Aristotelian terms, would garden and guard the world: we are not decent

---

[1] To say that it is *logically* possible, even if not physically, depends upon the assumption that we can identify creatures as of such and such a kind while simultaneously holding in abeyance the powers and potentialities that are logically connected to any proper account of those creatures.

[2] This is not a pretext for culling the herd, though it is a good reason for moving the herd along when we have eliminated wolves, lest it crop its pasture into desert. Contraception is better than culling (though total contraception would also be an evil, if a lesser one). And if we *must* kill we should not give ourselves any extra, corrupting motive. Those who kill seals, if it must be done (why?), should get no profit from the skins. It may be said that it would be criminal waste not to eat the animals we keep for milk or recreation: by the same token we should eat our human dead. But I would agree that we should not keep so many of such creatures as to present ourselves with the problem: veganism is a better project than lacto-vegetarianism, though we may in the end be able to take *some* milk from our kin without injustice.

men. Let us remember how dependent we are, and not so readily engage in fantasies of remaking the world. We have done enough remaking (see EISELEY p. 148).

Scepticism

Once again: I have not offered any consistent moral system in the course of my explorations. The first reason for this is purely practical: I am very much more interested in achieving a practical issue than in the details of abstract philosophy, and am willing to argue on almost any basis to achieve that end. The second reason is Aristotelian: I doubt if there is any set of rules, any clear and compendious system that does full justice to the vagaries and un-formalizable sensitivities of our moral experience (see *Nicomachean Ethics* 1.1094b11 f.), any more than there is such a system in the realm of science. It may be, as Aristotle believed, that there is a reconciliation of all value in the knowledge of God—a true being which makes sense of all physical phenomena, and a true good which comprehends all lesser goods. It may be that the good life consists in contemplating and serving that divinity (*Eudemian Ethics* 8.1248b19 f.; see CLARK pp. 174 f.): but such a knowledge and such a service are not matters for words. Either God and the sense of things is seen or He is not: argument can never do more than clear our eyes of self-induced blindness. Certainly no system is a good substitute for what sensibility we still retain.

No system is a good substitute. Indeed, systems are lethal.

I have argued at length that it is rationalism, moralism, scientism which have so often been responsible for our worst behaviour. Beside the self-justifying fury of the Elect, the occasional unruliness of the merely lustful has done little harm. It is for this reason, amongst others, that I have not offered very many *positive* suggestions as to what we should do. Certainly positive action will often be called for, but all that I dare to urge is negative: let us begin by *not* doing certain evil things.

But all preaching, even of the negative sort, stands in danger of becoming lethal. Even vegetarianism, which as a first step is almost a *sine qua nihil*, could easily become a menace to zoophily, and to animals. If it is engaged in the wrong spirit, the movement will find that it is presiding over the extinction of many genetic lines which are suddenly of no more value to the exploiter. The presently bloated populations of the food-animals certainly do no good either to the individuals concerned or to any hypothetical Great Pig, Great Cow and the rest. But it would be an equal and opposite error to allow their lines to end, or rather to compel them so to end. I say this not because of any hosts of potential cows, sheep, pigs thus deprived of the doubtful blessing of corporeal existence, but because of the injury done to living creatures in depriving them of the chance of offspring (which most creatures want), and because of the injury done the world in further depleting its variety.

I therefore decline to sum up my moral position in any finite set of rules. Morality, as I have remarked after Aristotle, cannot be wholly systematized. We should be very wary of any pretended system. And it is for this reason, amongst others, that I feel considerable sympathy with the amoralist whom I have occasionally depicted in the preceding pages. Do not moral systems present a sort of ghastly *reductio ad absurdum* of their own pretensions? We are urged that life will not be worth living unless we follow the preacher's will, but the institutions embodying that will have a strange faculty for preventing any worth-while life. Civilization will fall; wealth will decay; violence will multiply *unless*—unless what? Unless we ourselves commit violence; unless we make most men poorer than they ever were in any 'state of nature'; unless we make of civilization a thing that few experience and many detest. Are we not still promising our young that they may enjoy the thrills of sexual and civic adulthood only when they have undergone castration or its equivalents? You can have the good life when you no longer *want* it.

This picture may be too jaundiced: it is no part of my plan to advocate its truth. Indeed, it could not be. For the true amoralist is also the true sceptic. Once one abandons the insidious categories of what it is right or what it is wrong to do, one has also abandoned those equivalent myths: what it is right or wrong to believe—the true and the false. The true amoralist cannot defend his actions or beliefs on any general ground, cannot disavow his own absolute responsibility for what he does. It is not *morality*, nor *the common good*, nor *logic* that demands the act: it is he, and he only. He cannot ... Can he not? What is to stop him? The true amoralist can say what he pleases, even if he contradicts himself. Why not?

Such an approach to life is one whose attractions I can feel—to commit myself to it utterly would be to stop being utterly sceptical. And in feeling its attractions I am somewhat moved by a problem on which I have found little guidance. In the body of my work I have appealed to 'facts', and more particularly to 'realism'. It seems plausible enough to think that some scientists have adopted the inane belief that 'animals do not feel pain' in order to be able in moderately good conscience to go on torturing them. Similarly, at a more popular level, flesh-eaters pretend that their victims delight to serve them. I have suggested that flesh-eating itself is for most of the West of largely ritual significance, bearing very little relation even to real gastronomic pleasure. All this seems plausible: long may it continue so. But from a purely sceptical stance I can now ask what better credentials my own beliefs and practices have? I choose to believe that animals feel pain, for I wish to continue living (subjectively) in a world not wholly alien to me, not wholly devoid of companionship. I have similar 'grounds' for believing that my wife has feelings, or that my young son can really and truly be played with as a partner and not as an object. Every fact that I believe most strongly to be a fact I believe because it is felt to be the required context or content of some activity that I am loathe to abandon. There is no fact mentioned in the most authoritative text, no fact so familiar to all that I could not disbelieve if I were prepared to abandon my commitment to certain sorts of action, certain sorts of felt reality. It is the mark of the lunatic, or the dreamer, that he has abandoned, perhaps only briefly, the enterprise of our common life, or what we individually insist to be a common life, or what I insist to be a common life. What have I in the end to say but a bare *Credo*? Some things are forced upon me? Very few—maybe only the extremes of pain or pleasure (and how many of their foothills are reached only by the faithful?): and it is a 'known' feature of *them* that the patient may cease to experience anything. The moments when we are most at the mercy of the ineluctably given are the very moments when we are least conscious of what it is that is given. To say 'that is a *fact*' is only to reveal that there is some enterprise which the speaker chooses not to give up, whether the 'fact' be the Virgin Birth, or the non-existence of creatures before their bodily conception, or the date of Archilochus, or the atomic number of lithium. To admit that it may not be a fact is to admit the possibility of abandoning that particular enterprise.

I have sketched this total scepticism at some length because I find it a real possibility and a serious challenge to any moral philosopher, or any would-be honest man. The best part of morality, or of philosophy, lies in eliminating prejudice, bias, fantasy and wishful thinking. But if the sceptic's challenge is valid then such an elimination is a mere fantasy itself. All thought is wishful thinking—and it is no answer to remark that some of our 'facts' are in themselves distasteful (as that we are going to die): for such facts are believed as logically necessary consequences of other beliefs, which *are* wishful. That I am going to die counts as a fact because I am bound on pain of doubting my senses (or my common sense) to believe that other people die, and to believe (in public, at the least) that I am one with people. To doubt my death is to doubt logic, history and human companionship: in short it is to doubt of human companionship—and for most of the time I do indeed succeed in doubting it. To doubt it wholly would be to turn solipsist, or occultist. *Some* of the time I prefer to share humanity, and work till the night comes. To doubt my death would be to lose an agonizing beauty.

All thought is wishful thinking: how then shall I castigate the scientist, or sentimentalist for his dealings with those shapes I choose to take as kin? I hardly think that such scientists and sentimentalists are likely to bring this charge against me, but it should be met. Assuming that my readers are capable of conversing—and my writing of this book proclaims my allegiance to that faith—I can only ask that each man considers what reality he truly does desire: an alien world of unmeaning automata, a sycophantic consolation for the felt inadequacies of his human relationships (why need to torment beasts to prove our manhood unless that manhood is a source of grief?), or a cooperative, communicative assembly of living creatures each in its kind? Perhaps as a sceptic I cannot say that one is right, or even that one *is* enjoyable, as if these were matters of fact whose status did not depend on my choice (or our choice), but I can ask that each man should make his own decision. And it is of some interest to note that past amoralists have(?) been on the zoophiles' side: the Lokayata, those sceptical, amoralist, hedonists whom orthodox Hinduism did its best to forget were the ones to reject sacrifice. Diogenes the Cynic was the one to demonstrate, by eating a raw squid, the unfitness of such a diet for humankind (Julian Orat. 6.191 f.; PLUTARCH (1) 995d: though Plutarch takes a rather different point from the anecdote).

Either there are standards of right and wrong to which we must,

in some sense, bow; or there are not. If there are, then it is the
zoophile who has the best claim to realism. If there are not, then
all of us alike are fantasists, spinning our wish-dreams to our taste—
and if that be so and recognized as so, then those who recognize
it are likely enough to make a more enjoyable reality than the
mixture of dogma, sentiment and vague conceit which passes for
orthodox thought.

Is not the whole amoral relativism I have sketched itself a wishful
thought? Of course. Will not real unrealism be revealed in failure
to avoid pains, death, destruction? Maybe so: and if it is so, then
are we all unrealistic—for none of us will ever evade such things,
at least on any view that is commonly accepted as realistic.
'Morality' promises us the good life, if we only abandon all such
tastes as constitute the good for us; everyday realism promises us
safety, if only we abandon all such imaginative exercise and self-
abandoning love as makes our life worth protecting. Neither
'morality' nor everyday realism has ever kept its word. Perhaps we
might consider, briefly, from this view-point whether we might
attempt with profit(?) to do as Christ commanded. And what motive
could we have in such a state for treating anything as we now treat
such things as have a different shape?

Neo-platonism

Extreme amoralism is difficult to expound, not least because the
true amoralist cannot permit even his amoralism to become dogma
or doctrine. He does not claim to be right, either in detail or in
theory. He acts, but he does not, in acting, proclaim his right or
his truthfulness. Action and statement alike are, for him, very much
more gamesome than they are for natural dogmatists. This may
make him a somewhat irritating conversationalist, and an unnerving
ally. The moralist in all of us feels very sure that action is a serious
matter, that evil is all too real a fact and not to be erased by philo-
sophic fantasy. I do not deny it—I would hardly have written this
book if I did not feel the point deeply. But I have sketched the
amoralist at such length both to remind opponents who may be
tempted to deny the value of all moral discourse what true amoralists
are *like*, and to remind myself and my allies of the need to look to
one's own heart. It is not only *morality*, or not morality at all, which
demands a revolution in our treatment of the non-human: *I* demand
it, and employ morality as a device to get attention for the demands

I choose to make. It is not realism only that compels the recognition of what we currently do to the non-human as an evil not to be borne. It is an imaginative fantasy that offers both a possible ideal, and the prospect of a battle with the hordes of conventional hypocrisy. And this fantasy may well have roots in my own personality. I have castigated the orthodox for inventing a war against the beasts in order to give themselves a sense of their own identity as *human* beings. But the challenge can be reversed: do I not posit a war against the callous and unimaginative in order to give myself a purpose in being, in order to find a credible image in the phenomenal world of that war-in-heaven which we carry in our hearts? Do I not seek an enemy? Perhaps I do, though if I do I can at least claim that my warfare is Mental and not Corporeal, in Blake's terms:

> Our wars are wars of life, & wounds of love
> with intellectual spears, & long winged arrows of thought.
> ('Jerusalem', 38.14)

But all philosophers, and particularly philosophers with radical intentions, should remember themselves, and be humble.

'(Swedenborg) shews the folly of churches, & exposes hypocrites, till he imagines that all are religious, & himself the single one on earth that ever broke a net.' (BLAKE p. 157.)

The amoralist is a useful companion to speak against that 'confident insolence sprouting from systematic reasoning'. (BLAKE p. 157.) We should all remember that our beliefs of fact and of value spring from inner causes, and that those causes are not always as innocent as we would wish.

Nonetheless, for better or for worse, we must rely on that 'prefiguration of reality, interior imagery of nature' (DUBOS (3) p. 14) which exists in the human mind. It is these images which determine what we expect to meet in the phenomenal world, how we interpret our meetings, how we endeavour to transform the material by reinterpretation or by action. What is so surprising for any honest epistemology is that our images, our guesses so often prove reliable. It is as if there were entities which existed *first* in the inner world of consciousness and then were painted or reflected or took up residence in the outer realm of material event. Though this way of putting it, by its separation of the inner from the outer, may be misleading. We do not get knowledge purely from the five senses, but from the correspondence of such information with the images of our intellect: we do not accept what we *see*, but carefully prune our seeings to that shape we are assured is real. The being of things apart from us is not the being we see, or hear, or touch—for all such beings are dependent on our presence for their existence. Something exists in our absence—of that we are sure—and its being is such as to be realized on occasion and partly in our senses. But its being-itself is a matter, once again, for intellect. How is it that our intellect can ever hope to be even partly right? The only convincing answer known to me, though not one for which I intend to argue in this context, is that given by Neo-Platonists, and by shamans before them. We can 'see' into the Beginning of things, can grasp the principles on which the phenomenal world is founded, because it is founded on Spirit. The Forms are the eternal thoughts, activities of God, and we are shadows of God, or are, in some sense and at some level, identical with God. Or to put the point otherwise: the phenomenal world is the play, the multiplied and interwoven reflection of spiritual being—and *we* are spiritual beings, however lowly. We guess what will happen, because we can overhear the colloquy of the gods. Kekulé can dream of serpents that eat their tails, and know the benzene ring. MONOD can identify with the protein molecule (p. 146). Just so the shaman can dream himself into the presence of the ancestors, or the founding gods, and find the secret that unravels phenomenal mystery (on the analogy between science and shamanism see HORTON). Great scientists are great artists, seeing more clearly and with less idiosyncracy those archetypes of our psychology which are prototypes in cosmology.[3]

The strengths and undoubted weaknesses of this epistemology are not my present concern. It is, I suspect, the very same answer that Aristotle was inclined to give (see CLARK pp. 217 f.), and it is an answer that is closer to the common assumptions even of western man than most orthodox philosophers are prepared to admit. I mention it here in the interests of philosophical honesty, so as not to conceal a view which tempts me, and to see what ethical capital can be found in it.

The Aristotelianism from which I began is most in accord with the common sense of our society. It is under this tradition that I would appeal to common evolutionary ancestry, common abilities,

---

[3] 'Genius is revealed in a delicate feeling which correctly foresees the laws of natural phenomena.' (BERNARD (1) p. 43; see (2) p. 78.)

generous-heartedness towards our kin and benefactors. For better
or for worse we are all in the world together, and will do better
to remember this, allowing weight to our immediate loyalties but
not tyrannizing over other life. My occasional disenchantment with
all moral standards, and my impatience with all those thinkers who
are so *certain* (and often so mistaken) about the facts, allows me
Scepticism. This scepticism is not dogmatic even about itself, and
though I have offered, from that standpoint, as nearly consistent
an amoralism as I can manage, I am not committed to that amoralism. By envisaging it I am enabled to suspect that the only respectable version of non-scepticism is Neo-Platonic. If we are to trust
our judgement we must adopt an epistemology and an ontology
which makes it probable, or even plausible, that our judgement is
sometimes correct. We need to be able to believe that we have some
contact, or can have contact, with the world beyond sight. And it
is *only* of the world beyond sight that we can have the assurance
that we suppose ourselves to have: of the phenomenal world it is
simply false that we *know* that the sun will rise tomorrow—for we
do not know that we, that any of us, will live to see another dawn
(or even its aftermath). And if we are not there to see, how does
the sun *rise*? In the world beyond sight the earth (whatever that
is) will revolve maybe beneath the electro-magnetic radiance of the
sun (whatever that is). But our ability to say that this is so, and
to understand what we mean by saying it depends upon our intellectual grasp of or gesture at the noumenal reality. And such a gesture
is only possible because *we* are already in that realm. Science is only
possible if we can remember our being in the world beyond sight,
and any picture of the world that science devises must allow for
that fact.

If this be so, what ethical advice is there? True being lies in Spirit
that portrays itself in the phenomena, and at that level we are all
at one. Our office is to remember Spirit, whether by secluding ourselves from the phenomenal world or by seeing the phenomena as
fragments, reflections of the Truth. St. Hildegard's vision of the
Spirit:

'I am wisdom. Mine is the blast of the thundered word by which
all things were made. I permeate all things that they may not
die. I am life.' (MIGNE 197.743; C. SINGER I p. 33; see NASR
pp. 102 f.)

Our office is to remember Spirit, and to make its ways known in the phenomenal world. It has been part of the Neo-Platonic tradition that Spirit is in some way divided against itself—as we indeed know well; that the phenomenal world is in some measure the record, the arena of a struggle between the generous intercourse of Heaven and the self-aggrandizing of the fallen court. Instead of sharing and delighting in the blast of the thundered word, some elements, organs, spirits sought to keep life for themselves, and mastery. And this in turn was held to arise from having forgotten that they them-selves already *were* existing in full enjoyment of the divine being, and in coming to believe that value lay in the outward record of the divine creativeness. We saw our face in the water, and imagined that we must struggle to gain that good, and keep it from all others.

Whether this story is an accurate account of the coming-into-being of the world in which we now imagine we live, I do not profess to know, or even to guess. It has been the belief of many zoophiles in the past, and has as much claim to philosophical respectability as any other philosophy. The time is long past when philosophers or scientists could cast doubt on such theories by pointing to the difficulty of verbalizing them adequately, or to special problems of the tradition. No science and no philosophy is free of problems; no science and no philosophy can wholly avoid paradox or neolog-ism. But it is not my present intention to investigate the Neo-Pla-tonic universe: it is a life's study. What I do remark on is the fact that Neo-Platonic statements of cosmic unity have received con-firmation in modern science. PLOTINUS declared that in the world of Truth each being was all: 'There, the sun is all the stars, and every star is all the stars and sun' (v.8.4). In modern physics simi-larly every being is the entire universe from that particular point of view. The sun is not simply that gold guinea up aloft: we live in the sun. There are no absolute boundaries: when any organism acts the whole world acts in that organism. We are members of each other, and all of us are joined in making the whole world with which every one of us is coextensive. Is it not time that we remembered our loyalty to the world of truth, and forgot the delusive appearance of our being pure individuals in competition? In Neo-Platonic terms the spiritual universe of which we are natives has expressed itself in the phenomenal world: or to put it otherwise, the pheno-menal world, to the eyes of the spirit, is the arena in which we spirits can come to know our kin. We are not separate from the world,

nor are we its masters: if we men have an office 'higher' than those
of other creatures it is the office of care and understanding—understanding of cosmic unity, care for the diversity of creatures.

Neo-Platonists have been successful in practice to this extent:
they predicted that the universe would turn out to be mutually interdependent, that all things arise together, that there are many levels
of conscious being which all contribute to the life of all. And so
it is, they do, there are. We should perhaps give more honour, and
more attention to the imaginative philosophy that predicted it (for
an interesting beginning, though he deploys more Eastern parallels,
see CAPRA). And more loyalty to the single, beautiful and always-
to-be-completed universe that religion, poetry and science have
united in revealing (see also WARD AND DUBOS pp. 296 f.).[4]

Christianity

The three disparate but interrelated strands that I have laid out
are united for me in the tradition of the Christian Church, and I
make no apologies for the many occasions on which I have referred
to that tradition in the preceding pages. It is not my intention to
defend my allegiance in this context, or at all. But it is necessary
for me to say something about the Christian attitude to the non-
human.

There isn't one.

By this I mean that there is not, and never has been any general
agreement within the Church about the propriety of our dealings
with animals. All educated Christians should agree that they do not
belong to us. All should agree that there are limits on what we may
properly do with God's creatures. But all do not agree on the nature
or extent of those limits; nor do all agree on what office God
has designed for us. To glorify Him for ever, maybe—but the
manner of that glorification has not always been such as other
Christians, other believers would approve, or such as God would
approvè.

Some zoophiles have attempted to argue that Christ himself was

---

[4] 'Refrain at all times such Foods as cannot be procured without violence and oppression.
For know that all the inferior Creatures when hurt do cry and send forth their complaints
to their Maker or grand Fountain whence they proceeded. Be not insensible that every
Creature doth bear the Image of the great Creator according to the Nature of each, and
that he is the Vital Power in all things. Therefore let none take pleasure to offer violence
to that life, lest he awaken the fierce wrath and bring danger to his own soul.' (TRYON
p. 6, see p. 70.)

vegetarian (as TODD FERRIER or, by implication, E. WYNNE-TYSON), but the case cannot be sustained on the available evidence. He did speak, as I have mentioned, with courtesy and love of small creatures that the dogmas of His day despised and did drive the traders in sacrificial animals from the temple. But He assisted at the capture and the cooking of fish, certainly ate the Passover Lamb as a good Jew (even if there is some good ground for thinking that He fasted at the last supper: JEREMIAS (2) p. 208), and (crucially) distinguishes His own approach from that of the ascetic tradition of John Baptist (Matthew 11:18 f.). His alleged treatment of the Gerasene swine (Mark 5:1 f.) is not entirely relevant to the case, since even if it were correctly reported the story could be interpreted as the pigs' decision to drown rather than be slaughtered, once they had received the inspiration of a host of knowledgeable spirits. But I suspect that there is a parable lurking beneath the trivia (who, after all, was keeping *pigs*?).

Christ was not vegetarian. He could have been, but on the evidence was not. I would not commit the absurdity of seeking to justify Him, but the question is inevitable. Shall not the Judge of all the earth do right? But those who profess to follow Christ's example in this one point, ignoring the fact of His mission to the lost sheep of Israel, would carry more weight if they followed Him in others—like not having homes, or in giving themselves to the service of the poor. Those who do these things may be forgiven if they eat what they can share with others, even if they thereby fail to do all they theoretically might for the welfare of yet other creatures.

Some early Christians probably were vegetarian, for a variety of reasons. Matthew and James the Just are probable examples (CLEMENT pp. 107 f.). Some, as Paul makes clear (I Corinthians 8), refused the meat of idols. Ascetic practices accounted for others. Paul himself was a meat-eater. Now Paul was a great man, and a practical man. He was certainly not a misogynist, nor did he despise our sexual gifts, nor did he overlay the 'simple gospel' with scholastic theology—one could almost argue the contrary, that he unduly simplified the wild paradoxes and kindly muted the fearful threats of the gospel. But he never made the mistake of thinking himself infallible, and many of his letters show signs of a tendency to argue one point at a time, whatever the natural consequences for other issues of moment. When AQUINAS (*Summa* Ia 2ae q102 art 6 ad

8) deduces from Paul (I Corinthians 9:9) that God does not care for oxen, but that all the injunctions to the manifest contrary in the Old Testament are economic or symbolic in origin, he is taking the apostle far too literally. Paul, as a good Jew, knew well that God did care for oxen, though it is possible that the Rabbinic tradition of the day had forgotten it. When Paul was actually thinking about the fate of the non-human, as distinct from merely glancing at the topic in the course of a different argument, his judgement is that 'the universe itself is to be freed from the shackles of mortality and enter upon the liberty and splendour of the children of God. Up to the present, we know, the whole created universe groans in all its parts as if in the pangs of childbirth.' (Romans 8:21 f.)

The gravest damage was done to zoophily by the association of vegetarianism with Manichaean doctrine, beginning the long tradition whereby all who care for the non-human are instantly denounced as indifferent to the suffering of men. AUGUSTINE declares scornfully that Manichaean doctrine forbids feeding an unbeliever lest one be involved in his sin ((1) 36), and adopts himself the Stoic dogma that the irrational is beneath consideration. In those days it was perhaps understandable that most people had little sympathy left to spare for meat-animals. Even Augustine might perhaps have blanched at the treatment of animals by the Cartesian religious of Port Royal (see ROSENFIELD pp. 54 f.). And it is perhaps worth remembering the story of St. Eustace, who was converted to Christianity when the stag he was hunting turned at bay to reveal a crucifix between his antlers—by one of those incredible ironies of human hypocrisy, he is now the patron saint of hunters.

In short, the record of the Church has not been good—though it was in Julian the Apostate's day that hecatombs were sacrificed to revive Hellenism's sinking spirits. There have been pleas from time to time, from all branches of the Church (John Wesley to Cardinal Manning), but the general tradition has not been favourable to zoophily. For that matter it took eighteen hundred years for the conscience of Christendom to rouse itself against slavery. And it is perhaps notable that the same people who spoke against that were also active in the cause of animals (witness Martin, Wilberforce, and Shaftesbury: see LYNAM, TURNER). Christ promised his disciples that the Spirit would lead them into all truth (John 16:13), but the leading has indeed been long. Now that we have been led as far as here, it is hardly decent to deny what is now obvious merely on the grounds that it was not entirely obvious two thousand years ago.

All sacrifice has ended with the one oblation of the Lamb of God; all flesh-eating and almost all medical exploitation is for us mere greed; whatever moral standpoint is taken the same result is found, and hurriedly forgotten.

Envoy

Doubtless, we are all sinners. If I have offended I ask forgiveness. If I have omitted someone's favourite argument, consider it well: what matters, after all, is not what I have to say against it, but what you can in honesty find to say for it. If I have implied, or any still believe, that I think that there are no other moral issues than those which result in a commitment to dissociate oneself from animal-torture, I here state that of course there are many others—though many are related in practical and philosophical ways to our treatment of animals.

Other things can be said. It is axiomatic that other things can always be said. What matters in the end is not what we say, but what we do and do not do.

'Whoever has the will to do the will of God shall know whether my teaching comes from Him or is merely my own. Anyone whose teaching is merely his own, aims at honour for himself. But if a man aims at the honour of Him who sent him he is sincere, and there is nothing false in him.' (John 7:17 f.)

Such sincerity is not mine, not wholly so. But in some degree at least I speak beneath the eye of God the Truth-teller, that presence who is known to scholars in any field. I have sought, as far as I am able, to face the possibilities. If I am wrong, refute me. If I am right, must you not begin this further stage upon the royal road, the Way that has no ending?

> When,
> —at the mid of moon,
> at end of day—
> my lamp is lit,

grant me a boon,
I pray,
and do
so order it

—that the small creatures,
terrified and blind:
the gold and silvern moths
of lovely kind,
do not whirl to my taper,
nor, therein,
die, painfully,
and bring my light
to sin.

My light
is innocent!
Grant
—that it may be
harmless,
and helpful,
and remarked
of Thee.
James Stephens, 'Student Taper'
(*Collected Poems*, London 1954, p. 301)

LIST OF WORKS CITED

1. *Philosophical*

Philosophers are at last beginning to admit that the non-human creation is a proper object of moral concern. Recent work includes the following:

BROADIE, A. and PYBUS, E. A. 'Kant's treatment of animals', *Philosophy* 49, 1974, pp. 375 f.

DARLING, F. FRASER (2) 'Man's responsibility for the environment', *Biology and Ethics* (ed. F. J. Ebling), London 1969, pp. 117 f.

DISCH, R. (ed.) *The Ecological Conscience*, New Jersey 1970.

GODLOVITCH, R. 'Animals and morals', *Philosophy* 46, 1971, pp. 23 ff.

GODLOVITCH, R. and S. and HARRIS, J. (eds.) *Animals, Men and Morals*, London 1971.

LINZEY, A. *Animal Rights*, London 1976.

MACIVER, A. M. 'Ethics and the beetle', *Analysis* 8, 1948, pp. 65 ff.

MIDGLEY, M. 'Concept of beastliness', *Philosophy* 48, 1973, pp. 111 ff.

MORRIS, C. 'Rights and duties of beasts and trees', *Journal of Legal Education* 17, 1964–5, pp. 185 ff.

NELSON, L. *System of Ethics*, (tr. N. Guterman), New York 1956.

NOZICK, R. *Anarchy, State and Utopia*, New York 1974.

PASSMORE, J. *Man's Responsibility for Nature*, London 1974.

REGAN, T. 'The moral basis of vegetarianism', *Canadian Journal of Philosophy* 5, 1975, pp. 181 ff.

RYDER, R. *Victims of Science*, London 1975.

SAGOFF, M. 'On preserving the natural environment', *Yale Law Journal* 84, 1974, pp. 205 ff.

SINGER, P.
  (1) 'Animal liberation', *Moral Problems*, ed. J. Rachéls, New York 1975[2], pp. 163 f.
  (2) *Animal Liberation*, New York 1975.

SINGER, P. and REGAN, T. (eds) *Animal Rights and Human Obligations*, New York 1976.

TRIBE, L. H. 'Ways not to think about plastic trees', *Yale Law Journal* 83, 1974, pp. 1315 ff.

Yet more has been written, of considerable interest, on the relations between thought and (human) language, and on the mammalian and animal grounds of our ethical sense. Much of this writing is vitiated by a failure to apply our knowledge that there is no absolute divide

between species—in short by speciesism. It is not only our ethical
lives that are distorted by evil—we shall in the end lose also the good
of intellect.

2. General

ADDIS, W. E. and ARNOLD, F. *Catholic Dictionary*, London 1884
    (1957[16]), *s.v.* animals.
AGIUS, A. *God's Animals*, Westminster 1970.
AGAR, W. E. *Theory of the Living Organism*, Melbourne 1951[2].
ALEE, W. C. *Cooperation among Animals*, London 1951[2].
ALTMANN, S. A. 'Structure of primate social communication', *Social
    Communication among primates* (ed. Altmann), Chicago 1967, pp.
    325 ff.
APPLEY, M. H. 'Hedonic relativism and planning the good society'
    Adaptation-level theory (ed. P. Bickmann and D. T. Campbell),
    New York 1971.
AQUINAS, T. *Summa Theologica*, vol. 29 (ed. D. Bourke and A. Little-
    dale), London 1969.
ARMSTRONG, D. M. *Belief, Truth and Knowledge*, London 1973.
ASCLEPIUS *Corpus Hermeticum* (ed. A. D. Nock and A. J. Festugière),
    Paris 1945, vol. II pp. 257 ff.
AUGUSTINE, ST.
  (1) *De Moribus Manichaeorum*
  (2) *Civitas Dei*
AUSTIN, P. *Our Duty to Animals*, London 1885.
BALDRY, H. C. *Unity of Mankind in Greek Thought*, Cambridge 1965.
BARTH, K. *Church Dogmatics* (ed. G. W. Bromley and T. F. Torrance)
    Edinburgh 1961.
BATEMAN, M. (ed.) *This England*, London 1969.
BATESON, G. *Steps to an Ecology of Mind*, London 1972.
BENDER, L. 'Animals', *Dictionary of Moral Theology* (ed. P. Palazzini,
    tr. H. J. Yannone), London 1962.
BENNETT, J. *Rationality*, London 1964.
BENTHAM, J. *Principles of Morals and Legislation*, London 1789.
BERGER, J. and MOHR, J. *A Seventh Man*, Harmondsworth 1975.
BERNARD, C.
  (1) *Introduction to the Study of Experimental Medicine* (tr. H. C.
    Greene), New York 1949.
  (2) *Cahier Rouge* (tr. H. H. Hoff and L. and R. Guillemin), in GRANDE
    and VISSCHER.
BIERENS DE HAAN, J. A. *Animal Psychology*, London 1948.
BLAKE, W. *Collected Works* (ed. G. Keynes) Oxford 1966.
BOAS, G. *The Happy Beast*, Baltimore 1933.

BOONE, J. A. *Kinship with All Life*, New York 1954.

BOUGEANT, G. H. *A Philosophical Amusement upon the Language of Beasts*, London 1739.

BOSWELL, J. *Life of Johnson*, Oxford 1953.

BRADLEY, F. H. *Ethical Studies*, London 1927².

BROADIE and PYBUS: see section 1.

BRONOWSKI, J. and BELLUGI, U. 'Language, name and concept', *Science* 168, 1970, pp. 669 ff.

BROPHY, B. 'In pursuit of a fantasy', in GODLOVITCH AND HARRIS, pp. 125 ff.

BROWN, A. *Who Cares for Animals?* (story of the R.S.P.C.A.), London 1974.

BROWNE, T. *Religio Medici*, London 1642.

BUCHAN, J. *Memory Hold-The-Door*, London 1940.

CAMPBELL, C. A. Moral and non-moral values', *Mind* 44, 1935, pp. 273 ff.

CAPRA, F. *The Tao of Physics*, London 1975.

CARREL, A. *Man the Unknown*, New York 1935.

CARRIGHAR, S. *Wild Heritage*, London 1965.

CASTANEDA, C. *Journey to Ixtlan*, London 1972.

CHAN, W. T. (ed.) *Sourcebook in Chinese Philosophy*, Princeton 1963.

CHARLES, R. H. (ed.) *Apocrypha and Pseudepigrapha of the Old Testament in English*, Oxford 1913.

CHOMSKY, N. *American Power and the New Mandarins*, Harmondsworth 1969.

CHURCH, R. M. 'Emotional reactions of rats to the pain of others', *Journal of Comparative Physiological Psychology* 52, 1959, pp. 132 ff.

CLARK, S. R. L. *Aristotle's Man*, Oxford 1975.

CLARKE, J. *Man is the Prey*, London 1969.

CLEMENT *Christ the Educator* (tr. S. P. Wood), New York 1954.

COBBETT, W. *Political Register*, 1802.

COLERIDGE, S. J. *Complete Poetical Works* (ed. E. H. Coleridge), Oxford 1912.

COLLINS, A. W. 'How could one tell were a bee to guide his behaviour by a rule?' *Mind* 72, 1968, pp. 556 ff.

COMMONER, B. 'The ecological facts of life', in DISCH.

CYRANO DE BERGERAC, S. *Other worlds* (tr. G. Strachan), London 1965.

DARLING, F. FRASER
  (1) *Wilderness and Plenty*, London 1970.
  (2) see section 1.
  (3) *Pelican in the Wilderness*, London 1956.

DARLING, F. FRASER and MILTON, J. P. (eds.) *Future Environments of North America*, New York 1966.

DEAN, R. *The Future Life of Brutes*, Manchester 1777.

DEVEREUX, G.
(1) *From Anxiety to Method in the Behavioural Sciences*, The Hague 1967.
(2) 'Greek pseudo-homosexuality and the Greek miracle', *Symbolae Osloenses* 42, 1967, pp. 69 f.

DEVORE, I. and WASHBURN, S. L. 'Baboon ecology and human evolution' F. C. Howell and F. Bourlière (eds.) *African Ecology and Human Evolution*, London 1964, pp. 335 ff.

DEWAR, J. *The Rape of Noah's Ark*, London 1969.

DICKERMAN, S. O. 'Some stock illustrations of animal intelligence in Greek Psychology', *Transactions of American Philological Association* 42, 1911, pp. 123 ff.

DISCH: see Section 1.

DOGS, *The Vivisection of Dogs*, London 1933.

DOUGHTY, R. W. *Feather Fashions and Bird Preservation*, California 1975.

DOUGLAS, M.
(1) (ed.) *Rules and Meanings*, Harmondsworth 1973.
(2) 'Animals in Lele religious thought', *Africa* 27, 1957, pp. 46 ff.
(3) *Purity and Danger*, London 1966.
(4) 'Deciphering a meal', C. Geertz (ed.) *Myth, Symbol and Culture*, New York 1971, pp. 61 ff.
(5) *Natural Symbols*, Harmondsworth 1973[2].
(6) *Implicit Meanings*, London 1975, reprints (2) and (4).

DOWNIE, R. S. and TELFER, E. *Respect for Persons*, London 1969.

DUBOS, R.
(1) *Mirage of Health*, London 1960.
(2) *The Dreams of Reason*, New York 1961.
(3) *A God Within*, London 1973.

DU BOULAY, J. *Portrait of a Greek Mountain Village*, Oxford 1975.

DUFFY, M. 'Beasts for pleasure', GODLOVITCH and HARRIS, pp. 111 ff.

DUMONT, L. *Homo Hierarchicus*, London 1972.

EISELEY, L. *The Firmament of Time*, London 1961.

EVANS, E. P.
(1) *Criminal Prosecution and Capital Punishment of Animals*, London 1906.
(2) *Evolutionary Ethics and Animal Psychology*, New York 1867.

EVANS, H. E. *Life on a Little-known Planet*, London 1970.

FARBER, S. M. 'Quality of living—stress and creativity', in DARLING and MILTON pp. 342 ff.

FICHTELIUS, K. E. and SJOLANDER, S. *Man's Place: Intelligence in Dolphins, Whales and Humans*, London 1973.

FIRTH, V. M. *The Soya Bean*, London 1925.

FLUGEL, I. 'Some psychological aspects of a fox-hunting rite', *International Journal of Psychology* 12, 1931, pp. 483 ff.

FORTENBAUGH, W. W. 'Aristotle: animals, emotion and moral virtue', *Arethusa* 4, 1971, pp. 137 ff.

FOX, R. and TIGER, L. *The Imperial Animal*, London 1972.

FRANCIS, ST. *'Little Flowers of St. Francis'*, *'Mirror of perfection'* and *Bonaventura's 'Life'* (ed. T. Okey), London 1910.

FREUD, S. *Collected Works* (tr. J. Strachey), vol. XIV, London 1957.

FREUND, P. A. (ed.) *Experiments with Human Subjects*, London 1972.

FÜRER-HAIMENDORF, C. VON *Morals and Merit*, London 1967.

GALSWORTHY, J. *A Sheaf*, London 1916.

GARDNER, B. T. and GARDNER, R. A. 'Two-way communication with an infant chimpanzee', A. Schrier and F. Stollnitz (eds.), *Behaviour of Non-human Primates* vol. VI, London 1971, pp. 117 f.

GEWIRTH, A. 'Categorial consistency in ethics', *Philosophical Quarterly* 17, 1967, pp. 289 ff.

GODLOVITCH see section 1.

GODLOVITCH and HARRIS see section 1.

GODWIN, W. *Political Justice* (ed. H. S. Salt), London 1890.

GOMBRICH, R. *Precept and Practice*, Oxford 1971.

GOMPERTZ, L. *Fragments in Defence of Animals*, London 1852.

GOODALL, J. VAN LAWICK- *In the Shadow of Man*, London 1971.

GRAHAM, F. *Since Silent Spring*, London 1970.

GRANDE, F. and VISSCHER, M. E. (eds.) *Claude Bernard and Experimental Medicine*, Cambridge, Mass. 1967.

GRAY, C. 'Meaning of pain, death and consciousness', *Downside Review* 79, 1961, pp. 189 ff.

GRICE, G. R. *Grounds of Moral Judgment*, Cambridge 1967.

GUIRDHAM, A. *A Theory of Disease*, London 1972[2] (1957[1]).

GURNEY, E. *Tertium Quid*, London 1887 (see SHAW pp. 9 ff.).

HARDY, A.
 (1) *The Living Stream*, London 1965.
 (2) *The Divine Flame*, London 1966.

HARE, F. M. *Freedom and Reason*, Oxford 1963.

HARING, B. *Law of Christ* (tr. E. G. Kaiser), Cork 1963.

HARLOW, H. F. and HARLOW, M. K. 'The Affectional Systems', *Behaviour of Non-human Primates* (ed. A. M. Schrier, H. F. Harlow, F. Stolnitz), New York 1965 Vol. II.

HARRISON, R. *Animal Machines*, London 1964.

HART, H. L. A. *Law, Liberty and Morality*, London 1966.

HARTLEY, D. *Observations on Man*, London 1749.

HEDIGER, H. *Wild Animals in Captivity* (H. G. Sircom), London 1950.

HEGEL, G. W. F. *Philosophy of History* (tr. J. Sibree), London 1888.

HELPS, A. *Animals and their Masters*, London 1883².

HILDROP, J. *Free Thoughts upon the Brute Creation*, London 1742.

HILLS, J. H. 'On the evolutionary foundations of language', *American Anthropologist* 74, 1972, pp. 308 ff.

HINDE, R. A. (ed.) *Non-Verbal Communication*, Cambridge 1972.

HORTON, R. 'African traditional thought and western science', *Africa* 37, 1967, pp. 50 ff. and 155 ff.

HOWARD, L. *Birds as Individuals*, London 1952.

HOWELLS, W. *Evolution of the Genus Homo*, Reading, Mass. 1973.

HUI NENG, *The Platform Sutra of the Sixth Patriarch* (tr. P. B. Yampolsky), New York 1967.

HUME, C. W.
  (1) *Man and Beast*, London 1962.
  (2) *Status of Animals in the Christian Religion*, London 1957.
  (3) 'Animals', *Dictionary of Christian Ethics* (ed. J. Macquarrie), London 1967.

HUME, D. *A Treatise of Human Nature*, London 1739.

HUMPHREY, N. K. 'Vision in a monkey without striate cortex', *Perception* 3, 1974, pp. 241 ff.

HUTCHINGS, M. H. and CAVER, M. *Man's Dominion*, London 1970.

HUXLEY, J. *Religion without Revelation*, London 1967.

INGOLD, T. 'On reindeer and men', *Man* 9, 1974, pp. 523 ff.

JAMES, W.
  (1) *Will to Believe*, London 1897.
  (2) *Varieties of Religious Experience (1901–2)*, London 1960.
  (3) (ed. J. K. Roth) *Moral Philosophy of William James*, New York 1969.

JAMESON, A. *Commonplace Book*, London 1854.

JENYNS, S. *Free Inquiry into the Nature and Origin of Evil*, London 1757.

JEREMIAS, J.
  (1) *New Testament Theology* 1 (tr. J. Bowden), London 1971.
  (2) *The Eucharistic Words of Jesus* (tr. N. Perrin), London 1966.

JOHNSON, S.
  (1) *Commentary on Shakespeare's Plays*, London 1973, vol. 13.
  (2) *Complete Works* (ed. Hawkins), London 1787.

JOHNSON, S. and BOSWELL, J. *Tour to the Hebrides* (ed. R. V. Chapman), Oxford 1924.

JONAS, H. 'Philosophical reflections upon human experimentation', in FREUND, pp. 10 ff.

JONES, J. W. *Law and Legal Theory of the Greeks*, Oxford 1956.

KALGHATGI, T. G. *Jaina View of Life*, Sholapur 1969.

KAWAI, M. 'Newly-acquired pre-cultural behaviour of the Natural Troop of Japanese Monkeys on Koshima Islet' *Primates* 6, 1965, pp. 1 ff.

KAWAMURA, S. 'Process of sub-culture propagation among Japanese macaques', in SOUTHWICK pp. 82 ff.

KANT, I.
  (1) *Groundwork* (tr. H. J. Paton, *The Moral Law*), London 1948.
  (2) *Lectures on Ethics* (tr. L. Infield), London 1930.

KEITH, A. 'Stephen Paget Memorial lecture', *British Medical Journal* 1932[1], pp. 1184 ff.

KENNY, A. J. P. with Longuet-Higgins, H. C., Lucas, J. R., and Waddington, C. H., *The Development of Mind*, Gifford 1972–3, Edinburgh 1973.

KHAN, G. M. 'Muslim method of slaughter', *U.F.A.W. 1971: Humane Killing and Slaughter House Technique*.

KINGSFORD, A. and MAITLAND, E.
  (1) *Addresses and Essays on Vegetarianism* (ed. S. H. Hart), London 1912.
  (2) *The Perfect Way*, London 1890[3].

KIPLING, J. L. *Beast and Man in India*, London 1891.

KLINGENDER, F. (eds. E. Antal and J. Harthan) *Animals in Art and Thought*, London 1971.

KLUCKHOHN, C. and LEIGHTON, D. *The Navaho*, New York 1962[2].

KRIEGER, M. 'What's wrong with Plastic Trees?' *Science* 179, 1973, pp. 446 ff.

KROPOTKIN, P.
  (1) *Mutual Aid* (ed. P. Avrich), London 1972.
  (2) *Ethics* (tr. L. S. Friedland and J. R. Poroshnikoff), New York 1972.
  (3) *The Conquest of Bread* (ed. P. Avrich), London 1972.
  (4) *Fields, Factories and Workshops Tomorrow* (ed. C. Ward), London 1974.

LAIRD, J. *A Study in Moral Theory*, London 1926.

LANCASTER, J. B. 'Primate communications systems and the emergence of language', *Primates* (ed. P. C. Jay), New York 1968, pp. 439 ff.

LAPPÉ see section 1.

LAWRENCE, J. *A Philosophical Treatise on Horses and the Moral Duties of Man Toward the Brute Creation*, 1796[1], 1802[2], 1810[3] (see NICHOLSON: Nicholson's copy of the 3rd ed. is in the Bodleian Library, Oxford, with preliminary notes for a biography).

LEACH, E. 'Anthropological aspects of language: animal categories and verbal abuse', *New Directions in the study of language* (ed. E. H. Lenneberg), Cambridge, Mass. 1964, pp. 23 ff. (also in MARANDA).

LEACH, P. *Babyhood*, Harmondsworth 1975.

LECOMTE, J. *Animals in our World* (tr. L. Coghlan), London 1966.

LEFFINGWELL, A. *The Vivisection Controversy*, London 1908.

LEOPOLD, A. *Sand County Almanac*, Oxford 1966[2].

LEVI-STRAUSS, C.
   (1) *The Savage mind*, London 1966.
   (2) *Mythologiques* I–IV.
LEWIS, C. S.
   (1) *That Hideous Strength*, London 1945.
   (2) *Screwtape Proposes a Toast*, London 1965.
LIEBERMAN, P. (ed.) *The Speech of Primates*, The Hague 1972.
LILLY, J. C.
   (1) *Man and Dolphin*, London 1962.
   (2) *The Centre of the Cyclone*, London 1973.
LORENZ, K.
   (1) *Civilised Man's Eight Deadly Sins* (tr. M. Latzke), London 1974.
   (2) *On Aggression* (tr. M. Latzke), London 1966.
LINZEY, A. see section 1.
LOVELOCK, J. and EPTON, S. 'The quest for Gaia', *New Scientist* 65,
   1975, pp. 6 ff.
LYNAM, S. *Humanity Dick* (Richard Martin), London 1975.
MABEY, R. *Food for Free*, London 1972.
MCDONALD, A. D. *U.E.A.W. 1971: Rational Use of Living Systems in
   Biomedical Research* (Research Defence Society contribution).
MCHARG, I. L. *Design with Nature*, New York 1969.
MACIVER see section 1.
MAIMONIDES *Guide to the Perplexed* (tr. M. Friedlander), London
   1904[2].
MAITLAND, E. *Life of Anna Kingsford*, London 1913[3].
MARANDA, P. (ed.) *Mythology*, Harmondsworth 1972.
MARETT, R. R. *Faith, Hope and Charity in Primitive Religion*, Oxford
   1932.
MARTIN, P. S. and WRIGHT, H. E. (eds.) *Pleistocene Extinctions*, Con-
   necticut 1967.
MARTINENGO-CESARESCO, E. *The Place of Animals in Human
   Thought*, London 1909.
MAXWELL, G. *Ring of Bright Water*, London 1960.
MÉNARD, L. *Reveries d'un paien mystique*, Paris 1911.
MENNINGER, K. A. 'Totemic aspects of contemporary attitudes to ani-
   mals', *Psychoanalysis and culture: Essays in Honor of G. Roheim* (ed.
   G. B. Wilbur and W. Munsterberger).
MERTON, T. 'The wild places', in DISCH pp. 37 ff.
MIDGLEY see section 1.
MIGNE, J. P. *Patrologia Latina*.
MILGRAM, S. *Obedience to Authority*, London 1974.
MIRRLEES, H. *Lud-in-the-Mist*, London 1926 (1972[2]).
MITCHELL, B. *Law, Morality and Religion*, Oxford 1967.
MONEY-KYRLE, R. E. *Man's Picture of his World*, London 1961.

MONOD, J. *Chance and Necessity* (tr. A. Wainhouse), London 1972.

MONTAIGNE. *Collected Essays* (tr. J. Florio 1603), London 1892.

MOORE, P. (ed.) *Against Hunting*, London 1965.

MORRIS see section 1.

MOWAT, F. *A Whale for the Killing*, London 1972.

MUMFORD, L. 'Closing Statement', in DARLING and MILTON pp. 718 ff. (also DISCH).

MURRAY, J. 'Animals', *Catholic Dictionary of Theology* (ed. H. F. Davis), Edinburgh 1962.

NASR, S. H. *The Encounter of Man and Nature*, London 1968.

NELSON see section 1.

NEMESIUS, *Premnon Physikon* (tr. N. Alfanus, ed. Burkhard), Teubner 1917.

NIALL, I. *Around my House*, London 1973.

NICHOLSON, E. B. *The Rights of Animals*, London 1879 (including extracts from LAWRENCE. Nicholson's annotated copy is in the Bodleian Library, Oxford).

NORBU, T. J. and TURNBULL, C. *Tibet*, Harmondsworth 1972.

NOZICK see section 1.

PAPPWORTH, M. H. *Human Guinea Pigs*, London 1967.

PASSMORE, J.
 (1) See section 1.
 (2) 'The Treatment of Animals', *Journal of the History of Ideas* 36, 1975, pp. 195 ff.

PATON, H. J. *The Good Will*, London 1927.

PEMBROKE, S. L. 'Oikeiosis', *Problems in Stoicism* (ed. A. A. Long), London 1971, pp. 114 ff.

PETERS, C. R. 'Evolution of the capacity for language', *Man* 7, 1972, pp. 33 ff.

PFANNER, D. F. and INGERSOLL, J. 'Theravada Buddhism and village economic behaviour', *Journal of Asian Studies* 21, 1962, pp. 341 ff.

PHILO. *Opera* (tr. C. D. Yonge), London 1854.

PICKERING, G. 'The place of the experimental method in medicine', *Proceedings of the Royal Society of Medicine* 42, 1949, pp. 229 ff.

PIRIE, N. W. 'Leaf protein: a beneficiary of tribulation', *Nature* 253, 1975, pp. 239 ff.

PLOTINUS *Enneads* (tr. S. MacKenna), London 1969[4].

PLUTARCH
 (1) *Moralia* (tr. H. Cherniss and W. C. Helmbold), London and Cambridge, Mass. (especially vol. XII).
 (2) *De Iside et Osiride* (ed. J. G. Griffiths), Swansea 1970 (also *Moralia* vol. v).
 (3) *Lives* (tr. B. Perrin), London and Cambridge, Mass, 1914, vol. II.

POLLARD, J. *Wolves and Werewolves*, London 1964.

POPE, A. *An Essay on Man* (ed. M. Mack), London 1950.

POPPELBAUM, M. *Man and Animal* (ed. O. Barfield), London 1962[2].

PORPHYRY
(1) *On Abstinence* (tr. T. Taylor).
(2) *Life of Plotinus*.

PORTMANN, A. *Animals as Social Beings* (tr. O. Coburn), London 1961.

POWYS, J. C.
(1) *Morwyn*, London 1937.
(2) *Autobiography*, London 1967[2].

PRIMATT, H. *The Duty of Humanity to Inferior Creatures* (ed. A. Broome), London 1831.

R.D.S. *Memorandum of Research Defence Society*, London 1964.

RAMBURES, MARQUISE DE. *The Church and Kindness to Animals*, London 1906.

RAPHAEL, D. D. 'The standard of morals', *Proceedings of the Aristotelian Society* 96, 1974–5, pp. 1 ff.

RASHDALL, H. *Theory of Good and Evil*, Oxford 1924[2].

RAWLS, J. A. *Theory of Justice*, Boston 1971.

REES, A. and REES, B. *Celtic Heritage*, London 1961.

REGAN see section 1.

RENNER, H. D. *The Origin of Food Habits*, London 1944.

RHYS DAVIDS, T. W. (ed.) *Dialogues of the Buddha* (Dighanikaya), London 1890.

RICHARDS, D. A. J. *Theory of Reasons for Actions*, Oxford 1971.

RICKABY, J. *Moral Philosophy*, London 1888.

RITCHIE, D. G. *Natural Rights*, London 1916[3].

ROCHE, A.
(1) *These Animals of Ours*, London 1939.
(2) *Animals under the Rainbow*, London 1952.

ROSEN, S. *Nihilism*, New Haven 1969.

ROSENFIELD, L. C. *From Beast-machine to Man-machine*, New York 1968[2].

ROSZAK, T. *Where the Wasteland Ends*, London 1973.

RULAND, L. *Foundations of Morality* (tr. T. A. Rattler), London 1936.

RUSSELL, W. M. S. and BURCH, W. L. *The Principles of Humane Experimental Technique*, London 1959.

RYDER see section 1.

SAGOFF see section 1.

SAHLINS, M. *Stone Age Economics*, London 1974.

SALT, H. S.
(1) *Animals' Rights*, London 1922[2].
(2) *Seventy Years among Savages*, London 1921.

(3) 'Rights of animals', *Ethics* 10, 1899–1900, pp. 206 ff.

(4) *The Logic of Vegetarianism*, London 1933.

(5) (ed.) *The New Charter*, London 1896.

(6) (ed.) *Kith and Kin: Poems of Animal Life*, London 1901.

SARTRE, J-P. *Sketch for a Theory of the Emotions* (tr. P. Mairet), London 1962.

SCAIFE, M. and BRUNER, J. 'The capacity for joint visual attention in the infant', *Nature* 253, 1975, pp. 265 ff.

SCHAPIRO, M. 'Religious meaning of the Ruthwell Cross', *Art Bulletin* 26, 1944, pp. 232 ff.

SCHOPENHAUER, A. *World as Will and Representation* (tr. E. F. J. Payne), Colorado 1958.

SEJOURNE, L. *Burning Water: Thought and Religion in Ancient Mexico*, London 1957.

SELYE, H. *The Stress of Life*, London 1957.

SERENY, G. *Into that Darkness* (biography of F. Stangl), London 1974.

SEYMOUR, J. and SEYMOUR, S. *Self-Sufficiency*, London 1973.

SHALER, N. *Domesticated Animals*, London 1896.

SHAW, G. B. *Shaw on Vivisection* (ed. G. H. Bowker), London 1949.

SHELLEY, P. B. *Complete Poetical Works* (ed. N. Rogers), Oxford 1972.

SHERIDAN, C. L. and KING, R. G. 'Obedience to authority with an authentic victim', *Proceedings of the American Psychological Association*, 80, 1972, pp. 165 ff.

SINGER, C. *Studies in the History and Methods of Science*, Oxford 1917.

SINGER, P. see section 1.

SMART, C. *Jubilate Agno* (ed. W. H. Bond), London 1954.

SMITH, F. D. and WILCOX, B. *Sold for Two Farthings*, London 1950.

SMITH, V. L. 'The primitive hunter culture: pleistocene extinction and the rise of agriculture', *Journal of Political economy* 83, 1975, pp. 727 ff.

SNYDER, G., *Earth House Hold*, New York 1969.

SOUTHWICK, C. H. (ed.) *Primate Social Behaviour*, New York 1963.

SPEARMAN, D. (ed.) *The Animal Anthology*, London 1966.

SPINOZA, *Ethics*.

STEINER, G. *After Babel*, Oxford 1975.

STIRNER, M. *The Ego and his Own* (ed. J. Carroll), London 1971.

STRATO (ed. F. Wehrli) *Fragmenta*, Basle 1969.

SZALAY, F. S. 'Hunting-scavenging protohominids: a model for hominid origins', *Man* 10, 1975, pp. 420 ff.

SZENT-GYORGI, A. 'Science and ideas' (Report from Montreal conference), *Lancet*, 1961.1, p. 1394.

TAMBIAH, S. J. 'Animals are good to think and good to prohibit', *Ethnology* 8, 1969, pp. 424 ff. (also in DOUGLAS (1)).

TAYLOR, T. *Vindication of the Rights of Brutes*, London 1792.

TELEKI, G. 'The omnivorous chimpanzee', *Biological Anthropology* (ed. S. H. Katz), San Francisco 1975, pp. 91 f.

THORPE, W. H. *Animal Nature and Human Nature*, London 1974.

TINBERGEN, N. *The Study of Instinct*, Oxford 1951.

TODD FERRIER, J. *On Behalf of the Creatures*, London 1903, 1934[2].

TOLSTOY, L. *'A Confession', 'The Gospel in Brief', 'What I Believe'* (tr. A. Maude), London 1940.

TOMPKINS, P. and BIRD, C. *The Secret Life of Plants*, London 1974.

TRETHOWAN, I. *Absolute value*, London 1970.

TRIBE, L. H. see section 1.

TRYON, T. *Wisdom's Dictates*, London 1691.

TURNER, E. S. *All Heaven in a Rage*, London 1964.

UEXKUELL, J. VON. *Theoretical Biology* (tr. D. L. Mackinnon), New York 1926.

UTTLEY, A. *The Farm on the Hill*, London 1941.

VESEY-FITZGERALD, B.
  (1) *Town Fox, Country Fox*, London 1965.
  (2) *The Vanishing Wild Life of Britain*, London 1969.

VIRTANEN, R.
  (1) *Claude Bernard and his Place in the History of Ideas*, Lincoln, Nebraska 1960.
  (2) 'Claude Bernard and the history of ideas', in GRANDE pp. 9 ff.

VYVYAN, J.
  (1) *In Pity and Anger*, London 1969.
  (2) *The Dark Face of Science*, London 1971.

WADDELL, H. *Beasts and Saints*, London 1934.

WALLACE, A. H. *The World of Life*, London 1910.

WARD, B. and DUBOX, R. *Only One Earth*, Harmondsworth 1972.

WEIL, A. *The Natural Mind*, London 1973.

WELLBOURN, F. B. 'Man's dominion', *Theology* 78, 1975, pp. 561 ff.

WESTERMARK, E. *Christianity and Morals*, New York 1939.

WHEWELL, W. *Elements of Morality*, Cambridge 1964[4].

WHITE, L. 'Toward an ecological ethic', *Science* 155, 1967, pp. 1203 ff.

WHITE, T. H. (ed.) *The Book of Beasts*, London 1954.

WILLIAMS, L.
  (1) *Samba and the Monkey Mind*, London 1965.
  (2) *Man and Monkey*, London 1967.
  (3) *Challenge to Survival: a Philosophy of Evolution*, London 1971.

WILLIS, R. *Man and Beast*, London 1974.

WILSON, C. A. *Food and Drink in Britain*, London 1973.

WINSTEN, S. *Salt and his Circle*, London 1951.

WITTGENSTEIN, L. VON *Philosophical Investigations* (tr. G. E. M. Anscombe), Oxford 1958[2].

WOOD, J. G. *Man and Beast*, London 1874.

WOODS, J. H. 'Integration of consciousness in Buddhism', *Indian Studies presented to C. R. Lanman*, Cambridge, Mass. 1929 pp. 137–9.

WYNNE-EDWARDS, V. C. 'Ecology and the evolution of Social Ethics', *Biology and the Human Sciences* (ed. J. W. S. Pringle), Oxford 1972, pp. 49 ff.

WYNNE-TYSON, E. *The Philosophy of Compassion*, London 1962.

WYNNE, TYSON, J. *Food for a Future*, London 1975.

ZEND-AVESTA (tr. J. Darmesteter), Oxford 1885.

ZIMMER, H. *Philosophies of India* (ed. J. Campbell), London 1952.

NOTES FOR PROSELYTES

Vegetarian cooking does not consist of an endless round of cheese salads and omelettes: even those vegetarians who have not (yet) progressed to veganism are generally sparing in their use of eggs and dairy products, and have many more culinary resources than the orthodox seem to realize. Nor, in general, is it necessary to subsist on textured vegetable protein spun from soy-beans. Beans (including the much-maligned soy) and whole grains, particularly in combination, provide nutritious and tasty meals. Middle Eastern and Indian cookery books provide many interesting recipes; and French and Italian cooking traditions are not entirely ignorant of the possibilities. Even British cooking, with its porridges, breads and puddings, can be mined for useful hints. All traditional cooking, in fact, uses meat *sparingly*: the steak and chips régime is a very recent perversion.

We find the following particularly useful:

BIRCHER, R. *Eating your Way to Health* (tr. C. Loewenfeld), London 1961.

BROWN, E. E. *The Tassajara Bread Book*, Berkeley 1970.

FARMILANT, E. *Macrobiotic Cooking*, New York 1972.

LAPPÉ, F. M. *Diet for a Small Planet*, New York 1971[1], 1975[2]. This is essential reading, as it contains a clear account of how to balance grains and beans (and other things) to obtain the best protein use. Ms. Lappé is not a vegan, but her recipes are usually suitable for vegan households with very little adaptation. In fact, they provide too *much* protein.

RODEN, C. *A Book of Middle Eastern Food*, London 1968 (Harmondsworth 1970).

SINGH, D. *Indian Cookery*, Harmondsworth 1970.

Other, and more conventional vegetarian cookery books are usually either dull or wilfully exotic. W. and J. Fliess *Modern Vegetarian Cookery*, Harmondsworth 1964 is the former; A. Thomas *The Vegetarian Epicure*, Harmondsworth 1972, as well as being very non-vegan, is the latter. Further practical information, on food-stuffs and on other animal products, can be obtained from the Vegetarian Society at 53 Marloes Rd., Kensington, London W8 6LD, and from the Vegan Society at 47 Highlands Rd., Leatherhead, Surrey.

Suggestions on what can, practically, be done about the use of animals in laboratories, can be found in R. Ryder *Victims of Science*, London 1975. Organizations to contact include the Scottish Society for the Prevention of Vivisection; 10 Queensferry St., Edinburgh; the National Anti-vivisection Society; 51 Harley St., London W1N 1DD, and the Fund for the Replacement of Animals in Medical Experiments (F.R.A.M.E.), 312 Worple Rd., Wimbledon, London SW20 8QU. There is hardly any aspect of man's dealings with the non-human that does not require reform: zoophiles should find their own areas of effectiveness, and *act* in them—not to participate in evil is a good, but there are times when to seek to prevent that evil is a better.

INDEX

Italicized entries refer to works cited in the text by author's name